Co-operative Structures in Global Business

This volume explores how firms operating in industries as diverse as film making, shipping, engineering, mining, bottling and advertising have collaborated to develop innovative services, technologies and products to reach new markets. Using a series of twelve historical case studies that are based on extensive archival research, this book explains why firms succeeded or failed in communicating, transferring knowledge and discovering new expertise. By analysing how workable trade-offs between opposing forces have been achieved in the past, this study provides a set of guidelines for executives who embark upon inter-firm projects.

Gordon H. Boyce teaches courses in business history, management and economics at the Victoria University of Wellington, New Zealand. He is widely published on the topic of inter-firm collaboration.

Routledge International Studies in Business History
Series editor: Geoffrey Jones

Co-operative Structures in Global Business

Communicating, transferring knowledge and learning across the corporate frontier

Gordon H. Boyce

London and New York

First published 2001
by Routledge
11 New Fetter Lane, London EC4P 4EE

Simultaneously published in the USA and Canada
by Routledge
29 West 35th Street, New York, NY 10001

Routledge is an imprint of the Taylor & Francis Group

Typeset in Baskerville by
Prepress Projects Ltd, Perth, Scotland
Printed and bound in Great Britain by
Biddles Ltd, Guildford and King's Lynn

British Library Cataloguing in Publication Data
A catalogue record for this book is available
from the British Library

Library of Congress Cataloging in Publication Data
Boyce, Gordon, 1954–
   Co-operative structures in global business : communicating,
   transferring knowledge and learning across the corporate
   frontier / Gordon H. Boyce.
   p. cm.
   Includes bibliographical references and index.
   1. Business networks – Case studies. 2. International business
   enterprises – Management – Case studies. 3. Technology transfer
   – Case studies. 4. Strategic alliances (Business) – Case studies. I.
   Title.
   HD69.S8 B69 2000   338.8′7–dc21 00-035383

ISBN 0-415-21644-3 (hbk)

Contents

Figures and tables

Figures

Tables

Preface

This book is the outgrowth of an earlier study of business networks used by British shipowners between 1870 and 1919. After completing that work, I decided to cast the investigative net more widely and explore other forms of co-operative structures that had been used in the past by business leaders engaged in other industries. Teaching business history to management students in Australia and New Zealand also encouraged me to think about co-operative principles that could be distilled from historical experience and applied today.

I was also encouraged to pursue this project because Oliver Williamson's path-breaking work has intrigued me for years. I have read and re-read his books, and each time I have come away with new insights and additional questions. His work has provided a strong foundation for thinking about not only the economic logic beneath co-operative structures but also the processes within them. (Having worked in business, I was and am especially intrigued by how inter-firm relationships begin and develop.) Williamson made some tantalising comments about atmosphere, dignity and the benefits of arranging transactions, and it is towards these themes that this study is directed. Along with Williamson, Mark Granovetter, Walter Powell, and various sociological economists provided a basis for thinking about inter-organisational relationships in systemic terms.

Business historians never take for granted the knowledge of archivists and the wisdom of those business figures who ensure that corporate memories need to be preserved for future generations. Today, when financial resources and facilities are under such pressure from short-sighted 'leaders', these efforts deserve even greater recognition. Since all but one of the cases below are based primarily on archival sources, my gratitude is indeed considerable.

I acknowledge with thanks the assistance of Charlotte Havilland and John Swire & Sons Ltd; Noel Butlin Archives of Business & Labour at the Australian National University; Frank Strahan and Leigh Swancott and the University of Melbourne Archive; Mary J. Auckland and the School of Oriental & African Studies in London; the University Library Cambridge; Adrian Allan and the University of Liverpool; the Keeper of the Records of Scotland for permission to use the records of the John Brown Company, the Ellerman Lines papers, and the Babcock & Wilcox collection; Michael Moss and the University of Glasgow; the Merseyside Maritime Museum; Ellen Gartrell and Duke University; the History of Advertising Trust in Raveningham; Ken Scadden and the Wellington Maritime Museum; the National Maritime Museum in Greenwich; Furness Withy & Co., Ltd; Gilbert M. Ralph MBE and the Western Mining Corporation; Unilever; and the J. Walter Thompson Company.

I owe a great debt to Douglas Lowell, MSc, a treasured friend, who guided me through the workings of the Hollywood film industry, commented extensively on drafts of Chapter 12, and provided many friendly contacts in the industry. David Shaheen, vice-president of Chase Securities, and Tom McGuiness, post-production supervisor, provided specialised advice.

I am also grateful for the permission of the editors of the *Australian Economic History Review* and Blackwell Publishers to include here revised versions of 'The Western Mining Corporation–Hanna/Homestake joint venture: game theory and inter-organisational cooperation', Vol. 37, no. 3 (November 1997), pp. 202–21 and 'The Steel Manufacturers' Nickel Syndicate Ltd, 1901–39: assessing the conduct and performance of a co-operative purchasing organisation', Vol. 38, no. 2 (July 1998), pp. 155–75. Likewise, I thank Manchester University Press and the editors of the *Journal of Transport History* for permission to publish a rewritten version of 'Union Steam Shipping Company of New Zealand and the adoption of oil propulsion: learning by using effects' [3rd series, Vol. 18, no. 2 (September 1997), pp. 134–55].

I am fortunate to be able to work with John Singleton, who is collegiality itself; he read through drafts of nearly every chapter in this book and always provided insightful comments. At Victoria University, I am also grateful to Professor Gary Hawke for his encouragement over the past ten years. I acknowledge the assistance of Professor Athol Mann and Monica Cartner, who broke through the onerous regulations governing research funding and supported my application for a travel grant. Finally, I thank Victoria University of Wellington for funding a sabbatical leave and for the aforementioned travel grant.

The J. Walter Thompson Company generously awarded a research grant that enabled me to visit the John W. Hartman Centre for Sales, Advertising, and Marketing History at Duke University.

At other universities, Professors Simon Ville, Peter Townley, and Stephen Nicholas read chapters and provided opportunities for me test out ideas in seminars. At the LSE and the Business History Unit, Dudley Baines, Paul Johnson, and Terry Gourvish arranged seminars from which I gained helpful comments. Professor Tony Slaven offered the hospitality of the Centre of Business History in Scotland. The University of Glasgow and the University of Melbourne kindly provided fellowships and facilities. Over the years, I have benefited greatly from the academic leadership offered by Professors Charlotte Erickson, Leslie Hannah, Paul Robertson, Peter Davies, Skip Fischer, Geoff Jones, Mira Wilkins, Sarah Palmer, Frank Broeze, John Armstrong, Keith Trace, and John Perkins. Steve Jones, Diana Olein, Mary

Rose, and Will Hausman have also been loyal colleagues. In Canada, Professor Peter Townley and Dr Mark W. Bailey have always offered encouragement and support.

Most of the research for this book was carried out during a sabbatical leave from December 1995 to February 1997, when with my wife, Evelyn Stewart, I visited archives and historic sites in the UK, North America, and Australia. Throughout, she cheerfully provided indomitable records management and computing skills, research expertise, and proofreading. Of inestimable value, however, is how she helps me understand what co-operation is. I dedicate this book to her.

Gordon Boyce
August 2000

1 The theoretical and historical context

Introduction

This study examines inter-organisational structures as distinctive systems that support communication, knowledge transfers, and collaborative learning across corporate frontiers. It explores how participants in co-operative relationships exchange information efficiently, how they make transactions involving knowledge, and, in contrast to much of the literature that examines 'learning organisations' in terms of a single firm, how organisations learn by working together. These themes are examined using a series of eleven separate studies.

To provide an overarching framework for the cases, the book harnesses insights derived from economic theory and business history. Specifically, it applies and extends the economics of information to analyse these inter-firm structures explicitly in systemic terms. This approach exposes questions to guide an evaluation of past practices. Further, the study mobilises business history in order to reveal different devices and techniques that were employed in the past to support communication and co-operation in a variety of specific contexts. The findings provide a basis for filling gaps in the theory and for expanding its parameters.

The book has two main objectives. The first is to extend our knowledge of the wide range of inter-organisational structures. History exposes a startling variety of frameworks, some of which may strike present-day businessmen as innovative and subtle. Improved knowledge of the array of possible forms may make for better-informed choices and more effective designs. The second aim is to extract from historical experience concepts and principles that can be taken into account when forming or analysing inter-firm frameworks. History reveals a battery of surprisingly sophisticated techniques that were used to initiate and sustain co-operative endeavours. It also provides a context within which to assess outcomes. Each of the following chapters examines one or two variables that can influence performance. Together, the cases cumulatively assemble a set of concepts and considerations to guide business practitioners and institutional analysts in assessing the dynamics of inter-organisational relationships.

The book covers an extensive chronological period in order to show how changes in environmental conditions and relationship-specific factors shaped co-operative undertakings and determined their longevity. A long-term perspective also reveals patterns of learned behaviour and conditioned expectations which together set in train so-called 'path dependencies' that in turn channelled the course of institutional development. The chapters consider inter-organisational structures employed by economic actors from different countries to capture the dynamics of collaboration that unfolded across national and cultural frontiers. They also include examples of collaboration in the manufacturing and service sectors. Some of the participants in the projects examined below are widely known, but others are not; previously overlooked firms are included because they devised unusual frameworks or innovative techniques. In order to learn from success as well as from failure, these ventures consist of projects that achieved all of their founders' objectives, some that were marginally effective, and others that did poorly.

At present, there is an urgent need for an improved set of guidelines for those engaged in co-operative undertakings. Since the early 1980s, firms have made increasing use of inter-organisational frameworks in an attempt to penetrate new markets and to develop new technologies. Yet, these initiatives have sustained an alarmingly high rate of failure. Estimates vary considerably, but something like thirty to seventy per cent of all new joint ventures disappoint their founders (Deloitte 1989; Harrigan 1985). Perhaps, greater awareness of history and economic theory can improve the record. With this in mind, the book examines *why* a particular type of inter-organisational structure was devised and *how* it operated within a prevailing business environment.

Today's international economy is characterised by accelerating change and increasing turbulence. Technological innovation is unfolding at a growing pace and bringing forth new products and more efficient methods of production. Firms face intense competition on a global scale and must provide high-quality, low-cost goods with sophisticated options to retain their markets. They are compelled to provide better service and to develop greater innovative capabilities using fewer resources.

To contend with this increasingly complex and rapidly changing environment, firms are making a series of interrelated structural changes, just one of which is to rely more extensively on co-operative relations with other companies. In addition, large-scale enterprises are flattening their hierarchies to speed up information flows and seeking ways to improve the learning capabilities of staff. They are also focusing more on core businesses in order to develop a greater depth in their knowledge bases while they spin off previously sheltered units so that these face a market test. From a theoretical point of view, these adjustments compel us to reconsider our conception of the firm, but in terms of historical trends the structural forms appearing increasingly today are not entirely new. To place structural dynamics in a perspective needed to drive the analysis firmly toward communication, knowledge transfers, and learning, we must review the theoretical and historical literatures to isolate the salient themes.

Business history

Business history has made an important contribution to our understanding of both the internal organisation of modern corporations and changes in industrial structure. By providing a rich empirical base that supports institutional comparison, it has had a significant impact on the development of new economic theories of the firm. However, there is considerable scope for discovering new evidence about the range of co-operative structures employed in the past and for examining how they operated in actual practice.

From the perspective offered by mainstream American business history one might infer that the structures appearing today represent something of a retreat by hierarchical organisations. The pioneering work of Alfred D. Chandler Jr (1962, 1977, 1990) charted the initial rise of big business and bureaucratic management structures in the United States. These developments occurred as a result of dynamic interaction between firms and a new business environment that emerged following the completion of the national transport and communication systems in the 1870s. Within the context of a quickly growing national market, rapid product and process innovation, and from the 1890s unique anti-trust legislation, US enterprises could grow to great size by establishing strong capabilities based upon investment in executive resources, mass-marketing techniques, and mass-production facilities. Firms that were first movers in harnessing these new capabilities did so by integrating vertically and by building hierarchical structures and systems. Such administrative innovation made it possible to capture durable economies of scale and scope, especially in technologically advanced sectors. The extension of the visible hand of managerial control over activities that hitherto had been co-ordinated by market transactions between suppliers, manufacturers, and distributors arose as a consequence of a two-way process wherein firms were shaped by, and shaped, the wider business environment. By prising open the modern business institution and exposing the structures and systems inside, Chandler explained the logic behind the initial development of the hierarchical organisations that are being reformed today.

However, other segments of the business history literature have taken a complementary, more externally oriented, view of institutional growth. Interacting with a distinct segment of the American business arena, small businesses in the US, and indeed throughout the world, have relied heavily on informal, externally focused arrangements (Scranton 1989, 1997; Piore and Sabel 1984). Similarly, scholars of British business found that within the context of a slower growing, more fragmented market, with more craft-intensive production processes and lenient regulations, family-based networks endured for long periods. In Britain, these structures also sustained the emergence of large-scale operations, but they were not comprehensively transformed into extensive hierarchies (Payne 1967; Hannah 1976; Brown and Rose 1993; Boyce 1995a). Profound resource scarcities also induced Japanese business to rely upon alliances, and enterprise in many Asian countries still exhibits a similar constitution (Fruin 1991; Gerlach 1992; Numazaki 1986, 1993). In these environments, smaller and more flexible companies specialised in a particular production or marketing function, but relied on large co-operative frameworks – as an alternative to comprehensive hierarchical structures – to secure economies of scope and to win competitive advantages. However, this branch of business history has focused largely on alliances or network structures. Less work has been done on other types of inter-firm relationships.

Theory

Economists have outlined a strong framework for explaining why some business activities are conducted in markets and why others are co-ordinated within the firm. In recent years, more has been done to develop theories that explain how co-operative frameworks function and how they differ from markets and hierarchies. One way to advance this work is to focus directly upon the communicating processes that underpin inter-firm relationships.

Business historians, as well as executives who are reforming Western corporate hierarchies today, have been influenced by a variety of economic theories that explain the design and internal processes of business institutions. Agency theory, transaction cost economics, the voice-exit approach, game theory, and sociological economics provide an array of prescriptive and descriptive frameworks. (Management theory provides complementary and contrasting perspectives: the notes below consider some of the principal works in this vast literature.) Implicitly, all of these economic theories raise information, communication, and learning issues that, if treated in a more broadly based and a more explicit manner, will help to extend our understanding of inter-organisational structures.

Agency theory

Principal–agent theory stemmed from the work of Berle and Means (1932), who addressed the problem of how the divorce of ownership from the management of large-scale enterprises exposed serious incentive problems. The question revolved around how shareholders could be assured that professional executives, who owned little if any of the equity of the firms they ran, would safeguard the interests of the owners. Principal–agent theory assumes that economic actors are self-interested and have imperfect information. The challenge centres upon how *ex ante* (before the fact) contracts can be devised to ensure that agents (managers), who possess superior information relative to their principals (shareholders), act in the best interests of the principals when the latter cannot observe and assess their behaviour directly. This situation arises in many bilateral relationships within and beyond the firm's boundary. Essentially, agency theory is concerned with how to arrange contracts that include incentive structures and monitoring mechanisms in order to overcome the effects of the asymmetry in the information available to the two parties (Williamson 1975; Jensen and Meckling 1976; Arrow 1985).

By considering the contract as the basic unit of analysis, agency theory offers an austere view of economic action that is 'under socialised' in the sense that it ignores social context (Wrong 1961). Its behavioural assumptions are open to question; in some social and cultural settings people naturally exhibit co-operative propensities and share common values or expectations that reduce the effects of imperfect information. Even in the absence of such social and cultural affiliation, systems installed for monitoring purposes may also generate two-way exchanges that generate mutual trust. In contrast to the *ex ante* presumption of opportunistic propensities, *ex post* processes (adjustments that are made after a contract is signed) may give rise to co-operation. Thus, although information asymmetry lies at the heart of the agency problem, its effects can be reduced not only by cleverly designed legal provisions that convey incentives and by assessment mechanisms, but also by mobilising *ex ante* or creating *ex post* some form of social–cultural foundation. The *relationship*, rather than the *bare contract*, becomes the focus of attention once communicating activities and learning processes are incorporated into the analysis (see Powell 1990: 323).

Transaction cost economics

The so-called 'new institutional economics' of which Oliver Williamson (1975, 1981, 1985; Williamson and Ouchi 1981) is a pioneering proponent, offers a rigorous framework for understanding business structures. Building on Ronald Coase's (1937) insight that, in contrast to one of the assumptions of conventional microeconomics, there are costs involved in making transactions, Williamson developed a set of theoretical tools to explain why some exchanges are conducted through markets and some are not.[1] Williamson began by assuming that:

1   economic actors have a propensity towards opportunistic behaviour (their pursuit of self interest is not benign but is infused with calculating, guileful intent); and
2   they are afflicted by bounded rationality (they try to act rationally in an economic sense but lack the full information and the analytical capacity needed to determine with absolute accuracy the costs and benefits of their actions).

In light of these assumptions, exchanges will be affected by a number of transaction cost variables including the number of potential bargainers, the frequency of exchange, the presence or absence of highly specialised assets, and the degree of prevailing uncertainty. Interaction among these factors will determine whether a transaction is carried out through markets or corporate governance. Thus, when the number of bargainers is small, uncertainty and the frequency of exchange are both high, and transactions rely upon specialised assets that have few if any alternative uses, the transaction will be internalised within the firm.[2] Alternatively, when there are many potential bargainers available, uncertainly and the frequency of exchange are both low, and non-specialised assets are involved, the market will be used.[3] If these variables are aligned between these two extreme combinations, co-operative mechanisms – the so-called 'intermediate modes' – such as relational contracts or trilateral governance, that is third-party-mediated arrangements, will be employed. [In his later work (1985), Williamson indicated that intermediate structures were more widely used than he previously believed.] The selection of transacting mechanism – whether firm, market, or intermediate mode – will be based on which alternative offers the lowest cost in light of how the transaction cost variables listed above are configured.[4]

Williamson's analysis points to a number of themes that can be explored further to reach a fuller understanding of co-operative structures. First, his behavioural assumptions are 'under-socialised' and can be questioned in much the same way as those that underpin agency theory.[5] Moreover, his earlier work (1975: 37–9) indicates that 'atmosphere', or the extent to which parties derive non-pecuniary benefits from exchanges, shapes the interplay of the transacting variables he identifies. However, he leaves wide scope for business historians and practising managers to determine how social and cultural forces influence intermediate mode design and operation within particular contexts.

Second, even though Williamson emphasises the efficacy of hierarchical authority in facilitating *ex post* adjustment, he does recognise that relational contracts may have desirable attributes and distinctive processes of their own. For example, if sufficient trust is present co-operative structures can achieve learning-by-doing effects, considerable flexibility, and diminished opportunism.[6] These frameworks can also generate a specialised language that sustains close interpersonal relationships and thereby secures 'communicating economies' (Williamson 1985: 62). Our analysis focuses directly upon these communicating and trust-building processes and the purposes for which firms and individuals used them (see Doz 1996; Ring and Van der Ven 1994).

Third, Williamson's framework has a static, equilibrating character that focuses on the internal transacting efficiency of each institutional arrangement.[7] It provides a 'snapshot' perspective that does not come to grips fully with the dynamics of institutional change. There is little room for growth, learning, power, or other strategic factors to influence initial mode selection or subsequent shifts in arrangement.[8] These issues are explored in the cases that follow.

Finally, like conventional microeconomics, transaction cost analysis employs *calculative* rather than a *communicative rationality* (Lundvall 1993: 59). It is based mainly upon cold assessment of costs and benefits and ignores those less precisely determined motivations that influence relationship-building activities. (The latter include the long-term benefits of pursuing mutual growth, joint learning, sharing complementary resources, reputation gains, access to diverse information, and non-pecuniary benefits). From this angle, it is important to consider how particular cultural values shape conceptions of trust and how the social milieu in which transactions unfold support specific communicating mechanisms, or informal, inter-organis-ational systems. The nature of the social and cultural context will determine the extent to which it either creates transacting 'friction' or lubricates information exchange and learning, thereby reducing the cost of co-operation. One of the aims of the present study is to explore how business leaders can shape the outcome by creatively influencing social and cultural elements to facilitate joint initiatives (see Casson 1991; Powell 1990).

Intermediate modes, voice-exit, and game theory

Richardson (1972) was one of the first economists to recognise the ubiquity of intermediate modes. He suggested that firms should not be seen as 'islands of planned co-ordination in a sea of market relations', but rather as entities that are enveloped in webs of interdependence. Indeed, markets and firms – as transacting frameworks – represent points at opposite ends of a spectrum of institutional arrangements characterised by degrees of interdependence. At these poles price and managerial control provide co-ordinating mechanisms. Between these extremes Richardson saw an array of co-operative intermediate arrangements that function effectively when participants willingly sacrifice some degree of their sovereignty; the relevant co-ordinating mechanisms for them are trust and power. However, for Richardson, what draws participants in intermediate modes together is the opportunity to combine capabilities that are complementary but dissimilar. At issue, therefore, is how firms gather and process information to discover initially that they have capabilities which can be blended and subsequently how they learn jointly to create a broader set of complementary attributes to sustain further growth.[9] Moreover, how do firms communicate to build the trust needed to induce them to sacrifice a measure of their right to pursue self-interest? Following Richardson's perspective, Powell (1990) calls for studies that show how information is processed and learning unfolds within these frameworks. These concerns draw attention to the systems that underpin inter-organisational structures.

The idea that communication and learning processes support co-operative business ventures underlies Hirschman's (1970) contrast between voice- and exit-based relationships. Hirschman's framework explains inter-firm operations in terms of how economic actors respond to disagreements or problems. Partners in voice relations, as the name implies, communicate intensively to resolve difficulties and preserve long-term ties. In contrast, when discord arises those firms that pursue exit strategies will find another party to deal with and thus exit from an existing relationship. These different patterns of behaviour reflect the time horizon observed by participants, the degree of trust between them or the credibility of threats to exit, and their conceptions of the benefits derived from sharing knowledge. The voice-exit approach highlights the rigidities that arise from the underlying patterns of conditioned behaviour, especially those that impede a shift from exit to voice relations (see Helper 1990). An important feature of the voice strategy is its capacity to achieve greater learning from collaborative interaction. However, this benefit must be weighed against the cost of the extensive communication involved. This draws attention to the role of inter-organisational systems in containing communicating expenses. The cases below examine the efficiency properties of inter-firm channels and their role in shaping patterns of behaviour.

Game theory offers another valuable framework in which to consider issues of communication and conditioned action. There are many games that model bilateral and multilateral links, but probably the most basic and most popular one for depicting two-sided relations is the Prisoner's Dilemma game. This scenario revolves around whether or not a 'partner in crime' will remain silent during police interrogation or implicate a fellow criminal to save his own skin (Axelrod 1984; Kreps 1990; Parkhe 1993; Camerer and Knez 1996). When this game is played once, both parties will always behave opportunistically and defect from a co-operative arrangement because – in the absence of direct communication – they do not trust each other. However, if an infinite number of games are played, players will adopt a strategy of conditional co-operation wherein each will co-operate as long as the other did so in the preceding game but will defect as soon as the other acts opportunistically. Changes in external conditions as well as internal shocks will affect the players' behaviour. Based on incomplete information and uncertainty, the Prisoner's Dilemma is a useful framework for thinking about inter-firm relations. It highlights the conditional nature of co-operation, the impact of internal and external shocks, and the role of implicit communication – in the form of actions – in shaping behaviour. However, to apply this approach, investigators need to consider it within a broader social context that provides norms, precedents, and conventions which support other forms of implicit transmission and influence human action.

Sociological economics

Granovetter (1985) advances the social 'embeddedness' approach as a middle way between what Wrong refers to as 'over-' and 'under-socialised' views of human relations. Granovetter (1985) argues that transactions of all types are 'rife with ... social connections', but it is concrete social relations that matter. By using this approach we can avoid relying on the austere rationality of economics and generalised conceptions of culture that gloss over the dynamics of interpersonal ties. Order–disorder, honesty–malfeasance, and efficiency–inefficiency have more to do with the *details* of social relations than they do with formal structures. He suggests that 'future research on the markets–hierarchies question [should] pay careful attention to the actual patterns of personal relations by which economic transactions are carried out', and he indicates that such approach will 'make it easier to comprehend the various complex intermediate forms' (1985: 504).

Granovetter's recommendations strike a responsive chord that resonates in the background of the present study. In the forefront are the communicating processes that economic actors use to create and sustain social relationships that in turn support inter-organisational co-operation. The quality of these social connections reflects the efficacy of information exchange and interpersonal and inter-organisational learning. The context and the details of inter-firm knowledge assume decisive importance. Moreover, Granovetter's perspective raises serious implications regarding human resource development. It compels us to consider how organisations recruit and train individuals who display the communicative rationality needed to forge business relationships.

Fundamentally, issues concerning communication, knowledge, and learning lie at the heart of each of these theoretical approaches. However, the mechanics of inter-firm transmissions are treated in an implicit or generalised manner. Similarly, both branches of business history literature, the Chandlerian and studies of networks, recognise with varying degrees of explicitness that information-related issues provide the key to understanding institutions.

What this book does is to penetrate beneath the theory and the historical evidence to expose the communicating principles and procedures that underpin co-operative frameworks. It explicitly considers information exchanges which support relationships that involve transferring knowledge or collaborative learning. We begin by articulating and exploring two concepts, contracting capability and the communicating infrastructure, that serve as a foundation for the analysis.

'Contracts' and contracting capability

How economic actors arrange agreements or forge ongoing relationships in the presence of asymmetric information and uncertainty is a central concern for managers. 'Contracts' (used here in the broader sense of relationships) are the basic building blocks of business development. Designing agreements and eliciting co-operation are vital skills.

All *contracts*, whether internally focused (between firm and employees) or externally oriented (between firms) are based upon three elements:

1   formal legal terms,
2   monitoring mechanisms, and
3   a cultural foundation (Carlos and Nicholas 1990).

Intermediate frameworks provide channels through which parties can discuss formal prescriptions, assess performance, and either build a culture or signal that they observe particular values or patterns of behaviour. However, the use of these elements necessarily imposes costs: time costs involved in negotiating legal terms, investment in monitoring devices, and expenses entailed in creating and manipulating social/cultural foundations. The extent to which a contract relies on each of these components – and all contracts must employ all three to some extent – reflects the need to minimise these expenses while ensuring compliance in light of prevailing environmental circumstances and the degree of trust existing between participants. Getting the right balance among these contractual elements, interpreting environmental conditions, and determining the character of other constituents all require entrepreneurial judgement as well as considerable skill in gathering and assessing information.

From this description, it is obvious that contracts are, in actual operation, far more than just pieces of paper contrived by legal experts. These agreements need to be flexible or they should be interpreted in a judicious manner so that parties can accommodate internal tensions and external shocks that often arise after the signatures are dry. Thus, contracts are not merely conceived as one-off deals, but rather ongoing relationships that generate mutual benefits over the long term. Therefore, in addition to exhibiting ingenuity in initially configuring the three contractual elements, economic actors also have to display creativity in adjusting their alignment to changing conditions afterwards. Ongoing modification demands continuous information collection and interpretation.

Contracting capability refers to ingenuity in arranging and maintaining co-operative agreements by communicating in implicit and explicit ways. It consists of several skills:

1   the capacity to establish one's presence in an incipient bargaining flow,
2   the ability to forge with others the bonds of trust needed to conclude an initial agreement, and
3   the judgement needed to exert a creative influence upon contractual design within the prevailing social and cultural context.

In a multiple time period, contracting capability also encompasses the ability to sustain co-operation by making sequential adjustments to the initial agreement and to win a reputation as a reliable contractor. (In a private, directly apprehended form, such renown constitutes one's *relational capital*, whereas in a public context it – along with one's contacts, status, and position – represents *social capital*.) A favourable reputation reflects investment in a valuable intangible asset, built by consistent action over the long term, that is important in determining future business possibilities and in deterring opportunism. It is a vital form of transmission that implicitly conveys assurances to other parties.[10]

Communication takes a variety of forms depending on the extent to which the parties involved possess interpersonal knowledge and physical proximity, both of which determine the degree of prevailing information asymmetry. Information can be conveyed explicitly through face-to-face conversation, but implicit emissions may have greater impact ('actions speak louder than words'). Informal signals derived from how a party behaves reveal underlying motives, whereas common affiliation may reflect shared experience and the observance of similar values. Effective communication within the context of a culture, which shapes the imagery and impact of different types of transmissions, depends on the availability of a supporting construct.

The communicating infrastructure

Social and cultural forces shape both communicating processes and frameworks that facilitate exchanges of information required for contracting purposes. Often, economic actors implicitly recognise these supporting structures and employ them intuitively. However, awareness of the basic features and manifold functions of these constructs can enhance the creativity that an entrepreneur exhibits when exercising contracting capability.

Communicating infrastructures are frameworks that facilitate transmissions between prospective and actual contractors. The particular elements that make up these frameworks vary according to partner-specific attributes, the scope of contracting activity, and the types of information and learning effects needed to ensure the satisfactory performance of an intermediate mode. In general terms, however, they consist of several components:

1 recognised contractual principles or models that serve as precedents,
2 bargaining fora and consciously designed communication lines (including accounting systems),
3 communicating conventions (including accepted behavioural rules, procedures governing informal transmissions, signalling devices and indicators of personal or corporate reputation, as well as deliberately contrived devices intended to contain communicating costs), and
4 persons selected to occupy positions at the interfaces between firms.

The effective range of a communicating infrastructure depends upon the scope of contracting: it can be specific to a bilateral relationship, it may encompass a multilateral network of constituents, or it may be associated with a particular geographic area, occupational group, or industry. These frameworks are grounded in a social and cultural context. They may be like a public good that reduces the cost of finding parties to deal with, assessing their trustworthiness and stature, devising an agreement, and establishing consensus regarding methods for future adjustment of the contract. Economic actors who can rely on such a public framework incur some expenses in modifying it or adapting to it, but they face lower costs than those who have to install a customised structure to forge and sustain a specific relationship.

Communicating infrastructures may serve several functions. They can:

1   support low-cost transfers of commercial intelligence, valuable private information, and existing functional knowledge (technical, accounting, marketing, and managerial know-how) relevant to a particular project;[11]
2   convey interpersonal and inter-organisational knowledge, facilitate cross-cultural learning, or furnish a basis for building a relationship-specific culture (any one of these functions can assist partners in generating enough trust to enable them to assemble sets of complementary resources or intangible assets);[12]
3   sustain learning-by-using effects required to adapt technology to new environments and thus realise the full potential of an initial quasi-rent stream;
4   facilitate the creation of knowledge related to an initial venture and later projects in order to enhance the future quasi-rent stream;
5   provide feedback mechanisms that enable partners to learn how to learn more effectively in the future.

The attributes outlined above indicate that co-operative structures can do far more than play a role in reducing transaction *costs*. Instead, these functions focus attention more firmly on the wider *benefits* that arise from exchanges conducted through intermediate institutions.

To conclude, this study uses these three concepts – contract, contracting capability, and communicating infrastructure – to examine a series of inter-firm structures. The forms examined below include agency relations, several types of network, a purchasing syndicate, joint ventures, licensing agreements, and a supplier chain. The book does not cover some frameworks, such as consumer co-operatives, cartels, or franchising arrangements, because they have been the subject of intensive study and because I could not find sufficiently detailed archival records to support a close analysis that would yield fresh insights about their internal processes.

Using the cases below as building blocks, the book develops a set of considerations that can be taken into account when designing contracts and co-operative frameworks. It also highlights potentially conflicting forces that need to be balanced to produce workable trade-offs. Finally, it draws attention to a number of specific techniques that may or may not be appropriate in particular circumstances. The study does not provide a ready-made formula or a blueprint for co-operators. Rather, it offers a framework for guiding critical thinking about how co-operative structures support communication, knowledge transfers, and learning activities.

2 Agency agreements in international business

Dynamic model of shipowner–agent relations, 1870–1939

This chapter shows how shipowners and agents designed contracts and employed a public communicating infrastructure to support transactions involving trade-related knowledge. The type of knowledge generated quasi-rents that – if appropriated – were rapidly dissipated. A model shows how a set of variables might interact to preserve a stable bilateral arrangement, precipitate collapse, induce a shift to vertical integration, or cause vertical disintegration.

The history of shipping agents highlights their role in supporting the expansion of marine transport services, international trade, and economic development (Marriner and Hyde 1967; Ville 1981; Jones 1985; Fischer and Fon 1990). Situated at a distant port, agents booked cargo and handled related matters on behalf of shipowners. In return, agents received a commission in the form of a flat fee for each ship they dealt with or a percentage based on the value of the freight rates charged on cargo they secured.

The agent's position rested upon his possessing, relative to his shipowning clients, superior information about the trade in his local port. The shipowner, in turn, deployed expensive assets in part on the basis of information provided by the agent. Yet, the shipowner–agent relationship was usually much more than just that of principal and agent. Agents were often an integral part of the trust-based networks that sustained British maritime enterprise from the late eighteenth century until after World War II.

History reveals, however, that shipowner–agent ties were not static. This chapter presents a model that explains why and how shipowner–agent ties changed in response to exogenous and endogenous shocks. The present discussion also sets the stage for the book as a whole by examining how shipowners configured the three basic contractual elements and how a sector-specific communicating infrastructure that had public good properties helped them to reduce the cost of arranging contracts.

Transactions based on knowledge

Within the shipping business, agents and vessel owners provided services that were vertically adjacent. Although Williamson's framework does not tell us precisely what degree of asset specificity, frequency, or bargaining scope will induce a change from market mediation to internalised exchange (see Chapter 1), it is evident that conditions in shipping after 1870 changed in ways that would lead us to expect a greater degree of vertical integration. The widespread adoption of steam power increased the frequency of transactions, the greater specialisation of service brought about by the growth of world trade enhanced asset specificity (in the form of ship design), and the rise of giant groups reduced the number of bargainers. Yet comprehensive vertical integration did not occur.

This situation is all the more curious because, in effect, agents sold their shipowning clients route-specific knowledge, and transactions involving knowledge are fraught with risk. As the 'paradox of knowledge' reveals, it is impossible to determine the value of knowledge until it has been disclosed, but once it has been revealed to another party that party has in effect acquired the knowledge without paying for it. For this reason transactions involving knowledge are likely to encounter market failure. Usually, the solution is to internalise the transaction within a firm.

There is all the more reason to expect vertical integration between agent and shipowner because of the type of knowledge agents sold their clients. Knowledge yields a quasi-rent when it is used or sold, and most types of knowledge have public good properties, in that they can be sold without reducing their value in some original application. However, agents sold knowledge about merchants' requirements, commodity flows, and factors affecting the supply and demand for shipping between particular ports. Such route-specific knowledge generated a quasi-rent that *would be* dissipated in its original application if it was sold to another party competing in the same trade. The surprising persistence of relations between shipowners and agents is reflected by the way social norms and cultural constraints helped to generate trust between the two parties. To explain this fully it is necessary to examine the nature of contracts in the maritime sector.

The configuration of shipowner–agent contracts

As the introductory chapter highlighted, contracts consist of three components: legal provisions, monitoring mechanisms, and culture. The use of each component imposes costs, and every contract must rely upon all three to some degree. Shipowners minimised expenses by designing contracts that relied most heavily upon culture and to a lesser degree upon legal specifications and monitoring devices.

Legal provisions were based on the precedent set by the merchant–correspondent relationship. Before the invention of the telegraph enhanced the speed of communication and the span of centralised control, merchants relied on corresponding agents, who had local knowledge, to exercise wide discretion in conducting routine business as it was defined by mutual understanding. The corresponding agents used their best judgement and through regular correspondence informed their principals of action taken. However, when agents had to perform a task that went beyond previously agreed limits, they first sought guidance and permission from the merchant. Many shipowners were formerly merchants or the sons of merchants and thus recognised the legitimacy of this arrangement. Using it as a template eliminated the need to incur the cost of devising custom-made agreements that precisely specified all obligations. As time passed, the contracts used by shipowners and agents became standardised to the extent that they were printed with blank spaces where the signatories filled in details (RMSP 31/ 3). Eventually, commissions became more uniform reducing specification costs further [PSNC box 3 (C36)2/1].

Regarding monitoring mechanisms, shipowners and agents again drew upon precedents in the form of reporting and accounting methods set by their merchant forebears (Boyce 1995b). In addition, the densely knit information channels that permeated the maritime community were also used in an informal manner to assess conduct (Boyce 1995a). Moreover, the mercantile sector furnished a variety of formal and informal bonding mechanisms that deterred opportunism and reduced the need for close monitoring. Formal bonds were used more extensively early on in the period and gradually became less important as entrepreneurs achieved renown. Increasingly, informal devices, especially reputation-staking, assumed more significance. The use of existing accounting models, bonding instruments, and informal conduits reduced monitoring costs.

The third and most important contractual component – culture – also drew upon mercantile precedents. Culture is reflected by two elements: a system of values and patterns of cognition (Smircich 1983). Values influence expectations and conduct and thus elicit to varying degrees 'spontaneous co-operation' (Casson 1991). Cognitive processes are shaped by socialisation and other influences that establish 'the rules of the game' and condition patterns of thought (North 1990; Cremer 1993).

In the marine sector, exchanges were enveloped in a co-operative ethos (Boyce 1995a). Long-standing values and social norms placed a premium on trustworthiness and reciprocity. Shipowners adopted these beliefs from the mercantile community along with expectations that transactions were highly personalised, that family was the foundation of reputation, and that considerable social and economic mobility were attainable. In this context, opportunism was a form of extreme deviance: not only was it egregious, it was also self-destructive because it jeopardised network ties, undermined reputation, and severed links that furnished access to resources and information.

The cognitive dimension of the shipping community's culture was shaped by historical trends that showed how socially conditioned mechanisms supported patterns of business growth. Since shipping was overwhelmingly a family business, social position and ties determined by kinship, religion, and local affiliation facilitated contracting by conveying information about individuals' trustworthiness. Using these communication lines as a foundation, an entrepreneur extended his business by forming networks with trusted parties who could provide resources that complimented those that he commanded. By doing so, parties could reduce risk and achieve greater growth than they could by working independently. Their aim was to co-operate and secure mutual growth safely.

Social and economic mobility were inextricably linked. Rising up the social and business ladders brought access to ever larger contracting arenas where one could forge grander alliances and thus secure access to better-quality information, more extensive supplies of capital, and more prestigious contacts which conferred greater reputation by association. In a reinforcing manner, reputation as a trusted contractor was accentuated by upward mobility. In a service industry where transactions involved intangible assets and depended upon trust, investment in reputation was rational. Thus, the cultural element that played a vital role in facilitating shipowners' contracts also reflected a co-operative ethos and socially conditioned cognitive processes that together supported the enduring operation of intermediate institutional arrangements.

What really drove these agreements were not Williamson's variables, but rather reputation, resources, and information, three factors that occupy central positions in the model below. An entrepreneur's renown as a trustworthy contractor determined his scope for building progressively larger networks. The size of his wealth and the nature of his physical assets also determined his attractiveness as an ally. The quality of the trade-related information he possessed shaped his contracting options. Exchanges based on these three elements were supported by an elaborate information handling construct.

The communicating infrastructure

Shipowners were fortunate to have a communicating infrastructure that operated like a public good in facilitating transactions. It consisted of the elements outlined in the introductory chapter: contractual models, communication lines (including accounting systems), communicating conventions, and recognised personal attributes that conveyed assurances. How were these components arranged?

1   The contractual precedents drawn from the merchant community have been discussed. They articulated legal obligations as well as the Victorian conception of service, which shaped the 'spirit' of the agreement.
2   Shipowners installed formal reporting channels (including accounting systems) that supported mutual learning. In addition, informal communication lines followed business, political, religious, and family ties. (The densely interwoven nature of these channels also enabled businessmen to confirm or refute personal impressions derived from a single source and thus deterred opportunism.) As shipowners expanded

their businesses and rose in society, these channels could assume regional, national, and international dimensions. Such conduits helped economic actors make themselves known to prospective contractors, build wider reputations, and establish a presence in larger bargaining arenas. In addition, bargaining fora, such as shipping exchanges, occupational associations, and social venues generated communication that enhanced interpersonal knowledge.

3   A specialised occupational language, recognised communicating conventions, bargaining procedures, and devices for signalling commitment or indifference served to streamline contracting activities. These instruments enabled shipowners to work within or manipulate prevailing values and cognitive patterns in creative ways to engineer confidence.

4   Long-standing and immediately recognisable indicators of position within Britain's social hierarchy provided contractors with a ready-made set of media for signalling stature.[1] Titles, public offices, and maritime organisations provided a finely graduated system for ranking social capital. With a wealth of signalling instruments, men with superior attributes could occupy positions as intermediaries who could broker deals among parties who lacked direct knowledge of each other. By providing the necessary introductory and screening services, these figures acted as communicating nodes that facilitated transactions which in their absence might have failed.

Thus, the various parts of this infrastructure worked together to facilitate transmissions that lowered the cost of making both *ex ante* contractual specifications and *ex post* adjustments as conditions changed.

A dynamic model of shipowner–agent relations[2]

Figure 2.1 depicts the relationship between an agent in New York and a British shipowner who has hired the agent to represent his ships on one route, for example New York–London. (The general reader may chose to focus on the dynamic factors reflected in the company correspondence and overlook references to the Figures depicting the model.) Figure 2.2 represents the agent's wider business in New York, including related operations, such as stevedoring, and other agencies he holds with shipowners outside the New York–London trade. Figure 2.3 shows the shipowner's New York–London line, while Figure 2.4 depicts his overall operations which include other lines.

From the previous description of the historical context, it is assumed that these economic actors work in a commercial community which, although permeated by interrelated communication lines, is still subject to an asymmetric distribution of information. Thus, individuals have different trade-related intelligence and business contacts, whereas knowledge of commissions charged by agents to their various clients is private.

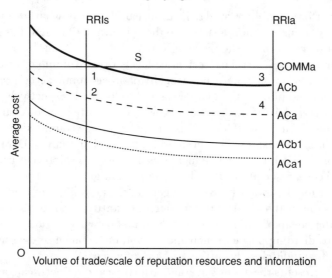

Figure 2.1 Dynamic model of shipowner–agent relationships (see legend to Figure 2.4 for abbreviations)

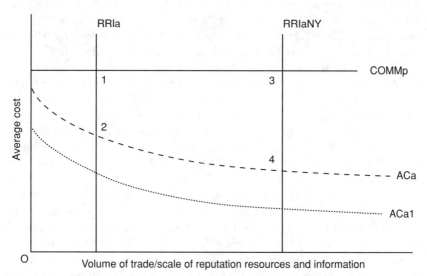

Figure 2.2 Agent's wider business in the Port of New York (see legend to Figure 2.4 for abbreviations)

The shipowner and agent each had a distinct combination of reputation, resources, and information, the three variables that shaped the contracts described above. Their reputations reflect records of past behaviour and social capital. The shipowner has vessels, funds, and knowledge of conditions beyond the New York to London trade. The agent has capital, assets, ancillary resources (for example related to insurance brokering or wharf owning), and contacts within New York. Relative to the shipowner, the agent has superior information concerning the trade of New York.

The four figures correlate cost/price levels to the volume of trade/scale, showing the business-generating capacity of an economic actor's resources, reputation, and information. COMMa and ACb show, respectively, the cost *to the shipowner* of using an agent or his own branch office to book cargo given any volume of business. (COMMa is a flat percentage commission.) When a small volume of business is generated ACb is higher than COMMa, but it declines as the volume of trade increases because the shipowner can spread the fixed costs associated with a branch over a larger amount of business. It is cheaper for the owner to use the agent until the volume of trade reaches O–S (S is the switch point), but for a larger quantity of cargo a branch office will be the cheaper option. Conversely, if a shipowner initially has a large enough trade to support a branch and the volume of business declines to the left of S, he might close his office and hire an agent.

ACa represents the agent's average cost curve and reflects scale and scope effects (agents often represented several owners and offered related ancillary services). The level of his costs relative to the shipowner's branch office costs (ACb) reflects the agent's first-mover advantages. However, the shipowner cannot estimate ACa, but the agent's local information enables him to approximate ACb. ACa1 and ACb1 represent lower-cost levels that the two parties can achieve as trade grows and as learning raises efficiency.

The shipowner and the agent possess reputations, resources, and information that attract a given volume of cargo. Initially, the owner's trade-generating capability is O–RRIs and for the agent RRIs–RRIa (the positions are reversed in Figures 2.3 and 2.4). By co-operating they can win a quantity of cargo equal to O–RRIa. The agent secures a quasi-rent equal to the area 1, 2, 3, 4 in Figure 2.1, and the shipowner gains a similar quasi-rent, shown in Figure 2.3. The initial positions of RRIs and RRIa in Figure 2.1 show the relative power of shipowner and agent.

Both parties also have wider resources, beyond New York and the New York–London trade, that enable them to generate other business and associated quasi-rents. Figure 2.2 shows that by working with the British shipowner who has deployed his vessels in the New York–London trade, the agent can attract a volume of cargo equal to RRIa (this is the same as RRIa in Figure 2.1). The agent's ties with other ship operators who run other lines to New York from other ports generate business equal to RRIa–RRIaNY. From these operations he wins a quasi-rent equal to the area 1, 2, 3, 4 in Figure 2.2. The shipowner also conducts other services using different agents. This additional business is shown as RRIa–RRIsS and the related quasi-rent 1, 2, 3, 4 in Figure 2.4.

Over time, the initial configurations of the lines in these diagrams will change as a result of several factors.

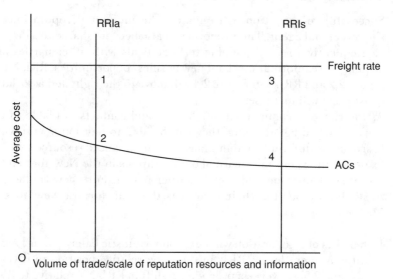

Figure 2.3 Shipowner's London–New York line (see legend to Figure 2.4 for abbreviations)

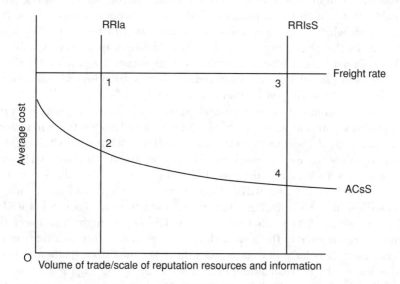

Figure 2.4 Shipowner's wider operations. COMMa, commission charged by agent to shipowner in New York–London trade; COMMp, commission charged by agent to all shipowner clients in New York; ACb, average cost of branch office; ACb1, average cost of branch office after learning effects; ACa, average cost of agent; ACa1, average cost of agent after learning effects; ACs, average cost of shipowner; RRIa/s, reputation resources and information of agent/shipowner

1   Successful co-operation will enhance the individual reputations of shipowner and agent. Their renown will also become shared to a degree. Consequently, they will be able to forge deals with other parties and acquire more information about new business opportunities. RRIaNY in Figure 2.2 and RRIsS in Figure 2.4 will move to the right and associated quasi-rents will increase.

2   As the range of commercial intelligence and contacts available to the shipowner and agent grows, they will be able to develop new services based on the different combinations of their enhanced resource sets. For example, the agent may learn about conditions in the New York end of the Australian trade and the shipowner may acquire new contacts in Australia; by pooling their resources they can form a New York to Melbourne service.

The benefits of co-operation will deter opportunistic behaviour as long as rightward movement leaves RRIs in the same relative position to RRIa in Figures 2.1 and 2.3. However, a pronounced shift in RRIaNY relative to RRIa in Figure 2.2 or a major change in the positions of RRIa and RRIsS in Figure 2.4 may destabilise the relationship. In these cases, the benefit of continued association will decline relative to other, wider ranging opportunities, but a break will diminish the reputation and resource combinations of the two parties on which their business-generating capabilities and quasi-rents depend. In the prevailing cultural context, a break in a long-established relationship will send adverse signals to other prospective or actual business contacts. Only in extreme situations, where the resultant loss is small relative to the gains of working with others, will a break occur.

In less extenuated circumstances, growth will create tensions between owner and agent. For example, as the New York to London trade increases, RRIs in Figure 2.1 will move to the right until it reaches the switch point S, where it will become economic for the shipowner to establish his own branch office in New York. Again, the loss of access to the agent's wider knowledge (RRIa in Figure 2.1 and RRIa–RRIaNY in Figure 2.2) and the resulting diminution in the shipowner's reputation (which would reduce his RRIa–RRIsS in Figure 2.4) tends to deter him. The agent might also lower the commission charged in the New York to London trade to retain a share of his RRIa (which may have moved to the right in the meantime), albeit at some reduction in the corresponding quasi-rent 1, 2, 3, 4 in Figure 2.1. On the other hand, ACa may also fall over time to ACa1 as the agent secures further economies of scale and scope from the growing size and range of operations. The outcome of these movements may not reduce the size of the agent's quasi-rent stream. However, even if ACa and quasi-rent 1, 2, 3, 4 do not change, the agent will tend to be willing to lower his commission to preserve the associated gains he wins in the port of New York (in Figure 2.2 RRIa–RRIaNY and quasi-rent 1, 2, 3, 4). In this case, COMMp will not fall by much because the commissions charged to other shipowners will remain the same (any fall in COMMp will reflect the concession made to the shipowner he serves in the London to New York trade). The switch point will recede as the shipowner obtains a lower commission. However, he will tend not to drive COMMa all the way to ACa for fear of jeopardising his access to future growth in RRIs–RRIa in Figure 2.1, RRIa–RRIaNY in Figure 2.2, and RRIa–RRIsS in Figure 2.4 along with the relevant quasi-rent streams. All of these considerations explain why, in the face of various tensions and shocks, shipowner–agent relationships tended to endure.

Correspondence between shipowners and agents

Company correspondence reveals how shipowners and agents interacted within the communicating infrastructure. The initial decision to use an agent or form a branch depended on whether the shipowner or the agent had the best cargo-generating capabilities, based on their reputations, resources, and information. Moreover, the volume of trade that either party could attract also had to be considered in relation to the agent's commission and a branch's fixed costs. Archival records support close analysis of three situations: stable bilateral relations, breaks in shipowner–agent ties, and take-overs of agents by shipowners. The fourth possibility – a shift from branch to agent – is only alluded to because letters discovered to date provide few details.

Instances of stable shipowner–agent relationships

Stable relationships persisted when agents' commissions remained below a certain threshold (point S) at which forming an office might become the lowest cost option for the vessel operator. An agent who raised his fees risked pushing his client beyond the switch point and signalled opportunistic tendencies. For example, when Furness Withy & Co.'s agent in Rotterdam raised his commissions, Frederick Lewis intimated to J. F. Lund 'that everything is tending towards our having our own office' (FW Lewis Papers, FWL to JFL 27 June 1903). Some impression of the value of commissions in relation to other sources of revenue can be obtained from Lewis's report on Furness's London–Halifax service. In 1902, for example, the fees Furness paid a Halifax agent were higher than the earnings of the ships deployed in the trade (Lewis Papers, Lewis to Furness 10 January 1902). However, no switch occurred at this time because it was still cheaper to use the agent than to run an office. Moreover, when trade was in recession or a client was in difficult circumstances, agents sometimes reduced their commissions on the expectation that long-term profits and gains in reputation derived from continued association would compensate for the short-term sacrifice (FW&Co. Early Correspondence, 1911 Report).

Furness Withy & Co. employed an agent called Mr McPherson to represent their Manchester–Quebec City line (FW&Co. Early Correspondence, Report 7 June 1899). In 1899, Stephen Furness advised his colleagues against setting up an office in Quebec because even though the volume of the firm's business had grown in recent years (RRIs had moved to the right) it was still not large enough to make a branch the lowest cost option. More importantly, McPherson was highly regarded locally and attracted considerable cargo (the balance between O–RRIs and RRIs–RRIa rested in his favour). Six years later trade had grown further, but another Furness manager, F. W. Lewis, felt that the firm should retain the agent:

> [H]aving been associated with Mr McPherson so long, and found him so straight forward, it would not be advantageous to [form an office]. Mr McPherson is a man who has considerable influence, and might be useful in ... subsidy or other negotiations.
>
> (Lewis Papers, Lewis to C. Furness, 19 April 1905)

The agent's reputation, contacts, and information had grown to sustain the relationship (RRIs–RRIa had moved further to the right). Moreover, McPherson's increasing influence within the port might in time support further expansion (based on rightward movement in RRIa–RRIaNY in Figure 2.2). In addition, Furness Withy was deterred from breaking with the agent for fear of undermining its own reputation (causing *leftward* movement in RRIs in Figure 2.1).

Over time, shipowners learned more about the trade of the ports they served, and their assessment of the advantages of agency or branch in relation to long-term business development could change. For example, in 1898, Lewis considered whether Furness Withy should form its own Liverpool office to serve its Newport News and Halifax lines that had been represented by Allan Brothers & Co. He had recently absorbed knowledge about Liverpool's wider trade (RRIa–RRIaNY in Figure 2.2), and this suggested the possibility of developing other routes that the new office could serve (which would lower ACb and bring the switch point closer). 'There is also a very good opening between Philadelphia and Liverpool which could be commenced for the benefit of such an office' (Lewis Papers, Lewis to S. W. Furness, 14 November 1898). In the end, the balance between the trade-generating resources of Allans and Furness did not justify a change.

In 1905, Lewis examined the costs and benefits of replacing Allans as the agent for Furness Withy's Liverpool–Newfoundland line. At the same time, he also considered shifting the booking of Newfoundland-bound cargo originating in London *from* Furness Withy's office at that port to an agency run by Allans:

> Allans could not obtain for us any [London] freight that we could not obtain for ourselves. In the Liverpool trade it is different. They have been running the ... business for a number of years, the connection of which we have no doubt had the advantage. In London, however, the Furness Line has been running this trade for nearly a quarter of a century

... [I]f we were to place the [London] outward business in their hands it would be putting a weapon and organisation into their possession and if we ever wanted to take the business [back] for ourselves ... we would be in a more difficult position on account of the *knowledge* they would have gained. [T]his inclines my opinion towards letting the arrangements stand as they are.

(Lewis Papers, Lewis to FW West Hartlepool office, 28 August 1905)

This letter provides two insights. First, Lewis knew that Allans and Furness Withy had distinct sets of reputations, resources, and information that sustained the use of an agency in Liverpool and an office in London (O–RRIs and RRIs–RRIa remained stable relative to each other in both cases). However, he also understood that changes in these sets could cause arrangements to shift in *either direction*, from agency to branch (if O–RRIs shifted in relation to RRIs–RRIa) or from office to agency (if RRIs–RRIa moved relative to O–RRIs). (Similarly, difficulties in maintaining its resource set in the 1890s led Furness Withy to replace its Baltimore and Chicago offices with agents.) Second, Lewis realised that a change from branch to agency or vice versa also posed risks. Displacing Allans in Liverpool could cost Furness cargo and a loss of reputation. Allowing agents, especially ones like Allans who possessed their own ships, to gain access to Furness Withy's London contacts could provide them with an opportunity to enlarge dramatically their London-based resource set (RRIs–RRIa in Figure 2.1 and RRIa–RRIaNY in Figure 2.2 both move decisively to the right). Consequently, Furness Withy might not be able to re-establish a branch at a later date if it wished to do so, or, more seriously, Allans might use their new-found advantage to set up their own shipping service and displace Furness Withy entirely. In the long run, an appropriate balance between the local advantages of each firm preserved the existing arrangements.

Such parity in itself generated interdependence, while concern for reputation also deterred opportunism. However, members of the shipping community also forged side deals, using their wider resource sets (RRIa–RRIaNY in Figure 2.2 and RRIa–RRIsS in Figure 2.4), to 'nest' their contracts (Tsebelis 1990). This standard tactic served to build a broader foundation for achieving mutual growth and for creating interlocking deterrents.

Examples of nesting activities are abundant. Using his knowledge of conditions in the Far East, John Swire, Alfred Holt's agent in China, induced his client to invest in a series of manufacturing and service sector ventures (see Chapter 3). Similarly, the agency firm Madura & Co. represented British India at six ports in order to build interdependence. Furness enmeshed Allans in a complex matrix of contracts including joint shipping services, overlapping agency ties, and finance for ship orders. Although 'nested' contracts served as a deterrent effect, they could also be used to punish opportunists.

Instances of breaks in shipowner–agent ties

In one case, Furness did use interrelated contracts to punish an unfaithful agent, Ronaldson, who, believing he could achieve greater growth by allying with a larger carrier, invited the Canadian Pacific Railway Company (CPR) into a Canada–Holland trade previously run jointly by Ronaldson, Furness, and Muller. Furness retaliated by calling in bills that were running on a vessel Ronaldson had purchased from his shipyard and bankrupted the agent (Boyce 1995a: 167). Furness's ability to translate the deterrent power of nested contracts into overt force depended upon the terms of the sales contract for the ship. Moreover, he had to demonstrate convincingly that he operated within established behavioural rules to avoid reputation loss; the fact that he abandoned forbearance only after Ronaldson had done so first probably enhanced Furness's renown, especially in Muller's view (see Buckley and Casson, 1988). Furness's capacity to inflict punishment also hinged on his having sufficient resources to substitute for the assets supplied by Ronaldson or withstand a short-term loss.

Disparity in resource sets was just one factor that could deter opportunism (it might also provoke aggression by the stronger party). The quality of resources is another. This point is illustrated by the contrasting case of Mr Darby, an agent whose association with the Bucknall family had been terminated for unknown reasons. Darby punished Bucknalls by providing Furness with information that this rival needed to invade the former client's Persian Gulf route. Like Ronaldsons, Bucknalls failed to recognise disparities in the quality and the extent of the resources that could be mobilised by those whom they betrayed. Such recognition was vital if nesting tactics were to prevent opportunism.

Apart from opportunism resulting from such miscalculation, agent–shipowner breaks occurred for a variety of other reasons. At the turn of the nineteenth century, Furness Withy transferred its Newfoundland agency from a Mr Schofield to Thomson & Co. because the former antagonised Furness representatives and because he was not sufficiently diligent (FW&Co, Early correspondence, reports 1899, 1901). Thomsons energetically solicited merchants for cargo and had strong contacts, including a link with the President of the Board of Trade (their capacity to expand RRIs–RRIa was much stronger than that of Schofield). Merchants and other agents who were aware of Schofield's poor reputation and Thomsons' influence and business-like methods would probably have more rather than less regard for Furness Withy after the change in their arrangements at St Johns.

Sudden accretions in a participant's resources could cause breaks. For example, when Sir John Ellerman purchased a new fleet his view of the advantages of his agency arrangements changed enough to induce him to displace Allans as his Liverpool cargo representative in 1905 (UGD 131/1/34/2/1). To understand this break, it is necessary to outline the growth of Ellerman's interests. In 1901, he acquired two shipping firms: the City Line, which ran from Glasgow to Bombay and Karachi with calls at Liverpool, and the Hall Line, which operated a service between Liverpool and Bombay and Karachi. The City Line had an office in Glasgow, but it relied upon Allans to represent it in Liverpool, whereas the Hall Line had its own Liverpool house (Taylor 1972).

Ellerman informed W. S. Workman, the Hall Line manager, that he had 'long felt that the steamers [of the two lines] would work to much greater advantage if [*cargo booking operations only*] were under one firm's management in Liverpool and that firm ours [sic], any commission made being earned by such firm' (7 November 1905). (Thus, he anticipated that combining booking arrangements in Liverpool would lower ACb relative to ACa.) Moreover, 'the loading and allocating of cargo to given steamers ought to be in the hands of one man' to increase operating efficiency. The real catalyst for change was a pronounced shift in Ellerman's resource set brought about by the purchase of five large passenger and cargo steamers 'which were never contemplated to be run in your service [but] are now being put on your berth'. (As a result, Ellerman's RRIs moved decisively to the right in relation to Allan's RRIa). Thus, although operating efficiencies had been available, he did not exploit them until his resources changed radically (movement in RRIs combined with a prospective decline in ACb took him beyond S).

To implement his decision, Ellerman had to manipulate prevailing cultural norms. He wrote to W. Beckett-Hill of Allan Brothers citing the legal terms of the formal agency contract 'I in no way recognise, and have never recognised, that an Agency agreement, of however long standing, is anything but an Agency agreement which can be terminated at will' subject to the provisions of the contract (7 November 1905). In keeping with recognised standards of conduct, however, he offered Allan Brothers compensation equal to six year's commission on the understanding 'that you will give your friendly co-operation where possible, and we should propose to continue advertising your firm as passenger agents' (in effect, he capitalised the portion of Allan Brothers' quasi-rent, 1, 2, 3, 4, corresponding to their cargo business). To Workman he confided 'I do feel that with the intimate relations that have existed for so long it would be equitable to give them a very liberal sum' (7 November 1905). Ellerman recognised that in truth agency agreements were not transient arrangements that could be terminated on efficiency grounds alone. He retained Allans as passenger agents in recognition of their strong position in this sector and their retaliatory capabilities based on possession of their own passenger vessels (p. 25).

Beckett-Hill was worried that his firm might lose Ellerman's passenger agency as well as the cargo business and that other clients might view Ellerman's actions as a signal that he lacked confidence in the Allan organisation. He replied to Ellerman that he understood the attraction of rationalising cargo booking arrangements. However, he did

> not think that it would be any particular advantage to your good self in expense or otherwise but a great disadvantage. Under the present

arrangement you get the benefit of both the 'Hall' Line connection and our connection, and there is a certain amount of rivalry in securing cargo, which keeps both firms on their mettle.

(Beckett-Hill to Ellerman, 8 November 1905)

In Beckett-Hill's view, rivalry based on the two firms' different cargo-generating capabilities gave rise to greater efficiency and a larger volume of business than Ellerman could win by rationalisation.

Beckett-Hill also warned Ellerman that concentration might encourage merchants to support a new entrant. 'Shippers at present have two Lines and two brokers to deal with, and do not see or feel a monopoly to which they would be bitterly opposed' (9 November 1905). Most merchants probably knew that Ellerman owned both the Hall and the City lines, but, in Beckett-Hill's view, they must have believed that an element of rivalry still existed. The consolidation of the freight agencies would dispel this belief and possibly attract other firms to the trade (causing Ellerman's O–RRIs to decline).

To dissuade Ellerman from rationalising his operation, Beckett-Hill pointed out:

> For the development of the passenger trade it is very desirable that the Agency at the port of departure should be a firm with a reputation – as I venture to think the 'Allan' Line has – for dealing handsomely with passengers ... [I]n order to make a success of the trade it is necessary to have experienced staff, used to the idiosyncrasies of passengers ... Such a staff is not readily obtained and would cost you much more than you pay us, as you can easily see on reference. But we work your business with our own.
>
> (8 November 1905)

Thus, Beckett-Hill argued that Allan Brothers' reputation and the service skills of its staff would generate more future business (represented by a growing O–RRIs) than Ellerman could win by hiring personnel to handle the business (O–RRIs). Moreover, Ellerman could not match Allan's costs, which were reduced by economies of scope secured by running their own passenger services to Canada in conjunction with his lines to India (AC_a was lower than AC_b; note how Beckett-Hill suggested that Ellerman could determine the positions of the two cost curves, indicating how learning effects could erode one of our assumptions above). By indicating his intention to retain Allans as passenger agent, Ellerman recognised the cost and business-generating advantages: Beckett-Hill wanted to re-enforce this point.

More bluntly, Beckett-Hill reminded Ellerman of Allan Brothers' capacity to employ its wider resources (Figure 2.2 RRIa–RRIaNY and, since Allans owned ships, in Figure 2.4 RRIa–RRIsS) to his disadvantage:

> With regard to Karachi we have done a good deal to develop this growing

trade, and I feel that if withdrawn from us, I could not pledge the Allans to give up a valuable business from this West coast [port] – specially useful when the St. Lawrence is closed and they have a parcel of passenger and cargo boats unemployed.

(8 November 1905)

Having accumulated considerable trade-specific knowledge and with suitable vessels idle on a seasonal basis, Allans could easily enter the trade (and reduce Ellerman's O–RRIs).

This threat clearly got Ellerman's attention. He confided to Workman that he wondered whether 'we have been quite wise in giving them [Allans] such control over the Liverpool portion of our business' (9 November 1905). Ellerman was therefore in the same position that Lewis of Furness Withy could foresee arising if his firm allowed Allans to represent their Canadian line at its London terminus.

To Workman he stated further that Beckett-Hill's letters 'are not written in quite the strain which I should have liked to receive from *a colleague* with whom we have worked so long' (emphasis added). In contrast to the view that agency ties could be 'terminated at will', a view that Ellerman put forward as a negotiating stance when he initially broached the possibility of a break, this quotation from an internal memo reveals how he really conceived of agency relations. Such links were founded on co-operation, give and take, accepted patterns of behaviour, and recognised efficiency criteria.

The two parties met and reached an amicable settlement whereby Ellerman would withdraw the cargo agency and pay compensation to Allans, and Allans would continue to book passengers for his line. In confirming the new arrangement, which would take effect at the end of 1906, Beckett-Hill wrote to Ellerman: 'I ... undertak[e] to make no difficulty should you then persist in the policy set forth in your favour of the 7th ultimo. I do this the more readily as I feel convinced that further reflection and another year's experience may perhaps lead you to reconsideration' (4 December 1905). He was willing to let time reveal whether the advantages of association proved to be greater than the internal efficiencies that Ellerman expected from consolidation. Beckett-Hill realised that long-term relations were based upon mutual advantages. Ellerman replied that Beckett-Hill's letter was:

Only what I should have expected from you as I feel sure you would at all times do everything you could to further what was believed to be in the general interests of the Line as a whole, even though such might be of a slight disadvantage to your good self. I thank you most sincerely again for coming to the arrangement and, if, during another year's experience, there should be any reason to change my present very strong feeling, I shall be only too pleased to do so. As you know, all I wish for is to work the Lines to best advantage.

(5 December 1905)

Thus, the two men established a new common perspective to support their business relationship in a modified form. Both recognised the fundamental importance of efficiency considerations in determining the best organisational structure for the service. They also understood that the institutional arrangements might shift in either direction – from agency to branch or vice versa – and they adopted a flexible stance towards making any future adjustments. However, Allans' position soon deteriorated, and in 1909 the CPR acquired control of the firm. The following year, Ellerman terminated Allan's passenger agency, but he paid them additional compensation [thereby capitalising the remaining RRIs–RRIa 1, 2, 3, 4 in Figure 2.1 (UGD 131/2/1/ 1, 30 May 1910)].

Examples of shipowners acquiring agencies

Company documents record instances in which shipowners bought out their agents. Usually, these acquisitions occurred when a senior partner in the agency died or retired or when the agency faced bankruptcy. In such circumstances, shipowners were quick to effect a take-over for fear that rivals might gain access to an agent's trade-specific knowledge or that agency staff might defect to other firms taking contacts and information with them.

Stephanie Jones's account of the reconstitution of the bankrupt Adamson Bell agency as Dodwell Carlill & Co. in 1892 confirms how imperative it was to protect contacts and information when an agency became vulnerable. Seeing the firm weakening, manager G. B. Dodwell planned in advance for the immediate transfer of agency connections and staff to a new firm should Adamson Bell fail. '[S]ealed instructions were drawn up and addressed to all constituents and agents, containing full instructions for carrying on transactions already in progress and advertising the new company, to be opened at the receipt of a single word by cable – "Haddock"' (Jones 1985: 33). So swift was the transformation that alert rivals, including John Swire, were unable to poach clients from the dying firm.

Instances of clients acquiring vulnerable agents abound. Holt bought Mansfields when a senior partner retired in 1903, and General Steam Navigation purchased four agencies when their founders died (Falkus 1990: 79; NMM GSN/1/38). Donaldsons and Thomsons jointly acquired Robert Reford & Co., and Cunard and Booth's took over Funch Edye when these agencies began to lose their viability (Boyce 1995a: 146). In most cases, shipowners preserved the house names of agencies in order to safeguard the goodwill and the reputations of the firms for which they generally had paid handsomely. The Furness records reveal in some detail why and how shipowners took over failing agents.

Furness Withy purchased the business of the Newfoundland agent, one Mr Pitt, who had replaced Thomsons, when Pitt's health deteriorated and business became 'of secondary interest to him' (Report 1911). Stephen Furness, who arranged the acquisition, assessed each employee's capability.

'The Kennedys [employees] know the whole of Pitt's business, and are specially familiar with the Liverpool business, and I think there are possibilities for the development of a Merchant business'. (These staff members could maintain RRIs–RRIa for the Liverpool trade and RRIa–RRIaNY for the business in St Johns). With access to Pitt's local information, Stephen could see potential for future growth (adding merchant operations would lower ACb and propel RRIaNY rightward by capturing scope effects).

Interestingly, Furness Withy did not preserve the identity of Pitt's agency. Instead, they used their own company title, because it was better recognised than Pitt's. The shipping firm also instated one of its own managers, Montgomerie, who 'possesses qualifications, which I believe will enable him to become respected by the best people in Newfoundland' (1911 Report). Stephen Furness apparently felt that Montgomerie had greater capabilities than the Kennedy brothers for developing high-level business contacts in the port. Stephen Furness's aim was to enhance the stature and contacts of the new branch while preserving the management skills and local knowledge of the Kennedy brothers. (Blending the capabilities of Montgomerie and the Kennedy brothers would extend RRIa and RRIaNY in Figure 2.2.)

By 1911, Furness Withy's Baltimore agent was vulnerable to staff defection (which would cause RRIa in Figure 2.1 and RRIaNY in 2.2 to shift left). Stephen Furness observed that the senior partners, 'Dresel and Rauschenberg practically do nothing, and ... it is just a question of time [before junior partner] Sidebotham ... start[s] on his own account, or take[s] ... a larger interest' in the firm (1911 Report). He took the precaution of entering into 'a private arrangement with [Sidebotham] that he make no agreements to bind his future without consulting me'. This informal undertaking – based on the word of both men – held until Furness Withy acquired the agency in 1915.

Furness Withy paid US$50,000 for the firm (the capitalisation of rent stream 1, 2, 3, 4), but of this sum Dresel – by then the only remaining senior partner – allowed Sidebotham only US$10,000 (FW Legal Lewis to Sidebotham, 9 March 1915). To safeguard the junior partner's co-operation Furness Withy 'privately allow[ed him] an additional $5,000'. The firm also raised Sidebotham's salary to US$10,000 (to assure his contribution to future growth in RRIa in Figure 2.1 and RRIaNY in Figure 2.2). To preserve goodwill and staff-specific reputation, Lewis asked H. Blackiston, head of Furness Withy's US operations, to 'put a suitable paragraph in the American papers to the effect that Furness Withy have acquired the business of Dresel Rauschenberg which will be under the management of A. F. Sidebotham who has been connected with the previous firm for so many years'.

Furness Withy also retained the identity of its Philadelphia agency, Charles H. Taylor & Sons, which it acquired in 1915. The sons of the founder, F. W. Taylor and J. S. Taylor, wished to retire and secured US$200,000 for the firm (FW Legal, 1916, Taylor & Sons). Initially, Blackiston feared that retaining the former owners would reduce future growth (cause RRIs–RRIa in Figure

2.1 and O–RRIaNY in Figure 2.2 to shift right). He was concerned lest 'there was … to be a feeling of dormant antagonism toward us by the Brothers Taylor and … the clerks would find it difficult to disassociate themselves from Taylor practices'. However, Blackiston soon changed his view: 'the Brothers Taylor have met us in a friendly aspect' and 'Mr F. W. Taylor would be a valuable asset if we could keep him …'.

Blackiston appraised the agency's other personnel for senior Furness executives:

> I had a long talk with Fred Taylor, after business hours at the hotel, and he speaks very complimentary [sic] of Barton and thinks he would be quite suitable for the position [of Office Manager]. He also thinks that we are fortunate in having Mr John A. Tait a very capable, energetic man, whom we have appointed General Manager of Stevedoring. [Tait] will be able to attend to the stevedoring organisation without any necessity for Barton's time to be taken up with these details, leaving the latter free to give his attention to office organisation, freight solicitation etc.

> (FW Legal, 1916, Taylor & Sons)

The combination of people at the agency suggested ways of lowering costs and promoting new business (ACb would fall to ACb1 and RRIa–RRIaNY would shift right).

Blackiston was pleased with the deal as a whole. 'The more I think of it the better pleased I am that we have been able to get hold of the business on such satisfactory terms, because, an open fight would have been a serious matter with serious possibilities'. He recognised that setting up a branch to displace Taylors and running the risk that a rival shipowner might acquire the firm could have resulted in Furness Withy not only losing the agency's local information but having this knowledge used against it.

These cases show that removing the information asymmetry by acquiring an agency exposed new sets of complementary resources within the newly integrated firm. (The same combinations could be exploited across firm boundaries when there was adequate trust, as it was within the network examined in the next chapter.) The capacity of the acquiring firm to harness the revealed resource mix depended on it reforming – as quickly as possible – the basis of trust with the vendor and his staff. This is precisely what Blackiston achieved after business hours in that timeless contracting forum, the hotel. He could do so because Furness Withy previously had had a strong relationship with Taylors and had acted honourably during the acquisition negotiations.

Conclusion

Our model presents reputation, resources, and information along with cost levels and prices (commissions) as an alternative set of factors to that advanced by Williamson to explain the dynamics of bilateral relationships. The main variables, shown as RRI, are important because they affect future growth directly while the communicating processes that reveal them shape institutional efficiency in ways that proceed beyond minimising transaction costs. Our principal factors also draw analysis closer towards the social and cultural context in which relationships unfold, and they emphasise human capital considerations, thereby highlighting the influence of power, learning effects, and changes in personal stature.

The framework used here may, with appropriate modifications, prove useful for analysts interested in the wider range of bilateral relations, including other forms of agency ties (see French 1994), preferential supply agreements, and joint ventures. Moreover, business leaders may find it useful to consider these variables when forming, revising, or assessing contractual arrangements. Thus, evaluation of their organisations' RRI may reveal qualitative or quantitative deficiencies, overdependence on one or two elements within the set, or areas that require further investment. (For example, today some travel agents are strengthening their positions in response to pricing pressure from airlines by investing in closer client relationships and information channels needed to assemble packages of services, *The Economist*, 10 January 1998.) Alternatively, such assessment may point to strengths that offer opportunities to contract with other firms.

The design of shipowner–agent agreements, with their heavy reliance on culture, represents just one possible configuration of the three basic elements of contracts. This particular combination was appropriate for the type of people involved, the broader context in which exchanges took place, and their contracting objectives. It was especially cost-effective for transactions involving people who shared particular values and cognitive processes. However, these cultural attributes were not associated with a specific national affiliation but rather with an international occupation that included, as our examples show, people from Britain, Canada, the US, and elsewhere. That economic actors may be affiliated with multiple cultures and subcultures draws attention to the broad scope for arranging contracts based on this mix.

The type of co-operation that unfolded within the marine sector was not of an altruistic or naïve nature. It was active and vigilant. Relationships reflected mutual awareness of each party's knowledge sets, resources, and renown. Participants knew that they had to deliberately manage their reputations in convincing ways, and they understood how others could interpret their signals. Indeed, their rich vocabulary provided a battery of nuances that were difficult for participants to misunderstand. The words they used reflected co-operative courtesy typical of 'gentlemanly conduct' but did not mask deterrent capability. One of their favourite, set-piece devises was the 'nested' contract, which compelled contractors to show commitment up front. For shipowners, requesting and agreeing to such an arrangement was a powerful form of emission.

The broader context in which this type of hard-headed deal making unfolded was shaped by a munificent communicating infrastructure. (The components of this framework deserve practitioners' attention; in a different garb they are relevant today, as Chapter 12 shows.) Maritime entrepreneurs were indeed fortunate in having at their disposal a ready-made, widely recognised, public construct. They did not have to learn how to use an unfamiliar framework, and they did not have to allocate resources to build one from scratch to span social or corporate frontiers. The elaborate yet flexible structure lowered the cost of engaging in the types of subtle exchanges needed to demonstrate observance of communicative rationality and above all to build trust. These attributes fitted the nature of the contracts shipowners and agents arranged. Trust was a prerequisite for making transactions involving a specific type of knowledge that generated quasi-rents which were vulnerable to swift dissipation in the event of disclosure. The form of contract examined here, and contracting processes in general, have fundamental implications for human resource development. This is one of the themes explored in the following chapter.

3 A family-based network

The Holt–Swire–Scott connection,
decision-support systems and staff
development, 1860–1970

This chapter extends the previous analysis of the links between contract design, communication, and transaction type beyond a bilateral agency relationship to a multilateral network. Specifically, it explores how new contractual threads can be created to build a diversified web of alliances. Treating the network explicitly as an information system, which is dependent upon complementary decision-making processes and personnel attributes, reveals a set of trade-offs that arise when co-operative activities are pursued.

In recent years, numerous historical and theoretical studies have developed a more refined definition of business networks and a more intimate description of their functions (Thorelli 1986; Powell 1990; Nohria and Eccles 1992; Boyce 1995a). In general terms, networks may be described as multilateral co-operative relationships that lack a central co-ordinating authority. Members (individuals or firms) influence each other in an interdependent manner. Accepting a long-term view of relationships, they engage in reciprocal exchange, share risks, and promote mutual growth. Networks exhibit some degree of exclusiveness as a guard against opportunism, and they mobilise reputation-based incentives and powerful sanctions that are administered directly and informally. As intermediate transacting frameworks, networks rely on reciprocity and trust to provide governance, facilitate knowledge transfers, and sustain collaborative learning.

Some investigators recognise that networks are in fact information systems that possess special properties (Powell 1990; Casson 1997). First, networks have more extensive lateral links than hierarchies. Second, they are very responsive to external stimuli because constituents are connected directly with one another: messages do not have to flow through prescribed channels to a central authority that interprets them before sub-units can use the information. Third, although they are to a degree exclusive, the communication lines of networks are more open-ended than those of hierarchies. Fourth, the contents of these conduits are very 'free-flowing' and much 'thicker' than that which circulates within hierarchies. Network information consists of high-quality, 'inside' intelligence as well as tacit knowledge. (Markets are not adept at handling transactions involving non-codified knowledge.) Moreover, as Powell (1990) suggests, information that circulates within networks is more likely to create new meanings or interpretations than data transmitted through markets or firms. Fifth, network information provides a stronger *context* for joint learning because it is not filtered as much as it is in firms nor as 'raw' as it is in markets. Thus, processing activities in networks are not as constrained as they are in hierarchies or as unfocused as they are in markets.

The circumstances in which networks exist will affect their capabilities as systems. Environmental conditions that give rise to high levels of uncertainty increase the demand for accurate, high-quality information. Moreover, external turbulence is more likely to dislocate network linkages, whereas excessive placidity will tend to cause ossification. Conversely, the internal composition of networks will affect how their systems operate. When membership is extremely homogeneous, communication will be more efficient, but over time the networks may become 'in-grown'. In contrast, when constituents are heterogeneous the variety of stimulation may increase bounded rationality and communicating difficulties. Effective network operations depend upon how these conflicting forces are aligned.

This chapter takes up Powell's (1990: 328) call for more investigation into how networks process information and sustain learning. The subject is the Holt–Scott–Swire (HSS) alliance, which, lasting for over a century, stands out as one of the most enduring networks in British business (Hyde 1957; Marriner and Hyde 1967; Drage 1970; Falkus 1990; Robb 1993). Of the three contractual elements discussed previously, the HSS network relied most heavily on culture, and to a lesser degree upon formal legal provisions and monitoring mechanisms. Member firms created a communicating infrastructure to reduce the cost of communicating. (The following case examines a part of this framework that was custom-made expressly to include a new constituent.) The aim of this chapter is to assess the information gathering and processing capabilities of the network using the principles of systems design.

The principles of system design

Virtually all systems are 'open' in the sense that they interact with an external environment; the 'closed' system is an abstraction (Senn 1989). Any type of system needs to have performance standards, methods for assessing operating efficiency, and feedback mechanisms that make it possible to compare actual performance against the standard and devise improvements. When creating these formal components, systems designers should also consider informal communication lines, interdependent linkages, and the roles of people who occupy nodes within the framework.

All of these design features are to be found in each of the three basic types of system. These are, first of all, transaction processing systems (TPS), which conduct bookkeeping functions. Second, management information systems (MIS) support 'structured' decisions that are routine in nature and which, being based upon known variables that interact in familiar ways, can be reported on in a standardised format. Third, Decision-support systems (DSSs) are used for strategic, non-routine decisions for which there are no readily apparent procedures and where all relevant variables are not obvious *ex ante*. Those conditions preclude standardised reporting and often necessitate sequential information searching and processing activities.

The operating requirements of the HSS network placed heavy demands on those who designed its systems. First, member firms jointly developed a wide range of businesses, including shipping, agency operations, shipbuilding, engineering, paint making, sugar refining, and airline operations. The fact that these units were run by managers who possessed specialised knowledge and skills posed assessment challenges for principals who lacked the same depth of expertise. Second, operations were dispersed as far afield as Greenock, London, Africa, the Caribbean, Australia, and the Far East. The geographic expanse of the business necessitated delegation to executives who had local knowledge that was not immediately available to their seniors in the UK. To harness such specialised knowledge over great distance and reduce the effect of information asymmetry required considerable systems expertise.

While developing their system, senior managers had to devise human resource policies that generated high levels of interpersonal knowledge and trust that would sustain inter-firm co-operation. Over time, they were compelled to develop methods for accommodating staff from diverse backgrounds in order to secure the specialised expertise needed to pursue diversified growth. Top level officials created interlocking feedback mechanisms that supported the ongoing assessment of executive talent.

This chapter consists of three parts. The first describes the network's structure, its interconnected lateral ties, and its open-ended nature. The second section uses a series of business development ventures undertaken by the HSS network to examine specifically its Decision-support system. Here, the aim is to show how the network attracted a flow of data that was free and thick in order to furnish members with a context for collaborative learning and for interpreting phenomena in new ways. The final segment considers the network's human resource policies. It explores how member firms used a social and cultural construct to sustain co-operation, and how they adjusted this framework to accommodate new constituents who had specialised knowledge that was needed to support diversification. Decision-makers took pains to strike a balance between homogeneity and heterogeneity in terms of staff composition.

Network structure

As Figure 3.1 shows, the core of the network consisted of three main nodes, Alfred Holt & Co. [Ocean Steam Ship Co. (OSS)], John Scott & Co. (JS), and John Swire & Sons (JSS). These firms established overlapping operating and

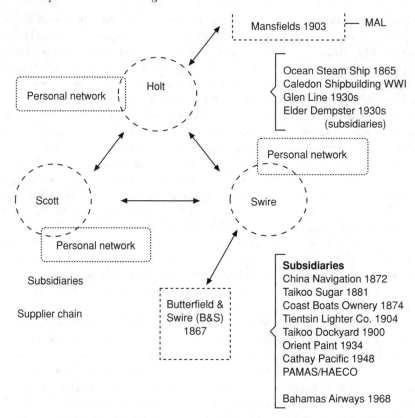

Figure 3.1 Links in the Holt–Swire–Scott network 1860s to 1970s. Other formal
contracts linked HSS constituents. These agreements served a variety of
purposes other than reinforcing pre-existing levels of trust. They acted as
a safeguard against intrusion by outsiders and directed non-dividend
revenue streams to specific affiliates (see Jones and Wale 1997)

financial ties in the 1860s to mobilise the set of complementary resources
that Holt needed to pioneer a new steam service to the Far East. Holts
contributed engineering and commercial expertise, Scotts built and helped
to finance Holts' ships, and Swires provided capital and acted as agent in
Shanghai and Hong Kong. Each founder of the three firms drew upon a
personal network in his home port to attract resources from outside the
network core. Over time, these private connections became intertwined.

   In the 1860s, the network also developed two secondary nodes, agency
firms Mansfields in Singapore and Butterfield & Swire, which established
branches throughout the Far East. These supporting units forged a wider
range of local contacts that were open-ended in terms of providing access to
external intelligence.

   The network's lateral links became more extensive as the three core firms
and the two secondary nodes formed subsidiaries. These new units formed

operating, financial, and managerial ties with primary and secondary nodes, members of the founders' personal networks, and outside interests. All network entities created direct links with each other to muster information and to promote collaboration.

Holts was initially backed by a personal network consisting of family members, Liverpool merchants, and shipowners, including Booths, Rathbones, and Lamports. OSS acquired an important rival, China Mutual in 1902–3, and took over three other shipping firms during World War I. Also, during the conflict the Holts invested in Scotts, Caledon Shipbuilding, and several engineering companies (Falkus 1990: 163). In the inter-war years, OSS took over the Glen Line and Elder Dempster, the latter being a broadly diversified business with airline interests. Mansfields, which Holts acquired in 1903, set up Malayan Airways (the forerunner of Singapore Air). Holts also invested in Bahamas Airways, which Swires took over in the late 1960s. By the early 1970s, OSS, which had been renamed Ocean Transport & Trading and listed on the London Stock Exchange, had become a diverse business group.

In its early years, merchant firm JSS drew support from a personal Liverpool-based network consisting of Ismay Imrie & Co., of White Star Line fame, insurance broker R. N. Dale, the Butterfield brothers, and sugar firms in London and Glasgow. After its formation in Shanghai in 1867, Butterfield & Swire (B&S) had set up fifteen branches in Asia by the 1890s. In league with other merchants, Swire also established agencies in Australia to represent shipping lines (including White Star). With the aid of insurance agents, merchant allies, and Scott, Swire founded the China Navigation Co. (CN) in 1872 to provide steam services on the Yangtse and act as a feeder for OSS. In 1874, Butterfield, Scott, and Swire formed the Coast Boats Ownery to run coastal services, and merged the new line with CN in 1883. The Tientsin Lighter Company, a joint venture with A. Holt & Co. followed in 1904. Swires founded its first industrial enterprise in the East, the Taikoo Sugar Refinery (TSR) in 1881 with support from Holts and other allies. The Taikoo Dockyard and Engineering Co. (TD&E) was set up in Hong Kong in 1900. TSR provided cargoes for CN, and TD&E built ships for CN, OSS, and Elder Dempster. B&S set up a paint factory in 1934 in alliance with an outside firm, Pinchin & Johnson, and later merged this with the Hong Kong interests of another non-network firm, Duro Paint. Swires entered the air in 1948 by acquiring a large interest in Cathay Pacific Airways with assistance from the Holymans, who ran Australian National Airways (ANA). TD&E and ANA collaborated to form the Pacific Air Maintenance and Supply Co. Ltd (PAMAS), which serviced aircraft. Swires also acquired Bahamas Airways Ltd in 1968 but was unable to make a success of the venture.

The third pillar of the network, Scotts of Greenock acted as lead shipbuilder for both Holts and Swires. Between 1868 and 1920 these two shipowners ordered 138 ships representing forty-four per cent of the value of all Scotts' contracts. Scotts also built vessels for Swires' Liverpool allies, Lamport & Holt, Rathbones, and Booths as well as for Elder Dempster after it was taken over by OSS (GD 319/11/1/20). Scotts became TD&E's technical adviser and with its extensive supplier chain in Scotland acted as purchasing agent for the Hong Kong yard. Scotts disappeared from the network in 1970, when it was included in a government rationalisation scheme.

Over a century, the network grew in a cumulative and interdependent fashion, despite the fact that Asia was a highly turbulent environment. (JSS's business and parts of Holts' operations were severely dislocated during World War II and to a lesser extent during the Communist take-over of China.) Despite these difficulties, the network successfully handled technological transitions ranging from steam engines to jet aircraft and expanded its operations from shipping to manufacturing and air services. The information and resources needed to support diversification were drawn through open-ended communication lines that connected affiliates with outside interests and through extensive lateral links within the network itself.

Decision-support systems

This section analyses three non-routine business development decisions that propelled the network in new directions. The ventures are TSR (1881), TD&E (1900), and air operations, including Cathay Pacific Airways (1948) and PAMAS (1947). All of the enterprises were situated in the Far East, a turbulent environment where high levels of uncertainty called for accurate information and rapid processing capabilities. The initiative for these projects came from within the Swire organisation.

JSS partners, who were based in London after 1871, had final responsibility for business development decisions. In order to obtain the local intelligence and specialised knowledge needed to diversify beyond the network's core capabilities, they consulted with affiliates and built a progressively wider set of communication lines with outside firms. London officials conducted ongoing dialogues with these interests to learn collaboratively and to develop fresh interpretations of phenomena. The following sections show how the network's DSS expanded and operated.

The Taikoo Sugar Refinery

TSR was supported by many of Swire's personal allies who had invested in CN, which JSS formed ten years earlier. Other figures who possessed specialised knowledge needed to assist the project gravitated to the network. Thus, TSR was an outgrowth of existing links and a device for extending Swire's contacts.

John Swire studied the sugar refinery proposal for three years before he approached 'friends who have been fortunate in their (previous) investments through us' to commit their funds in June 1881 (JSSIX 1/5 box 1087 J. Swire to Butterfield, 18 June 1881). JSS and B&S had investigated production costs, technological alternatives, and sales prospects. Swire based his projections on Richardson's refinery, which was the most up to date in the UK (Marriner and Hyde 1957: 98–9). Plans, staffing estimates, and fuel consumption data were sent to B&S, which calculated costs under local conditions. B&S also evaluated Eastern markets and forwarded local sugar for analysis to the Fairries, the family of Swire's first wife, who were sugar refiners in Greenock. B&S found out that the Hong Kong refinery run by a rival trading house, Jardine Matheson, was in a weak competitive position since it was 'burdened with a large capital, thro' [sic] having bought up some plant that ... proved to be unsuited to the sugar' (ibid. JSS to P. H. Holt, 10 June 1881). Swire also asked his Far East partners to find out about Jardines' suppliers and selling practices (ibid. JSS to Lang, Scott, and MacIntosh, 20 May 1881).

In a private circular letter, Swire gave prospective investors a strong signal about the incentive structure underlying the project when he told them that B&S would handle TSR's commercial operations business free of commission until specific profit targets were attained (ibid., 13 June 1881 ff.). Personal invitations to invest included information needed to assess risk and signals of commitment from core network members. Indeed, Swire, the Holts, and their close allies had reserved for themselves seventy-two per cent of the capital. In framing his proposal, Swire suggested 'anyone who wants a safe 8 or 10 per cent per annum to comfort his declining years, may, I believe calculate on that' (ibid. JSS to P. H. Holt, 10 June 1881). The implication was clear; Swire accepted the heavy responsibility for directing the funds of ageing allies towards a safe haven capable of generating a dependable retirement income. By mid-November all the shares had been allotted.

Between the time Swire issued the circular in June and mid-November, the network was mobilised to put the remaining pieces of the project in place. Securing an experienced manager was the most important concern, and B&S, Scott, James Barrow (see below), and J. Muir, another ally, all made inquiries. Ultimately, they offered the post to John McIntyre 'who was A1 – hard working + very prudent, [and] knows Chinese' (ibid. JSS to Ismay Imrie, 14 June 1881 and JSS to J. Scott, 6 September 1881). In turn, McIntyre provided access to skilled staff. Swire cautioned him 'we shall be guided by you somewhat in these matters although we have our Hong Kong partners' views thereon ... but as you are answerable ... it is in your interest to see that your staff be properly organised' (ibid., 21 September 1881). By relying on a newly recruited specialist who had passed through the network's screening machinery to hire other skilled staff members, Swire got around the difficulty of judging their abilities directly. Yet, as Swire contracted for specialised knowledge, he nested agreements by forming interlocking incentives and (through B&S) dual-monitoring mechanisms.

Through Thomas Ismay, JSS made contact with James Barrow, a major sugar refiner, who was willing to invest in TSR and, in cumulative fashion, bring in his partners. Barrow was an ally of such high repute that Swire mentioned him in the prospectus sent to other potential shareholders. Moreover, Swire warned his new contact 'I shall always be pumping you for information, and you will soon wish that you had never been born' (1 July 1881). Barrow provided financial, commercial, and technical advice, as well as more contacts.

Following John Scott's local connections in Greenock, Swire contracted with 'Blake Barclay & Co. [of the same port] who built Richardson's House + have a great reputation' (ibid. JSS to Lang, Scott & MacIntosh, 26 August 1881). However, not trusting to reputation and existing channels alone, Swire sought the views of Barrow and MacIntyre on Blake Barclay's plans (ibid. JSS to Barrow, 6 September 1881). To provide further assurances, Swire asked Scotts to arrange to have its superintendent, who usually oversaw JSS's, Holts', and Rathbones' contracts, monitor Blake Barclay's work (ibid. JSS to J. Scott, 14 October 1881). Swire mobilised additional interlocking incentives by telling Blakes that Barrow was observing their performance and by indicating that 'Sugar Refining in the East must be a great industry, and your names will be made there if our House is a success' (ibid. JSS to Blake Barclay, 8 July and 14 October 1881).

With these details arranged, the development of TSR went forward. Within two years, however, the firm needed more capital, and Swire sought to make another private placement in order 'to keep finance secret from Jardines'. He wrote to Imrie, who was associated with White Star, 'you and Holt seem to be our only friends with loose cash. I should like to get my fingers into Schwabe's pocket' (JSSI 1/6 JSS to Imrie, 29 September 1883). Imrie did not respond to the invitation to interest Gustavus Schwabe, White Star's wealthy supporter, but Swire, Imrie, and the Holts were able to raise the required £40,000. The episode confirms that networks were exclusive: for unknown reasons Imrie would not help Swire form a link with Schwabe, although Imrie was confident enough to commit his own funds.

The DSS needed to evaluate the TSR venture expanded as Swire's network grew within the limits determined by exclusiveness. Ever more extensive and interrelated linkages drew a wide range of intelligence from further afield, and Swire built interlocking incentives to bind the various threads. Numerous network units and new contacts collaborated in processing the growing stream of information.

The Taikoo Dockyard & Engineering Co.

For many years Swire's Eastern partners pressed him to set up a ship repair yard in Hong Kong to service CN's fleet. Although the project would have enabled him to compete in another field with Jardine Matheson, he resisted the temptation because 'we don't think that there is room for another dock Co.' (JSSI 1/5 1087 JSS to Lang, Scott & MacIntosh, 11 February 1881). As he elaborated to his partners:

> ... we could not speak in its favour, not having mastered the pros and cons, [and] not having any means of becoming acquainted with them, we

did not care to injure our reputation by suggesting such an investment to friends even had we believed they would have taken it up ... We should lose our power over others, if we attempted to float schemes of which we ourselves were not in a position to master details. The Sugar Co. was in a different position; some of our friends were refiners, + one, who has a reputation in the trade, had taken a favourable view of prospects when in China.

(JSSI 1/6 JSS to Lang, Scott and MacIntosh, 10 December 1881)

Swire's stated concern was the limited information that his contacts could furnish. He feared that if the venture failed it would undermine his capacity to draw support from the network over the long term. However, the distinction he made between TSR and the yard was not accurate because John Scott could advise on shipbuilding matters. Perhaps Scott was not confident in the venture, and Swire was following his guidance.

Whatever his real reasons, John Swire opposed the scheme, but after his death in 1898 his successors pressed ahead with it. E. V. Belilios, who was associated with the China Sugar Refining Co. for which Jardines' acted as agent and who invested jointly with B&S in a Hong Kong wharf, confirmed to JSS that there was ample demand to support a new entrant alongside Jardines' Hong Kong & Whampoa Dockyard (HK&WD) which levied 'exorbitant charges' (JSSI 2/9 Belilios to MacIntosh, 20 May 1899). Belilios – himself also a shipowner – reported that the expansion of steam services from Hong Kong and a huge rise in the publicly quoted shares of HK&WD indicated that investors would welcome a second yard. He promised his financial support and that of other shipowners he knew. Finally, he pointed out some of the weaknesses of HK&WD, whose docks were small and whose 'machinery [was] becoming obsolete'. Belilios's report shows that JSS had dual sources of local information on which to base its decision to proceed with the yard.

Out of concern for its reputation, JSS financed this project differently from its earlier ventures. It put up all of the initial funds, but promised to let interested parties in later. By 1908, Swires had solved serious construction problems and invited CN, TSR, and OSS shareholders to invest. JSS's chairman, J. H. Scott, stated 'we do not advertise to get shareholders. We have always found people who have trusted us and believed in us' (JSSVI 5/1 box 2016E, 28 May 1908). Having contained risks before exposing its allies, JSS preserved the confidence of network members.

In pursuing the dockyard project Swires relied heavily upon Scott & Co. Three members of the Scott family directed the planning and construction of the facility. John Scott IV acted as technical adviser from 1899 until his death in 1903. His brother Robin Sinclair Scott held the reins until he passed away in 1905, and from then until the completion of the works in 1908 Charles C. Scott directed the programme.

Scott & Co. formally contracted to act as expert adviser to TD&E because as R. L. Scott wrote to G. W. Swire: 'we cannot agree to put all the information + experience of our "brains" into your "archives" with the possibility of being "paid off"' (GD 319/12/2/1, 6 December 1912). Knowing that this type of knowledge-based transaction involved to a significant degree the integration of the two firms' systems and organisational memories, even such close allies as Scotts required a safeguard. The outcome was a viable long-term arrangement. Acting as advisor until at least 1961, Scotts offered guidance on operating procedures, developed ship designs, inspected plans, and selected new staff, including TD&E's first manager.

That Scotts was to serve the Hong Kong yard for so long in such a variety of capacities reveals an important determinant of network longevity. Fundamentally, the capacity of Scotts to play a long-term advisory role depended on their ability to learn more quickly than TD&E. From the start, JSS recognised Scott & Co.'s superior capabilities plus its client- and trade-specific knowledge. As G. W. Swire wrote to R. L. Scott in 1914 'we were not altogether satisfied that the Dockyard could design vessels up to our class and … thought it was as well to have some such provision for designs by you, who had extensive knowledge of China coast conditions and of our fleet' (ibid., 26 May 1914). Scott & Co.'s persistent lead in maritime technology manifested itself in many ways, and their reputation enabled them to secure licences for new engine types on TD&E's behalf. Through its commercial connections, Scott & Co. provided the Hong Kong yard with access to research and testing facilities as well as a chain of trusted suppliers. Scotts literally repeated the task of building the TD&E works from the ground up after World War II (GD 319/12/2/16 letters 1943–6).

Financially and operationally TD&E represented another link in the chain of Eastern enterprises founded by the network. Existing businesses and investment ties provided a foundation for the new shipyard. The decision to press ahead with the project was based on local information gathered from internal as well as external sources. Moreover, the network supported transactions for the knowledge and skills needed to bring the difficult scheme into operation. The long history of the Scotts–TD&E connection reveals that enduring network links depended on the ability of constituents to sustain advantages through continuous learning.

Air-related businesses

Existing network links provided some of the information JSS needed to enter air-related businesses, but it had to build new ties to secure specialised knowledge. For example, CN and B&S provided agencies, and TD&E had engineering expertise. OSS's Singapore agent, Mansfields, which formed Malayan Airlines (MAL), offered advice. However, to acquire repair know-how and operating experience, Swires forged ties with Ivan Holyman, of the Australian National Airline (ANA), and Syd de Kantzow and Roy Farell, the founders of Cathay Pacific Airways (CPA).

JSS first considered entering the business in 1933. They approached Holts and Mansfields for advice on how to obtain contacts to secure agency work for CN from Imperial Airways (JSSXI 1/8 box 59 JSS to Wurtzberg, 13 November 1933). 'In the belief that the future lies with co-ordination between the various forms of transport, and that in China especially airways will become of increasing importance,' CN took up an agency for China National Airlines and offered participation to Holts (ibid. JSS to AH&Co., 18 December 1933). In 1939, Swires thought about setting up an aircraft maintenance operation as an adjunct to TD&E's business, but abandoned the idea on the advice of its manager who felt it called for a distinct type of knowledge (PAMAS JSS to C. C. Roberts, 6 June 1947). Development was put on hold when war broke out.

In 1945, CN's Australian agent, R. A. Colyer, provided G. W. Swire with the initial contact with Holyman who was planning a service between Hong Kong and Australia (CPA Colyer to GWS, 25 July and 13 August 1945). (This link also brought a connection with P&O, which was part-owner in ANA and later acquired interests in CPA and MAL from JSS.) Quickly establishing rapport, John Scott and Jock Swire considered Holyman to be 'quite the most outstanding man we have yet met' (Jock Swire's diary, 9 June 1946). B&S secured ANA agencies in Asia and provided ANA with government contacts, which were vital in the highly regulated airline business. JSS offered its ties with MAL and Holts Wharf to help ANA build an air freight business (Diary, 6 May 1947). In return, Holyman promised to 'assist … in drawing up plans' for Swire's Hong Kong repair unit (CPA JSS to B&S, 1 August 1947).

JSS turned its internal information gathering capabilities to studying the market for aircraft repair services. TD&E's manager, J. Finnie, reported:

> A well organised company getting in early with efficient plant and personnel would get the work. It is apparent that at present a good deal of air maintenance is very haphazard and … many airlines would welcome a reliable … service which would give their passengers greater confidence and the line higher prestige.
>
> (CPA Finnie to Roberts (B&S), 30 June 1947)

Finnie evaluated the volume of air traffic at Hong Kong, the existing facilities at Kai Tek airport, maintenance procedures, and the cost of setting up a repair subsidiary (CPA, 8 August and 19 September 1947). On the basis of these studies and a tour of ANA's facilities by TD&E staff, JSS and Holyman arranged for the new repair unit to do basic work, while ANA's depots dealt with more complex repairs (PAMAS JSS to B&S, 5 September 1947). ANA seconded technical staff to Swires' service unit which was ultimately called PAMAS (CPA Ford to Finnie, 29 November 1947).

These newly extended inter-organisational ties provided mutual advantages. TD&E's link with ANA strengthened its position during merger talks with Jardines, who were also setting up a repair facility (PAMAS JSS to

B&S, 5 September 1947). B&S furnished ANA with the government contacts it needed to develop services to mainland China under an arrangement with CNAC, the national carrier (CPA JSS to B&S, 5 and 12 September 1947; and B&S to JSS, 14 May 1948). B&S also offered ANA advice on Chinese law, while JSS helped ANA extend its range of contacts after meeting Chinese officials at a civil aviation conference held in London.

From its allies, both old and new, Swires discovered what was entailed in taking on aircraft repair work and developed a more accurate assessment of the risks:

> We must not forget that for ten years before the war Mansfields lost money heavily on their Air Dept. and it is only since they became big enough to carry the very considerable minimum staff which is necessary to meet aircraft at all hours ... that they have been able to make the thing pay at all. It is now paying handsomely. On a long-term view, therefore, it does seem that unless we can get the hard core of a regular established (air)liner service such as ANA ... it is not really an economic proposition.
>
> (CPA JSS to B&S, 24 January 1947)

Swires also noted that ANA provided maintenance services of the highest standard, even if it meant a short-term financial loss, and concluded that PAMAS 'could not do better than emulate many of their methods'. Thus, Swires blended details of the experience of Mansfields that had been embedded in its own corporate memory with complementary information from ANA to determine an initial business development strategy. They had to carry out first-class work from the start, take a long-term perspective, and work hard to attract regular carriers. Above all, they could not afford to have an accident damage their reputation.

In late 1947, the direction of JSS's strategy changed suddenly when it became apparent that the Hong Kong administration was compelling the American owners of CPA to reduce their majority holding in the firm. This exposed a chance for B&S to take over an existing air operation that already owned maintenance facilities. B&S rapidly began gathering information to assess this acquisition target. They observed directly that 'the condition of Cathay Pacific aircraft in appearance is excellent and stands out in comparison to other aircraft [and the] Civil Aviation Dept. thinks very highly of their record, particularly in operations and maintenance' (CPA Grabowsky to Walsh, 12 December 1947). From CPA's agents, Mansfields and the Borneo Company, B&S learned that the firm was a 'very satisfactory' principal (CPA B&S to JSS, 12 March 1948). However, B&S warned JSS of rumours that CPA was engaged in gold carrying and that it flew without proper documents (CPA Roberts to JKS, 13 April 1948). Finally, the Hong Kong branch assessed CPA's owners as managers and prospective partners (CPA B&S to JSS, 7 May 1948).

Swires concluded the acquisition in 1948. CN took up a thirty-five per cent interest and JSS ten per cent, whereas ANA acquired thirty-five per cent and the vendors retained twenty per cent. B&S concluded a General Agency Agreement with CPA to handle its finances, purchasing, and passenger booking, while de Kantzow attended to flying operations. TD&E became general agents for PAMAS (eighty per cent owned by CPA and twenty per cent by TD&E). In 1950, PAMAS merged with Jardines' repair subsidiary, Jardine Aircraft Maintenance Company (JAMCO), to form the Hong Kong Aviation Engineering Company (HAECO), which still operates in Hong Kong today.

To conclude this section, these three instances of new business development in the sugar, shipbuilding, and air sectors all show that diversification policies depended on a DSS that not only could gather information from within the network but also could be expanded to obtain intelligence from new allies. This information was 'free' in the sense that it circulated directly and often (but not always) without the need for formal contracts. It was also 'thick' in terms of its quality, accuracy, and preferential character. Indeed, the data stream frequently included intelligence about competitors. Moreover, Barrow, Belilos, and Holyman worked with HSS affiliates to process the enlarged information flow, learn collaboratively, and interpret business conditions in new ways. Since all of these relationships involved transferring and generating knowledge, the capacity of Swire personnel to win the confidence of new allies was important in sustaining the network's capacity to expand into new sectors.

Human resource development

To enhance the capacity of the network's DSS over time, members cultivated human resources with three attributes. First, they needed trustworthy persons to whom they could delegate managerial tasks. Second, officials in England depended on Eastern staff to find and process information needed to support dialogues that enabled the former to appreciate the local context in which decisions were made, and the latter to absorb points of wider significance to those at home. (These exchanges were conditioned by interpersonal knowledge and the experience that JSS partners had gained while working in the East or visiting branches, and, conversely, by impressions formed by B&S men while they worked in the parent firm before going overseas or during home leaves.) Third, the network had to develop managers who could treat with Chinese officials and businessmen. 'Experience and local "face" are important assets', along with language skills (JSSI 3/9 A. S. Scott to JSS, 3 March 1936).

The HSS network developed overlapping channels to identify and evaluate personnel. This was vital because diversification depended upon arranging contracts with staff who possessed technical knowledge – often tacit in form – the quality of which was difficult for senior executives to assess independently. As we have seen, Swire secured references on McIntyre, the leading candidate for the post of TSR's manager, from no fewer than six people in the sugar industry to obtain corroborating opinions, while Scotts assessed engineering talent for TD&E.

Taking advantage of the dense web of contacts that characterised Britain's marine-related industries, Scotts could obtain impressions that reflected different contexts in which an individual's conduct had been observed. Of an applicant for the general manger of TD&E, they wrote 'a most reliable man whose works are not far distant from those of which Mr. [alias] was the Manager ... says that Mr. [alias] is not suited to fill the position ... owing to his temperament, [but] would be quite suitable for a more subordinate position' (GD 319 11/2/2 JS to JSS, 30 April 1907). Such evaluations enabled Scotts to match with some precision Swires' personnel requirements with the attributes of individual candidates.

The Greenock yard also enhanced the capabilities of Swire and TD&E staff. Scotts provided specialised training for new TD&E recruits before they were sent to the East and helped TD&E engineers to upgrade their skills while on home leave. Scotts gave summer jobs to Chinese men who won TD&E's prize apprenticeships.

Staff exchanges enabled JS, JSS, and TD&E to share personal information. Swires informed Scotts that the father of one apprentice was a 'Grade 1 Draughtsman employed in our Ship Drawing Office for the past 35 years [and] ... can be relied upon to ensure the best possible results from his son. The family live in our quarters at Saiwanho' (GD 319 12/2/196 JSS to JS, 22 June 1960). Swires also drew to Scotts' attention a man whose father who had worked at the Greenock yard for ten years before joining TD&E and whose 'elder brother is working for us on the airways side, and is doing well' [GD 319/12/2/266 John Scott (JSS) to J. Lee (JS), 25 October 1965]. Across industries and organisational interfaces, the network relied on family ties to furnish implicit guarantees and interlocking incentives when it contracted with staff.

Exchanges of knowledge about staff served other functions. First, they made network firms aware of each other's personnel expectations. Scotts wrote to Swires:

> knowing the nature of your work in Hong Kong we attach considerable importance to getting the right type of man for the job. Mr Greig [whom Scotts recruited for TD&E] used to say that what was required was a good working knowledge of the repairing side of shipbuilding plus considerable imagination.
>
> (GD 319 12/2/48 JS to JSS, 16 January 1947)

This type of knowledge, fused with extensive knowledge of each other's operations and experiences, gave the network a holographic quality, in that any part could replicate other parts that were destroyed. This was invaluable when TD&E's works had to be completely rebuilt after the war. To the suggestion by Swires that they should recruit an entirely new staff, Scotts replied 'having had in the early days of the Dockyard such unfortunate experience of a completely new staff unused to Eastern conditions, I think it cannot be your intention to embark on this, if it can be avoided'. With TD&E's history embedded in its own corporate memory as a result of being involved in the original recruiting process, Scotts then drew up a phased personnel plan to avoid repeating mistakes (GD 319/12/2/16 JS to JSS, 18 February 1944).

The second benefit stemming from exchanges of personnel knowledge was the creation of a private market for staff based on inter-firm ties among middle managers. Indeed, these links were deliberately cultivated. Thus, when Holts no longer required J. C. Murie's services, JSS hired him and requested Scotts to allow him to visit its works 'before we send him out [to the East, in order to enable him] to become thoroughly acquainted with the Doxford [diesel] Engine you are building for us, and *probably what is more important*, to get to know those ... who are responsible for the design and construction of these engines' (GD 319 12/2/75 JSS to JS, 31 October 1949 emphasis added). Thus, Murie carried advanced technical information, tacit know-how, and interpersonal knowledge between three firms and built new links as he went.

Temporary secondments served the same purposes and enabled companies to attain a degree of staff interchangeability while generating feedback on personnel. In response to a letter from Y. Fiennes of JSS commenting on how well a Scott man filled in for a TD&E manager who had been ill, George Hilton replied 'I am so glad that Taikoo found him useful, and I am sure he will have benefited greatly from his experience there. I haven't seen you for quite a long time and hope to be able to call in the near future' (GD 319 12/2/196, 27 February 1961). While commenting on the results of one exchange, the correspondents revealed that they were close friends.

Indeed, the network was interlaced with links between middle managers. J. Moulsdale (OSS) and J. Cairns (Scotts) dined together, visited each other's homes, knew each other's families, and corresponded in hand like senior HSS partners. Indicating that they were enveloped in a comprehensive culture, these managers even shared a similar sense of humour with the founding families. Requesting another loan from OSS, Cairns inquired of Moulsdale: 'How's the Exchequer? I hope you are in funds. We could use a little more' (GD 319 11/2/5, 19 September 1914). Such friendships smoothed many kinds of inter-organisational transfers.

Forming network-wide contacts enabled managers, who were being groomed for senior positions, to gain a wealth of interpersonal knowledge they could take with them as they rose. For example, in 1935–6, John Nicolson spent eighteen months touring the overseas organisations of OSS and JSS. JSS drew up a detailed itinerary that would 'give him the best possible education'. Nicolson's trip assured Swire personnel that he would continue the co-operative traditions of his forebears: he was 'clearly imbued with the R. D. H[olt] tradition and [would] carry it with him to the top' [JSSI 3/9 J. S. Scott (B&S) to JSS, 18 April 1936]. The visit also led to more systematic exchanges of lower level staff in the hope of avoiding 'bickering [and] unnecessary time wasting'. Nicolson made many 'friends with our younger men' many of whom were recent university graduates. Perhaps being more comfortable confiding in him, they expressed concern over their promotion prospects relative to less well-educated but more experienced long-serving B&S staff members. Having gained a more accurate impression of its own staff's expectations from an impartial figure who worked for an allied firm, B&S then provided the necessary reassurance in the hope of safeguarding its new talent.

JSS devoted considerable attention to managerial succession. It made a point of having two dependable men at each overseas office: a senior man and an 'understudy' who could temporarily fill in for the former and who was being groomed to succeed him. Indicating how carefully it prepared for change, the firm began planning the installation of two new management teams in Shanghai and Hong Kong in 1937 as early as 1933 (JSSI 3/8 box A33 J. Scott to JSS, 17 February 1933). Senior partners requested to see 'reports by younger men, on whom they sometimes throw light ... by revealing an unusual point of view' (JSSI 3/9 box A11 J. Scott to JSS, 1 February 1936). Their aim was to monitor the progress of 'understudies'.

In the process, senior executives developed an understanding of the way talent grew. Of one promising young manager they observed 'he is just at the stage where a man makes up his mind whether to chuck it in or stay', and they promoted him 'in the hope that that will give him a fillip over the next couple of years which are the dangerous time' (ibid. J. Scott to JSS, 18 April 1936). Knowing how expectations change enabled top executives to offer staff appropriate challenges and rewards.

Swires built a cohesive culture by hiring personnel with similar backgrounds. Moreover, indicating that network members who assisted with recruitment were aware of this aim, Scotts knew that TD&E 'prefer[red] to engage Scotsmen' (GD 319/12/2/121 JSS to JS, 23 June 1953). JSS recognised that staff who were part of a small expatriate community in China would develop close bonds. Today, new recruits often share a similar education, undergo induction and language courses together, and take meals with each other during their first year with the firm. The aim is to create opportunities for personal relationships to develop (C. Havilland, 10 December 1997).

At times when the constituent firms pursued a new course of growth by hiring people whose backgrounds differed from existing staff, they took deliberate steps to accommodate the newcomers. The infusion of university graduates, a policy that the Holts and Jock Swire supported during the inter-war years, called for assurances from senior staff (JSSI 3/9 box A33 J. Scott to Jock Swire, 24 April 1936). At Orient Paint, B&S had a problem integrating one man from its partner, Pinchin Johnson & Co. John Scott 'tried to get him in among our people as much as possible by giving him lunch in the staff room every day and in other ways' (ibid., J. Scott to Jock Swire, 24 April 1936). Scott found that the man became more co-operative as he absorbed 'the Taikoo atmosphere'. In the margin of the letter a London partner wrote that the B&S culture 'seems to have a wonderfully asphyxiating effect. Carbon monoxide', revealing that he wanted dynamic interaction between staff not one-way soporific infusions of culture. Similarly, managers who stayed on with acquired firms also needed to be accommodated. B&S worried about whether it would be able to retain de Kantzow, the founder of CPA, who was an individualist more suited to building up a business than to working for a large organisation. B&S's aim was 'to keep him fighting but by our rules, without blunting his claws' (CPA B&S to JSS, 27 August 1948). In the end, B&S could not keep this talented figure, but not because its managers failed to understand the nature of the challenge involved.

That network members did not consider personnel matters in an instinctive way, but rather used systematic deliberation, is confirmed by an address written by OSS's Cripps and circulated among the allied firms [attached to JSSXI 1/8 box 59 B. Heathcote (OSS) to G. W. Swire, 12 May 1933]. Composed in 1933, Cripps's paper addressed a number of the concerns explored in the present study. He distinguished between routine and unprecedented problem solving, discussed the nature of decision-making processes, and examined the roles of 'ideals' in motivating all levels of an organisation. Moreover, Cripps explicitly considered the role of standards from a systemic perspective. The 'Written Standard Practice Instructions' served as a corporate memory, and a records system provided a 'tool for the use of management'. For Cripps, a manager was one 'who has to make decisions of all sorts [routine and unprecedented]. These decisions must be based on live facts ... He must collect round him a small staff of business scientists, always at work keeping facts up to date by experiment and measurement'. He also suggested that teamwork was 'a principle, probably the oldest which runs through and connects up practically all principles'.

Probably the most striking instance of team-based knowledge, in the sense of knowing what others know and how they will react to situations, occurred at the outbreak of the Pacific War. Fearing that a Nazi invasion would prevent JSS from directing operations from London, it had given instructions to B&S that, upon receiving a single word message 'interregnum', the subsidiary was to assume overall control. In 1942, the London office received such a telegram from a Hong Kong manager who, on his own initiative, reversed the logic of the parent firm's directive when the port fell to the Japanese. Cripps's address and the actions of other network executives reveal that they had a deep understanding of the links between decision-making, systems, and personnel attributes.

Conclusion

The growth of the HSS network was sustained by related investments in DSSs and personnel. Any organisation's systems, especially its DSS, are only as good as the people who use them, but for HSS members achieving an effective fit between these two elements was a complex undertaking. After all, the DSS in question was an inter-organisational construct and the common approach to staff development spanned the boundaries of constituent firms. The purpose of the complementary dual investment made by all network members was not only to lower the cost of transactions, especially those involving knowledge, but more importantly to support learning activities needed to undertake diversification.

The HSS network, and especially JSS, successfully fused strategic decision-making processes, systems design, and personnel development to move into new business fields. It diversified cautiously and with careful deliberation. TSR, TD&E, and the air projects followed or moved in tandem with Jardines' course of expansion, indicating that JSS used a 'second entrant' strategy to contain risk. Moreover, each project was the outcome of prolonged deliberation. The slowness with which JSS diversified was a function of the need to build a progressively wider range of communication channels and alliances so that it could gain the information needed to assess risk and future prospects. Each thread in its web represented a relationship, like the shipowner–agent contact examined above, except that these links became intertwined.

The HSS case suggests several refinements to theoretical studies that indicate networks have distinctively configured communication channels that transmit specific types of information. The HSS construct was laced with lateral channels, but these were far more extensive – appearing at senior, middle, and lower management levels – than the literature suggests. Moreover, the example of Nicolson making friends with junior JSS staff also reveals that diagonal links grew across firm boundaries. In this instance the new channel helped JSS learn about the expectations of its new university recruits whom it needed to sustain growth. These ties grew out of socialisation processes that spanned different constituencies, succeeding generations, and diverse businesses.

Network channels are characterised as responsive to external stimuli. HSS staff exercised wide initiative in gathering outside information and autonomously processed it. Succession planning and the development of 'understudies' at subsidiaries, which acted like listening posts and primary processing units, lent continuity to these capabilities. The HSS network's communication lines were open ended yet exclusive. John Swire and other senior men were adept at balancing these features by generating the trust needed to build new channels, but at the same time they nested contracts and built overlapping links to provide deterrence.

Network information is depicted in the literature as 'free flowing', but our findings suggest that there were in practice limitations placed on its circulation. Imrie was unwilling to introduce Schwabe to Swire, and JS required contractual safeguards before it would act as TD&E's advisor. These constraints reflected the need to protect core capabilities and vital contacts on which future contracting options were based.

Our findings suggest a more refined definition of what the literature calls 'thick' network information. Data transferred within the HSS alliance were thick in the sense that they were not transferred in a raw state, but rather were partly processed by managers at affiliates before transmission and then refined further in a collaborative fashion during the dialogues conducted by London partners and Far East staff. Indeed, as they cultivated young talent, senior managers watched for those who, by interpreting phenomena in unusual ways, added substance to the intelligence stream. Network information was also thick because it was funnelled through several channels to generate feedback effects. Finally, network intelligence was thick in that it included tacit knowledge embodied in personnel who were transferred between affiliates.

The HSS case also confirms that network information can create new meaning and fresh interpretations of phenomena. A development not detected in the literature, but revealed in the HSS case, is that the construction of an inter-firm DSS in turn may stimulate the emergence of an inter-organisational memory. Having a shared knowledge of each other's experiences, helped member firms to enhance the accuracy of decision-making. Thus, with a memory of MAL's early history, JSS could see more acutely the challenges involved in forming its air maintenance unit. Instances, such as when Scotts warned TD&E against recruiting an entire new staff after World War II, reveal that a shared corporate memory can impart a holographic quality to networks. The 'interregnum' episode also shows creative, lateral-thinking processes in operation as well as an accurate awareness of what other constituents actually know. With an inter-organisational memory the learning capacity of the HSS network came to exceed the sum of the capabilities of the individual members.

While networks, like any organisational form, depend upon systems and staff that complement each other, because these related features span corporate boundaries, networks pose a variety of different trade-offs and balances between conflicting forces. First, while networks are described as very flexible structures, this case shows that the serial extension of information channels posed a trade-off between the rate of growth and time needed to cement contracts. Second, the time required for each agreement to solidify depended upon the ingenuity with which each contractual thread was tailor-made to strike a different balance between trust and deterrent capability to accommodate a particular new entrant. Third, the knowledge that circulated within the HSS network and joint learning activities reveals that network members have to strike a balance between maintaining their own knowledge advantage and sharing expertise to build joint capabilities with other affiliates. The final trade-off HSS had to grapple with was maintaining sufficient staff homogeneity to facilitate communication and enough heterogeneity to generate new knowledge. Senior partners demonstrated convincingly that they welcomed and earnestly tried to accommodate recruits from different backgrounds and the former managers of acquired units. Team building – the central principle isolated by Cripps – is also a vital factor in the case that follows.

4 A multinational joint venture

The Orient Paint, Varnish and Colour Co., 1932–49

When it diversified into paint making, JSS formed a joint venture with Pinchin Johnson & Co. (PJ) and custom designed a private communicating infrastructure to blend its capabilities with those of its new partner. Subsequently, internal and external shocks compelled the firms to modify this framework to sustain transfers of knowledge and to create new project-specific expertise. What Cripps called team building was a critical factor in the success of the venture: Orient Paint, Varnish and Colour Co. (OP)

A growing body of theoretical work is striving to identify those variables that determine the outcome of joint ventures. The ability to establish 'complementarity' between partners is seen as being crucial to a successful relationship. In response to the imprecise way much of the literature treats the concept of 'complementarity', Geringer (1988, 1991) studied an extensive list of task- and partner-specific attributes that influence initial partner selection and found the former to be the most important. Proceeding further, Lorange (1988) identified five key factors that determine the effectiveness of both planning and controlling joint ventures: a clear organisation, a viable competitive strategy, value-enhancing roles for each partner, compatible behaviour, and a balance of power. Following a different angle, Casson (1990) recognised that a joint venture may be the outcome of existing trust or an instrument for invoking co-operation. He suggested that a venture based upon sharing intangible assets in a dynamic market provides a chance for participants to demonstrate forbearance and thus become known as dependable partners.

These studies indicate that 'complementarity', which may be reflected in partners' assets, capabilities, size, and behaviour, is initially perceived by potential allies, refuted or confirmed after a project is launched, and develops further or erodes as events unfold (also see Ring and Van der Ven 1994). Yet, the literature does not reveal *how*, in practice, joint venturers communicate and learn about each other's attributes. Nor does it indicate how participants in a voice-based relationship contain the cost of the intensive communication that may be needed to make *ex post* changes.

The OP case reveals that the main partners, JSS and PJ, consciously installed a communicating infrastructure to facilitate inter-organisational information sharing and joint learning. This custom-built framework, which differed slightly from the public good type of construct examined in Chapter 2, consisted of four elements:

1 an agreement that clearly articulated each member's responsibilities,
2 inter-organisational communication lines (a bargaining fora was not needed),
3 a set of communicating procedures and aids, including an accounting system,
4 carefully selected people placed at the interfaces between the participating firms.

This construct supported the interpersonal and inter-organisational learning needed to build trust and recognise complementary attributes; it facilitated transfers of technical, managerial, and organisational knowledge; and it helped participants to collaborate in the creation of new, project-specific expertise. Over time, internal and external shocks compelled JSS and PJ to modify parts of the infrastructure to sustain these functions. In terms of the analysis presented in Chapter 3, this case shows in detail how by means of sequential adjustment, the partners created an enduring thread that connected the HSS network to new allies. The mix of contractual elements devised for the initial agreement between PJ and JSS favoured culture over legal specifications and monitoring mechanisms, and thus was consistent with contracts arranged between HSS constituents.

In the 1930s and 1940s, China was certainly a turbulent business environment. Western firms that had established operations in China before the communist revolution faced a number of common challenges: they had to secure the co-operation of the Chinese people, cope with local competition, and contend with uncertainty arising from unstable political and military conditions (Cheng 1986; Cochran 1986; Wilkins 1986; Osterhammel 1989; Cox 1995). Sharing and developing intangible assets within such an uncertain context afforded OP's founding partners many opportunities to demonstrate forbearance and thus enhance their reputations along the lines Casson suggested. Remarkably, the project survived the Japanese occupation of Shanghai, the Pacific War, and the Chinese Revolution. In the late 1940s, it became – in a different form – the basis of an extensive Hong Kong-based paint business, which is still operated by JSS today.

The first section below describes how the resources of JSS, PJ, Pinchin's China agent, Wilkinson, Heywood & Clark (WH&C), and Chinese allies complemented each other, and it outlines the strategy that the two main partners devised for OP in 1932–4. The second part examines the initial communicating infrastructure they created to support the foundation of the business and the construction of the factory that began operations in July 1935. Third, the discussion considers how the partners adjusted the infrastructure to accommodate shocks from mid-1935 to the end of 1937 when

OP and WH&C merged. The last section analyses developments from 1937, when the Japanese occupied Shanghai, to 1946, when OP moved to Hong Kong.

Background and strategy formulation

In contrast to JSS's highly diversified interests, PJ specialised solely in paint manufacturing and selling. Little is known about the origins and early history of PJ, but it expanded rapidly in the 1920s by absorbing thirteen other firms (Chandler 1990: 370). By 1935 the company was Britain's largest paint producer, and it earned profits of over £320,000 on assets worth more than £1.4 million (*The Economist*, 30 March 1935). PJ's extensive UK factories, which were supported by large laboratory facilities, produced a wide range of paints for the domestic market and for customers in Europe, Asia, and South America. It also had subsidiaries in India, Australia, New Zealand, Italy, and Argentina (Chandler 1990: 373; *The Economist*, 25 March 1933).

It was the Shanghai branch of Butterfield & Swire (B&S) that suggested the group produce paint in China. Shanghai's population was growing rapidly (it doubled between 1914 and 1936), creating strong demand for construction and maintenance materials. Having already built up a business selling paint to various customers, including other JSS affiliates, B&S recognised that an import-substituting opportunity existed in this expanding business field. China and Hong Kong bought increasing amounts of mostly high-quality paint from Japan and Britain (B&S to JSS, 23 December 1932). Even though tariffs ranged from fourteen to seventeen per cent no foreign manufacturer had yet set up operations in the country. Paint made by local Chinese manufacturers was priced well below imports, but it was of inferior quality. Thus, B&S identified a niche for a product of slightly higher quality than Chinese products but priced below imports. The Shanghai house believed that after it had succeeded in making low-quality paint it could establish brand identity, educate Chinese customers in the benefits of using a higher-quality article, and move up-market to displace imports as economic development progressed. Anticipating the construction of a factory with a 1,000 ton per annum capacity (about five per cent of the paint trade in China and Hong Kong) at a cost of £13,350 with a further £9,000 for working capital, B&S projected a yearly return of twenty-five per cent.

Based on full utilisation of an optimally scaled plant, this strategy required Chinese investment to help build up outside sales to local clients and obscure the venture's foreign identity. However, JSS recognised that the venture had to be 'more or less' successful before outsiders were invited to participate: '…we cannot afford to make a mess of things for more than a very short time without damage to our reputation' (JSS to B&S, 7 April 1933). Parent company officials suggested that a plant of 300 tons annual capacity be built initially [JSS affiliate China Navigation Co. (CN) alone consumed 45 tons annually]. After the new company had perfected the production of cheap, low-quality paints, Chinese investors would be brought in to help expand sales and capacity could be enlarged.

The main obstacle to executing this strategy was Swires' lack of paint-making expertise. Producing a cheap, low-quality article required considerable knowledge of chemistry because local raw materials, which varied widely in consistency, would have to be used to avoid tariffs and to achieve cost competitiveness. B&S needed a distinct type of manager 'not ... the ordinary sort of old time paint maker, but rather an educated man who has gone into the mills to gain practical experience with a view to advancement to the management end of the business' (B&S to JSS, 23 December 1932). Such a man would have to experiment with Chinese materials if not carry out basic research (B&S to JSS, 12 May 1933). JSS advertised for this type of manager in the British technical journals.

JSS's notices were observed by PJ officials who instructed C. G. Heywood, the head of their sales agents in China, WH&C, to approach B&S (B&S to JSS, 8 December 1933). Heywood had been thinking about setting up a factory in China with PJ, and to avoid conflict he suggested that JSS and PJ set up a joint venture with WH&C providing sales support.

As a result of Heywood's intervention, JSS's thinking regarding what type of framework to employ changed from forming a new subsidiary and inviting outside participation, after the project proved its viability (along the same lines as TD&E), to forming a joint venture. The latter course offered a way to secure vital technical and managerial talent and avoid competition. Once Swires began considering this institutional possibility, they evaluated at least one other possible partner, ICI, which also sold paint in China. The ICI link promised wider advantages 'other than purely commercial ones', but the breadth of ICI's interests might prove a distraction to its management. Moreover, ICI might try to prevent B&S from exercising managerial control over the venture, a matter of vital concern to the Swire group as a whole. Since PJ were paint makers only and had a strong supporting organisation, teaming up with them offered a more focused approach to overcoming the technical deficiencies of Swires. JSS and PJ were also both experienced international joint-venturers who understood the subtleties of dealing with foreign businessmen and who had long-standing reputations to protect. Thus, Heywood's initial approach led to the discovery of complementary attributes of a general nature.

Moreover, despite the implicit threat that PJ might set up a rival paint factory, Heywood managed to initiate contact with JSS in a non-intrusive, non-threatening way, and the parties established a degree of mutual trust. Heywood assured B&S:

> it is not the PJ policy to dispose of their interests in any sub-enterprise, and therefore they would not be prepared to enter into any co-operative plan unless they were assured that such a plan was one likely to be a permanent success, and one that was likely to continue.
>
> (memo appended to B&S to JSS, 8 December 1933)

Heywood's words indicated that PJ and Swires shared the same approach to business development. Thus, in terms of size, experience, and strategic outlook, Swires and PJ were a good match.

During these initial talks, the prospective partners also discovered that their resource sets were very complementary (Heywood memo). PJ possessed formulae, process expertise, and chemical knowledge. It had gained diverse experience operating in international markets, and it could furnish inputs on attractive terms through its preferential ties with suppliers. B&S offered 'prestige', valuable political contacts, and extensive knowledge of Chinese customs. In addition to these attributes that could help OP to build up local sales and to attract Chinese local investors, B&S also had construction expertise, a large network of offices in China, and experience in distributing paint in the country. The Swire group had a large internal demand for paint, which was probably very attractive to PJ. For its part, WH&C, with its forty years of experience selling paint in China, provided access to customers B&S could not reach.

Having established a basis of trust and discovered that their resources were very complementary during their initial negotiations, WH&C, JSS, and PJ had to settle two important matters: first, accommodating Chinese participants, and, second, organising inter-firm relations. Heywood saw Chinese interests playing a subordinate role financially and operationally, but based on their knowledge of the people JSS thought this would be inadequate. 'Co-operation with Chinese is not a matter of shareholding and dividends. Real co-operation means that they must in some way and to some extent be associated with management' (Heywood memo comment by a JSS director in the margin). In order to play down the venture's foreign image and to help it win the goodwill of local customers, the Chinese had to become actively involved but not allowed to assume control.

All four firms had distinct views about inter-company relations. PJ envisioned close operating ties between B&S, WH&C, and OP. Heywood suggested that WH&C have the exclusive right to sell OP's paint and that the two firms establish reinforcing board and shareholding links. This course would leave no scope for taking advantage of B&S's paint-distributing expertise and contacts. B&S felt that OP should absorb B&S's selling capabilities and use these to sell its own brands while making WH&C brands for that affiliate to distribute. The two firms could then tap different markets. Preferring that OP form non-exclusive agencies with WH&S and B&S, JSS wanted market-mediated relations supported by co-operation. The paint-making venture should be a stand-alone unit free to transact and/or compete on price and quality with PJ, WH&C, and local producers. One JSS partner felt the whole matter was too complicated 'I don't see how its going to work. Either the [OP] Co doesn't sell anything, or it sells in competition with [WH&C] and makes and sells the same stuff under a different [brand] name'. Although it correctly saw the second course as a source of future confusion, JSS pursued it to accommodate B&S's views and allow room for WH&C to participate.

Having provisionally bound themselves by what they called 'the Gentleman's Agreement', the parties signed a formal contract that laid down lines of inter-company constitutional authority (JSSIX 2/1 agreement, 11 July 1934). PJ and JSS each invested HK$450,000 in the shares of OP and reserved an initial tranche of shares worth HK$80,000 (capable of being increased later to HK$680,000) for Chinese investors. Each British partner could nominate two directors in Shanghai and one in London, and these men would liase in their respective locations. Later, the Chinese participants could appoint one director to the Shanghai board. The agreement explicitly encouraged consultative decision-making in order to avoid 'voting contests'. JSS and PJ agreed 'not to court the favour of the "Irish Party" in the form of the Chinese directors [sic]' and to settle 'any material differences of opinion … prior to formal Directors' Meeting'. At the same time, '[t]he impression of a secret cabal working behind the Chinese directors' [sic] back must, however, at all costs be avoided'. Although ownership and voting power were not initially divided equally with the Chinese, the partners intended to elicit real co-operation and trust.

The complementary resources of the two main participants were harnessed by two supplementary agreements (JSSIX 2/1). The Expert Advice Agreement bound PJ to provide full chemical and technical back-up and to furnish a plant manager in return for an annual fee of HK$30,000 and a five per cent commission on net profits. The General Agents Agreement committed B&S to providing management and other services for the same remuneration. The contracts created symmetrical rewards to avoid conflict.

In terms of its operating status, however, OP was placed in an ambivalent position. Its purchasing activities were subject to market mediation: acting on OP's behalf B&S were 'free to buy in the best market', but it was anticipated that PJ or B&S would be able to offer the most favourable terms. On the selling side, OP and WH&Co would distribute 'products of an exactly similar nature … under different marks' (JSSIX 2/1 General Agents Agreement). OP would run its own sales organisation but it would enjoy a ten per cent price advantage over WH&C, which had the offsetting benefit of established brands. Thus, in contrast to the cost-based principles that governed OP's purchasing, it received artificial price protection. The asymmetric incentives underlying OP's purchasing and selling activities and the dual distribution system provided potential sources of disputes.

To summarise this section, PJ and JSS were attracted to each other by both task- and partner-specific attributes. It is impossible to determine with any precision the relative importance of the two types of characteristics, but the correspondence gives the impression that – in contrast to Geringer's findings – the latter were more significant. Both parties clearly took a long-term view of the project and recognised that partner-specific attributes would influence the ease with which *ex post* modifications would be achieved. The OP project did not appear to be placed on a promising footing according to Lorange's five criteria for success. Each partner did have a value-enhancing role to play, but the organisation and competitive stance of the joint venture were unclear, the parent firms had different management styles, and the distribution of power among PJ, JSS, and Chinese interests was asymmetric. In Casson's terms, these were not necessarily defects, but rather areas in which JSS and PJ could demonstrate forbearance and build trust. It is clear that executives at the two senior companies had established mutual confidence; the form of the 'Gentleman's Agreement' confirms that of the three basic contractual elements, their agreement relied most heavily on culture. The next step they took was to create a communicating infrastructure that would enable them to adjust the overall arrangement in order to support transmissions of knowledge.

The initial communicating infrastructure: developments, 1934–35

This section describes how the partners built the initial communicating framework to facilitate planning, plant construction, and the development of a sales organisation. These activities required interpersonal/inter-organisational learning and transfers of expertise but the creation of only a small amount of project-specific knowledge. To show how these processes unfolded during the project's initial development phase, which concluded in July 1935 when the plant commenced operations, the discussion examines each part of the communicating infrastructure: areas of responsibility, inter-firm communication lines, communicating procedures and aids, and personnel placed at corporate interfaces.

Areas of responsibility

As we have seen, the formal contracts assigned specific responsibilities to individual participants. PJ was to act as expert adviser while B&S would manage OP subject to the instruction of the OP board (B&S to JSS, 31 August 1934). As technical adviser, PJ drew up a list of tasks that had to be completed so that production could start as soon as the plant was finished (JSS to PJ, 22 May 1934, PJ to JSS, 25 May 1934; and B&S to JSS, 13 July 1934). PJ determined the type of equipment required and ordered it from UK suppliers. PJ transferred staff to OP to analyse Chinese raw materials and devise formulae for paint that met local conditions. As it proceeded, PJ provided Swire personnel with technical instruction and sought to impart the benefits of its experience in planning other facilities (PJ to JSS, 30 August 1934). To learn about factory layout and processes, JSS sent H. F. C. Coleman to PJ's Silvertown plant. He modified PJ's factory design to suit the Shanghai climate. Using Coleman's findings and PJ's guidance, B&S built the factory. When the plant was ready both parent firms were pleased with the result, but after acquiring sufficient knowledge to develop a more informed critical faculty JSS later questioned some of PJ's equipment purchases (JSSI 3/9 J. J. Scott to JSS, 13 March 1936).

As we have seen, B&S were to manage OP. However, the agency firm had divided loyalties in that it was subject to the authority of the OP board as well as its parent, JSS. The danger was that JSS could circumvent PJ by using its influence as parent firm over B&S. Preventing mistrust or confusion from developing depended upon whether JSS's behaviour demonstrated convincingly that it would not work behind PJ's back and how communication lines between participants were arranged. JSS was aware of this potential problem, as its design of communication channels revealed.

Inter-firm communication lines

To elicit trust and mobilise participants' specialised knowledge, PJ and JSS established formal information channels. JSS initially asked PJ to send letters addressed to B&S through JSS's London office so that it could monitor transmissions directly (JSS to PJ, 22 May 1934; PJ to JSS, 25 May 1934). However, to enhance the speed of communication, JSS later encouraged PJ to correspond directly with B&S and send copies to JSS, which would follow the same procedure. JSS suggested that if misunderstandings arose between PJ and B&S, the former should consult with JSS to work out a solution (PJ to JSS, 22 September 1934). The 'definite rules as regards correspondence' also enjoined that PJ would communicate to OP through B&S so as not to bypass the managing agents (JSS to B&S, 28 September 1934; JSS to PJ, 1 October 1934). While unintentional deviations occurred, they were quickly rectified to prevent mistrust from developing.

Important Chinese interests that were mobilised through B&S's connections were given access to board level information. A government minister, T. V. Soong, and an official, Tse Tsok Kai, invested in OP, and Tse joined the board. They were given full information so that a relationship of trust could support the enduring Chinese presence that OP needed to break into a wider market.

As part of their inter-firm communication system, the partners also developed an accounting system. The challenge was for JSS, which possessed accounting expertise related to less complex sugar-refining operations, to learn about specific procedures relevant to paint making. PJ had proven systems that could provide a model for OP. However, Swire staff had to obtain not only a firm grasp of the underlying logic, but also an understanding of why certain financial ratios were very different from other businesses with which they were familiar (PJ to JSS, 22 July 1935, and PJ to JSS, 20 December 1935). PJ provided instruction to ensure that JSS was not alarmed by unexpected financial data.

Apart from arriving at an informed consensus on accounting procedures unique to paint operations, the parent firms also had to decide how to treat financial items that arise in any business. In this regard, JSS was anxious to ensure that preliminary expenses were allocated in a way that did not demoralise *PJ staff* who had been transferred to OP (JSS to PJ, 16 July 1935).

Harmonising accounting practices was necessary, but the way in which this was done was also important especially in reassuring sub-managers and nurturing bonds of trust at the new subsidiary.

Communicating procedures, aids, and accounting methods

To enable this formal system to build mutual confidence, PJ and JSS eschewed private transmissions. To overcome the suspicion that B&S and JSS might correspond informally behind PJ's back, JSS sent PJ copies of all its letters to B&S 'as a matter of routine'. At the same time, the Swire organisation attempted to head off private communication between PJ officials in China and PJ's head office in London. Thus, having heard that a PJ engineer, Mr Scase, would report unfavourably on their construction work, B&S officials laid out their case in a letter to JSS with a copy to PJ. B&S's aim was to 'avoid, if possible, any controversial correspondence resulting from Mr Scase's report' and to avoid giving 'an unfavourable impression' of Mr. Scase (B&S to JSS, 19 July 1935). How well the formal system supported inter-firm transfers depended upon whether parties acted in a transparent manner consistent with the etiquette of co-operation.

The parent companies devised a set of communicating aids so that they could co-ordinate the activities of the participants involved in the project. All affiliates were given a set of blueprints for the factory to use as a reference guide when discussing modifications to the facility. JSS and PJ provided each constituent firm with a set of telegraph codes that referred to precisely defined terms so as to prevent confusion from arising from multilateral communication (JSS to PJ, 7 December 1934). Later, the firms devised a set of accounting codes and an organisational chart that acted as 'a sort of 'bible' for future reference' (JSS to B&S, 22 November 1935). In these ways members sought to make their communication more precise and create an inter-organisational memory in order to build mutual confidence and to facilitate transfers of knowledge and collaborative learning.

Personnel selection

The initial selection of staff was important in creating a co-operative climate that could facilitate transfers of industry-specific technical, commercial, and production knowledge. PJ started with a very good appointment when it suggested that WH&C should send one of its managers, a Mr Maxted, to advise B&S staff, to investigate local materials, and to determine the types of inputs OP should import through PJ. (B&S to JSS, 27 July 1934; PJ to JSS, 13 August 1934). Maxted also acted as a channel for liasing with PJ's UK laboratory staff. Maxted quickly secured the confidence of B&S people who informed JSS that '[w]e are receiving from Mr Maxted the fullest co-operation, and we in turn are being perfectly open and frank with him' (B&S to JSS, 2 November 1934). Maxted formed 'a very favourable' impression of R. J. Tippin, whom JSS sent to study WH&C's selling methods and advise on how to organise OP's sales department (ibid. and B&S to JSS, 19 October 1934). The Maxted–Tippin axis created an initial co-operative bond between PJ, JSS, B&S, and WH&C around which other relationships would later develop to support further transfers of specialised knowledge (JSSI 3/9 A33 J. S. Scott to JSS, 21 April 1936).

OP mobilised complementary selling capabilities by appointing Woo Hong Chao as Chinese adviser to its sales department. Moreover, to win the goodwill of Chinese customers and allies, JSS knew that OP had to demonstrate 'real co-operation' by employing local men in the management of the business. OP took a decisive step in this direction by setting up a programme to train Chinese salesmen in the technical side of the business so that they could offer informed advice to customers. This 'consulting' sales approach was vital in convincing clients that the benefits of using better-quality paint more than justified a price that was slightly higher than that charged for locally made products.

Concerning technical and production knowledge, some of which was tacit, PJ sent A. Radford to China to run the factory. Radford had heavy responsibilities to bear: he was to train Chinese factory staff, install a plant costing system, and develop formulae based on local materials. Much time and effort would be expended accommodating Radford.

To promote co-operation among the staff they transferred to OP, the parent firms had to work together and intervene in the joint venture's affairs in a judicious manner. PJ and JSS could not force OP personnel to co-operate, but rather had to let them develop interpersonal knowledge. Allowing local staff the time to recognise their own interdependence would generate the right ethos through the power of suction rather than in response to outside pressure. However, definite indications that the parent firms had established a strong rapport and expected OP staff to do the same were required from time to time. Moreover, by informing one another that they would apply pressure in a restrained fashion, the parent companies reassured each other. As JSS admitted to PJ, B&S's 'first letter ... I am sorry to say does not show quite the right spirit ... [and] we are taking steps to rectify it' (JSS to PJ, 19 October 1934). Knowledge transfers and the generation of project-specific expertise hinged on co-operative interpersonal relations.

In conclusion, by the time the plant was ready, PJ and JSS had installed the communicating infrastructure, and they had gained some experience in using it. This framework enabled the partners to demonstrate forbearance by making *ex post* adjustments for which the initial agreement left wide scope. The actual design of the infrastructure was important but so too was how the partners used it. At this developmental stage, it successfully supported interpersonal learning and some knowledge transfers. However, the parent firms would have to modify their communicating framework in a more comprehensive manner to accommodate more intensive learning and the creation of project-specific knowledge after production commenced.

Early operations, 1935–38: adjusting the infrastructure

After the factory started operations in July 1935, disagreements broke out among the staff that the parent firms had transferred to OP. Difficulties also arose between JSS and PJ over staffing matters, relations between OP and Swire affiliates (CN and TD&E), and the dual distribution arrangement run by OP and WH&C. These internal shocks compelled PJ and JSS to adjust their arrangements in order to enhance interpersonal/inter-organisational learning and re-establish a strategic consensus. This section examines how the partners modified the communicating infrastructure to support interpersonal learning, inter-organisational co-operation, transfers of technical and sales expertise, and the creation of new project-specific knowledge between 1935 and 1938.

Interpersonal learning

At OP, trouble first arose from the suspicion that PJ was unloading underqualified staff on the joint venture. To strengthen the new firm's sales capabilities, Maxted suggested that OP recruit A. G. Howe, who had worked for WH&C, and H. O. Bramble, one of PJ's junior salesmen. Although Maxted, whom JSS and B&S trusted, wrote that Bramble was 'a good type' and provided a copy of his service record, B&S heard from Mr Martin, a PJ official in Shanghai, and WH&C's Heywood that Bramble was 'definitely second rate' (JSS to PJ, 19 July 1935). JSS confronted PJ's head office staff, who replied that they considered Bramble to be fully trained and suggested that Warren Swire meet him (PJ to JSS, 27 August 1935). Reassured by the interview, Swire agreed to the transfer. It was natural for the joint venturers to suspect each other of exploiting the project and from time to time to doubt intermediary figures, like Maxted, who had a closer affiliation with one party. Direct communication was necessary on both accounts to enable local staff to gain confidence in each other's abilities and to facilitate transfers of embodied knowledge. Confirmation of Maxted's judgement enhanced his future intermediary capabilities.

Problems also arose with Mr Radford, whom PJ sent to OP to occupy the key position of factory manager. B&S complained that Radford was cantankerous, he had not set up an efficient records system, and he did not delegate (B&S to JSS, 6 September 1935). In response, PJ instructed Radford to decentralise. Warren Swire reassured PJ by saying that 'Radford is intrinsically a good fellow [but h]e has had a very tough time ... getting ... the work started' (JSS to PJ, 28 October 1935). Martin, whom PJ sent to Shanghai to fill in while Maxted went on leave, suggested that the parent firms' distinct management styles explained Radford's behaviour: he was not used to the type of close control exerted by B&S (B&S to JSS, 8 and 15 May 1936). Recognising that Radford was overworked and better suited to factory management rather than paper work, B&S lightened his duties by transferring Mr Baggallay to set up OP's accounting system.

The crux of the matter was that Radford had not had time to transfer PJ's costing system to OP as PJ had promised, and B&S felt insecure as a result. Martin did not help matters when he indicated that he thought that Baggallay was too highly paid! B&S countered that 'we do not yet trust Mr Radford's managerial ability sufficiently well for us to remove the [only] avenue [i.e. Baggallay] we have' for obtaining cost data (B&S to JSS, 15 May 1936). JSS told B&S that Mr McLaren, who was known for his tact, would act as their 'watch dog' as soon as he had acquired knowledge of the paint business.

In response to further complaints, JSS told B&S that PJ recognised that Radford was temperamental but able. By September, B&S were convinced that Radford would have to go. JSS suggested they see how he behaved once he had help from a foreman whom PJ had promised to send to China. JSS informed B&S that, like PJ, it had 'to consider the matter in all its aspects' meaning that inter-parent relations might be affected if Radford was let go, but blamed no one for the problem, which was the result of 'bad luck and incompatible personalities' (JSS to B&S, 14 September 1936).

At this point, however, the problem spread: Radford and Offord, a chemist transferred from PJ, came into conflict. A JSS official sagely speculated 'I wouldn't mind betting the [source] of the trouble is Offord' (Comment in margin B&S to JSS, 11 September 1936). A week later, B&S again complained about Radford. Exhausted, JSS replied that Radford had gained valuable experience which should not be thrown away, suggested that Offord was the problem, and stated that B&S *must* retain Radford. To reassure B&S, however, JSS stated that Radford would be placed under McLaren, 'one of our best handlers of men' (JSS to B&S, 2 October 1936). Realising that Maxted's absence also contributed to the problem, JSS suggested that OP hire him.

B&S felt that JSS's comments were an unjustified 'censure' of their approach to the situation (B&S to JSS, 30 October 1936). In the margin JSS staff wrote: 'B&S are as perfect as they always have been' but felt that the stratagem had worked. 'The correspondence will have given Maxted the chance he wanted to clear the air and make a clean start on a more satisfactory basis.' Indeed, with Maxted's return, the arrival of Aplin (PJ's paint foreman), the departure of Offord, and McLaren in control, the situation began to right itself. By the new year, B&S reported that Aplin was working well with Radford, who had become a 'changed man' (B&S to JSS, 15 January 1937).

Personality conflicts, understaffing, and differences in management style could have cost OP the experience Radford had gained working under Chinese conditions. These factors did hinder the transfer of PJ's accounting system, and the absence of this vital part of the communicating infrastructure compelled B&S to employ an expensive 'watch dog'. Moreover, OP's personnel difficulties also delayed the creation of new project-specific knowledge (pp. 72–73). Both parent companies tried to solve contributory problems, especially overwork, hoping that relations would improve. PJ and JSS also communicated directly with their own people to encourage co-operation, and they showed forbearance towards each other's staff. Yet, when it appeared that parent company relations might be affected by conflict at OP, JSS, knowing that its affiliate was partly to blame, 'censured' B&S to push local management together. In this instance, managerial attraction by 'suction' had to be 'primed'. JSS's intervention also gave Maxted the chance to refocus the attention of all staff at OP. To prepare his way, the parent firms adjusted the managerial team to get the right mix of skills and personalities. It is remarkable that so acute was their knowledge of each other's staff that PJ and JSS were able to do so from London.

Inter-firm relations: PJ and JSS

While JSS and PJ were trying to resolve these personnel problems, PJ's Martin tried to undermine B&S's position as manager. The problem arose from the different ways PJ and JSS ran their subsidiaries. PJ treated its units like 'watertight compartments', whereas JSS affiliates collaborated intensively. The storm broke at a dinner party that B&S's G. E. Mitchell hosted to welcome John S. Scott, a JSS director, who was conducting an inspection tour of Swires' Far East interests. Apparently, Martin insulted Mitchell 'over his own dinner table'. Scott talked to Martin in private afterwards and pressed upon him that 'he must recognise that we have to manage the show and … [he must] not dictate to us as we don't respond well to that sort of thing' (JSSI 3/9 A33 J. S. Scott to JSS, 18 April 1936). Scott then made a determined effort to encourage interpersonal learning and co-operation by providing opportunities for Martin to mix with Swire personnel. Scott felt that 'the famous dinner at Mitchell's was a turning point', after which Martin had come to accept B&S's position and Swires' management approach.

However, after Scott's departure, Martin reverted to form. While filling in for Maxted who was on leave, Martin suggested that OP was straying from its original marketing strategy. B&S staff felt that Martin was 'trying to run the OP Co …' (comment in margin PJ to JSS, 27 June 1936). JSS reassured B&S by providing copies of its correspondence with PJ and by saying that it would guard against any attempt by PJ to run OP. However, when PJ staff offered advice in Maxted's absence B&S should be 'politic' (JSS to B&S, 3 July 1936). JSS stated that PJ's advice was objective – Maxted (whom all parties trusted) would say the same thing if he were in China – it was not 'the thin edge of the wedge' (JSS to B&S, 24 July 1936). JSS told B&S staff that they should accept suggestions. 'It [OP] is a joint concern and, however full the powers of the management may be, you cannot run a joint concern successfully, unless the parties in it feel themselves free to express their opinions' (JSS to B&S, 28 August 1936). B&S remained unconvinced, and JSS felt that B&S 'have got the *atmosphere* all wrong'. However, privately one JSS London partner admitted:

> we shall sooner or later have to put all our cards on the table and have a show down with PJ. The *sine qua non* of our getting into this show was that

we managed it and they are [sic] the expert advisers. There is no doubt at all that Martin regards the OP Co as PJ&Co's Shanghai subsidiary ... and we have got to make it quite plain to them that this is not so or we shall quietly drift into the position of it being so.

(comment in margin B&S to JSS, 31 July 1936 JSS)

With Maxted's return JSS's fear of losing control receded somewhat.

The episode shows how the failure to maintain one vital part of the communicating infrastructure – a clear understanding of each partner's responsibilities – could create concern for the future of the project. As JSS saw, open communication and the ability to *listen* to the other party were vital. Creating the right 'atmosphere' was also important, and here crisis resolution skills, such as those PJ and JSS exercised from London and those that Scott applied after the Mitchell dinner, could play key roles. The contrast between Martin and Maxted was poignant, and Swire officials remained suspicious of the former.

Inter-firm relations: OP and Swire affiliates, CN and TD&E

For PJ, one of the chief attractions of allying with the Swire group was the chance to gain access to demand from CN and TD&E. For Swires, it made no sense for its units to buy from OP unless its paint was competitive in terms of price and quality. This issue was another source of difficulty for the partners, especially while OP struggled to build up the volume of output and lower the burden of overheads to reduce its prices.

OP could not secure CN's business because it could not match the prices of high-quality imports. (JSS to B&S, 13 March 1936). PJ confirmed this but found that OP could compete with low-quality Chinese paint (OP to JSS, 24 April 1936). PJ pressed JSS to secure for OP CN's requirements for the inferior article, but Swires did not want CN to tie itself to OP (PJ to JSS, 16 July 1936). CN saw no advantage in buying from OP (CN to JSS, 28 August 1936). Maxted then suggested that CN give OP a one-year trial, but JSS at once recognised that this idea had been planted in his mind by the 'little schemer', Martin. To bypass this untrustworthy figure, JSS and PJ officials met in London and agreed that CN would buy from OP at market prices free from any long-term commitment.

The Swire link with TD&E, which possessed a small paint factory in Hong Kong, offered an opportunity for OP to tap foreign markets while avoiding Chinese export tariffs. The idea was that TD&E would buy raw materials from OP at market prices, make paint for OP using OP formulae, and pay a fee based on OP's gate cost (B&S to JSS, 4 September and 9 October 1936). The start of the operation was delayed because OP did not have an accounting system that provided the required cost data (PJ to JSS, 26 November 1936).

In these instances, defects in personnel relations and accounting capabilities hindered the development of mutually beneficial inter-firm ties through which proprietary knowledge, such as formulae, could be transferred. These weaknesses also prevented the quick resolution of *policy* differences between the parent firms concerning inter-unit transactions. The CN–OP case also shows how partners had to be on guard against opportunists, such as Martin, who might try to manipulate intermediary channels of trust.

Inter-firm relations: OP and WH&C

Under the original agreement, OP was to make paint for WH&C under that firm's brand names at gate cost plus ten per cent profit, and it was to develop its own brands that would compete with those of WH&C. Relations between the two firms were strained because OP's costs were high and its staff could not estimate gate cost. However, the basic problem was that at the outset OP and WH&C had been placed in a very difficult position.

The parent firms wanted OP and WH&C to co-operate rather than compete. JSS foresaw that OP would succeed to the point where WH&C would retreat into a small, high-quality market niche, but in the meantime it hoped that the two firms could work together. (JSS to PJ, 22 October; PJ to JSS, 9 October 1936). PJ did not want WH&C to 'fade away' but instead wished that it would grow alongside of OP (PJ to JSS, 20 November 1936).

B&S complained that 'the channels of business are so few that all sellers necessarily crowd in on all of them' and large customers were angered when they discovered that the two firms colluded (B&S to JSS, 11 December 1936). B&S also felt that WH&C must 'fade away' to avoid the duplication of expensive sales forces. Acquiescing to its partner's preferences, JSS wrote to PJ that OP and WH&C must 'work out their own salvation' but felt that constructive letters from the parent firms might help induce co-operation.

In October 1936 OP and WH&C staff hammered out a price agreement, but when it proved defective, officials from the parent firms met the following January. After making two more attempts to resolve the pricing issue in October 1936 and January 1937, JSS pressed PJ for a merger between OP and WH&C (JSS to PJ ,22 October 1936, memo, 5 January 1937; and JSS to PJ 4 February 1937). Maxted and B&S provided data showing that amalgamation would reduce overheads to the point that if combined sales reached 120 tons per month, OP would at last be able to pay the technical advisers' and general agent's fees (B&S to JSS, 12 February 1937). After working out royalty payments, the parent firms approved the merger, subject to stock valuations and the input prices PJ charged OP being negotiated satisfactorily (PJ to JSS, 16 June 1937). Martin could not resist an opportunity to suggest that further savings might be won if OP had its own management. B&S replied that it had lost £4,000 running OP, and, in some embarrassment, PJ's Mr R. Partridge replied that 'the question was raised by our Mr Martin, [but] had not previously had any discussion [by] Mr Heywood or myself' (PJ to JSS, 25 June 1937). As Martin's actions became more transparent, other PJ staff distanced themselves from him.

Initially sceptical that the dual distribution system would work, JSS had agreed to it to ensure that PJ would sign the original contract and that WH&C would not be alienated. Recognising that the disappearance of WH&C would leave PJ without an independent outlet in China, JSS gave the dual selling scheme a fair trial. Swires let experience gradually lead PJ to see the logic of a merger, albeit at the cost of a financial loss to B&S. This approach ensured that the resolution of this point, once achieved, would represent real consensus. Adjusting inter-firm relations was in this case, like the OP and CN–TD&E instances, delayed by defects in the accounting system and interpersonal ties, defects that could also impede knowledge transfers.

Knowledge transfers

The initial communicating framework helped organisational expertise to flow quite freely across the boundaries of the firms. PJ provided OP with an administrative model consisting of three units – accounting, sales, and general office – in addition to the factory department (PJ to JSS, 20 December 1935 and 4 January 1936). PJ provided organisational charts showing the relationships between these units and described in detail the tasks each had to perform, the type of knowledge needed, and the kind of manager required. Thus, PJ sought to *instruct* its partner in the administrative subtleties of making and selling paint, and as it did so it drew contrasts with sugar refining, with which JSS and B&S were familiar.

JSS urged B&S 'to *translate* [PJ's ideas] into terms with which you are already conversant in your management of TSR' (JSS to B&S, 17 January 1936). B&S responded with a modified version of PJ's organisational chart (B&S to JSS, 20 March 1936). Thus, the Swire group absorbed new organisational knowledge, reprocessed it into familiar terms, and finally applied it to meet the specific requirements of the paint business.

To transfer accounting information, which was to a degree tacit in nature, the partners had to modify the personnel component of the communicating infrastructure. Radford was supposed to have imparted such knowledge but had been unable to do so. B&S assigned one of its accountants, a Mr Lock, to help with the task. However, feeling 'the need of more knowledge of the scientific background to PJ's costing and pricing methods and their methods for control of production', Lock visited PJ's UK works to absorb this specialised knowledge (B&S to JSS, 29 November 1935).

PJ described the general principles on which the accounting system should operate. It advocated a cost-plus-pricing approach which like 'an automaton … works on predetermined lines until exceptions to the rule arise' (PJ to JSS, 4 January 1936). However, JSS wanted pricing separated from costs because it felt that the expense of making paint had no relation to what it could be sold for (JSS to B&S, 17 January 1936). The sales manager, Mr Tippin, 'should know nothing' of costs otherwise he might be 'psychologically liable to accept a lower price than he need'. It was up to the managing director to monitor prices in relation to costs and when necessary to instruct the factory to cut expenses. Thus, JSS modified PJ's principles to align incentives in a way consistent with both its market-based, decentralised approach and the local paint market.

OP began adjusting the system further so that it could show the profitability of each brand. B&S sent an accounting expert, F. D. Hunter, to OP to help with this task (B&S to JSS, 7 March 1937). When OP began to produce a large enough volume consistently, it could at last calculate overheads on a meaningful basis. JSS provided instructions about how these expenses should be loaded on to different products (JSS to B&S, 16 July 1937). Always with an eye on the incentive implications of systems design, JSS suggested that the procedures should not encourage salesmen to push some products at the expense of others and thereby undermine OP's overall market strategy. Hunter and Radford, who possessed the required industry-specific accounting knowledge, then worked out machine hours and allocated factory expenses to each department (Advisory Committee, 25 November 1937).

Thus, by 1938, OP had finally perfected its accounting system. The task took so long for a variety of reasons, but among these the most important was that such a system could not be adopted 'off the shelf'. Swire staff had to learn about the peculiarities of the paint business and then modify procedures in light of project-specific circumstances, some of which were revealed only after operations began. Even the incentive implications of the system's design could only be discovered by gaining experience in selling paint in what was a distinctive market. Finally, harmonious relations between Hunter and Radford were crucial in supporting transfers of tacit knowledge.

Just as B&S staff had to learn about and modify accounting systems, so they had to absorb and adapt new sales methods to suit the paint business and meet OP's marketing objectives. Getting the right mix of personnel was also important. B&S recognised that its experience in selling sugar was of little value to the paint business, which required much closer consultation with customers (B&S to JSS, 29 November 1935). JSS asked WH&C whether OP men could accompany WH&C staff on their sales tours in order to learn about sales consulting (JSS to B&S and B&S to JSS, 29 November 1935).

PJ could offer general advice on how it conducted sales in overseas markets that shared some of the same characteristics as China, but it recognised that OP's market was distinctive. It stressed the importance of having a sales manager who had intimate knowledge of the country and considered technical know-how to be of secondary significance. What OP needed in its sales manager was an 'inspiring force capable of partially moulding the sales activities ...' (PJ to JSS, 4 January 1936). It was also vital for salesmen to learn the technical side of the business at OP's factory rather than at one of PJ's more advanced plants in England. PJ strongly recommended that OP recruit and train Chinese salesmen who had BSc degrees in chemistry:

[T]he national characteristics of a concern are, largely, more closely determined by actual contact between salesmen and buyers. Management and factory operations are, so far as the buyer is concerned, impersonal activities in which they ... are not interested. The buyer knows the products through the actual salesman who calls upon them ... It is this conception which made us, in India, develop quite a large and successful staff of native salesmen to deal with native business. There would appear to be a parallel here for the [OP Co. to follow]

(ibid.)

JSS and B&S adapted these ideas to OP's operations (JSS to B&S, 17 January 1936). They decided to put Tippin in overall charge of the sales department and assigned management of the Chinese sales force to a Mr Hutchinson, who could provide the 'inspiring force' needed. Tippin went to WH&C to study its sales organisation, and ten men were put through a training programme in the factory and in the field (OP to JSS, 31 January 1936).

OP wanted its sales force to educate customers in the benefits of higher quality, but additional steps were taken to develop complementary distribution channels. Tippin conceived of the idea of having a parallel string of Chinese sales agencies, modelled on BAT Industries' local distribution chain, in order to overcome 'buy Chinese' sentiments (Cox 1995; Report, 18 July 1936). OP set this up in association with Wing Tai Vo, who also represented BAT, to win the custom of Shanghai dealers who supplied the up-country trade (B&S to JSS, 26 March 1937). Through T. V. Soong's contacts, OP arranged for MSI Co. to sell paint under different brands in northern China, where OP's salesmen had not been able to break through local distribution channels (Committee, 3 June 1937). WH&C's comprador, H. C. Woo, offered retail outlets for small lot sales in Shanghai (B&S to JSS, 15 January 1937).

OP modified PJ's ideas to develop a multiple distribution system that reached different market sectors and avoided a repeat of the OP–WH&C problem. To support its strategy of beating low-quality local paint and displacing imports, OP established a Chinese sales force that could educate customers in the merits of superior-quality paint and developed local outlets to meet culturally and geographically determined market segments. In building the Chinese side of the dual distribution system, B&S's local contacts, as well as its knowledge of existing distribution arrangements and trading customs, were vital. This intelligence enabled it to avoid bad debts, to determine the different types of security that merchants would provide, and to work with – instead of antagonise – local interests. Technical sales expertise was absorbed and blended with local marketing knowledge.

The communicating infrastructure and co-operative links within the Swire group also sustained transfers of proprietary information. As we have seen, PJ and WH&C provided OP with the formulae of their brands. Later, PJ granted OP the right to sell its brands in Singapore and, following the merger of OP and WH&C, gave OP an exclusive licence covering China and Hong Kong (memo, 12 August 1937). Thus, PJ and WH&C sacrificed to OP more of their sovereignty, in the form of independent marketing capabilities.

OP staff also provided TD&E with formulae so it could make paint for OP for sale through B&S in Hong Kong and Southern Asia (B&S to JSS, 4 September 1936; JSS to B&S, 20 November 1936). However, TD&E officials feared that OP might absorb *their trade secrets* and terminate the manufacturing agreement. Although both parties recognised that when the volume of business became large enough OP would set up its own Hong Kong factory, they had no formal agreement to cover how this development would be handled. JSS understood the fears of TD&E managers and assured them of fair dealing when the time came. The demonstration effect of previous transfers from PJ and WH&C to OP made this promise credible. Over time, co-operation gathered cumulatively to broaden the flow of proprietary information.

Creating new project-specific knowledge

The most important type of project-specific knowledge that the partners sought to develop was how to make cheap, low-quality paint. This was the key to OP's strategy until customers could be drawn to higher-quality products. It was also vital for financial success because only by producing in bulk could OP cover its overheads and make a profit (PJ to B&S, 24 July 1937). Although PJ modified its high-quality paints to use local raw materials, it could not instruct OP how to make the inexpensive product. It was up to OP staff to find the right formula, a quest that was difficult because of the variable nature of local inputs.

Radford's first attempt failed miserably: the paint hardened in the tins (B&S to JSS, 28 August 1936). JSS suggested that OP buy the required formula, possibly through T. V. Soong's contacts, but the stratagem did not work (JSS to B&S, 2 October 1936). OP also tried but failed to obtain formulae from a local manufacturer whose factory had been bombed. Then, acting on its own OP struck on the right formula in June 1938.

The delay in discovering how to make cheap paint reflected defects in the joint venture's set-up. First, it is possible that responsibility for this task had been incorrectly assigned to PJ. Instead of using Radford, perhaps a Chinese paint maker should have been recruited. Second, overwork and an atmosphere of tension impeded Radford's progress. Indeed, the failure of August 1936 occurred when B&S's opinion of his ability was at a low ebb. Although discovery always involves an element of luck, the fact that Radford found the formula after interpersonal relations had improved and when OP was near to proving its financial viability might suggest that a climate of growing confidence played a role.

To conclude this section as a whole, the parent firms were compelled to adjust parts of the initial communicating infrastructure to overcome a variety of problems that impeded interpersonal learning, knowledge transfers, and the creation of project-specific expertise. The responsibilities assigned at first to each affiliated enterprise had to be clarified and the contours of inter-firm communication lines had to be adjusted. PJ and JSS had to install and adapt their accounting system to build trust, to meet the requirements of the paint business, and to mobilise specific incentives. The partners needed to modify OP's management team to promote compatibility and to harness the right mix of skills needed to apply existing knowledge to meet Chinese conditions. Because defects in one component affected other parts of the infrastructure, all elements within the set had to be adjusted in an interrelated manner to strengthen the relationship.

Developments from 1938 to 1949

The final section examines developments from January 1938 until the move to Hong Kong in the late 1940s. During this period, a spirit of growing trust between the parent firms became more apparent, but B&S remained suspicious of PJ, indicating that inter-firm learning processes were still incomplete. The communicating infrastructure did not undergo further change, and it continued to support successful transfers of knowledge.

The bonds of trust between PJ and JSS show themselves most clearly during the completion of the OP–WH&C merger, which had been agreed to in principle in late 1937. Maxted, now managing director of OP, wrote to B&S confidentially outlining PJ's position on the merger (JSS to B&S, 7 January 1938). What prompted Maxted's letter is uncertain, but it made JSS feel uneasy '[it] is not the way in which we like doing business'. It was unnecessary and possibly diminished Maxted's reputation:

> In view of our present relations with PJ & Co, it is surely only common sense that he should show us such letters, but unless he can do so openly, we should rather that you [B&S] passed on their contents to us in the form of a letter from yourselves.
>
> (JSS to B&S, 7 January 1938)

JSS trusted Maxted's information but was concerned lest such informal communication, which the partners had hitherto eschewed, might jeopardise his position, which JSS valued highly. Above all, JSS preferred to resolve differences openly to retain PJ's trust.

Since it held shares in WH&C, PJ was concerned about the valuation of WH&C stock that OP would take over as part of the merger contract. Respecting this concern, JSS instructed OP not to use the war as an excuse for refusing to accept WH&C's goods:

> This is certainly not *our* intention as ... OP&Co. are paying nothing for the goodwill of the Company [WH&C] and it is only fair and reasonable that ... they should pay for the thick with the thin except only in so far as the incidence of the war has rendered this unreasonable ... [OP will take over all goods except] physically damaged stocks and stock of

industrial specialities imported for industries that no longer exist or are unlikely to be [re]established in the next twelve months.

(JSS to B&S, 7 January 1938)

Thus, JSS laid down a clear, rational basis for accepting WH&C stock.

PJ was also responsible for bad debts incurred by WH&C, and these rose alarmingly during the Japanese occupation. Fearing that such an unexpected financial blow might damage PJ's commitment to the venture, JSS wrote to B&S 'Bad Debt This is truly an alarming figure, and we are really quite ashamed at having to enforce the [merger] bargain under the terms of our Agreement' (JSS to B&S, 7 October 1938). Perhaps fortuitously, OP staff discovered that PJ had not been credited for WH&C's stationery worth $10,000, and JSS passed this information on to PJ at the same time that it informed its partner of the bad debts. PJ replied that this 'information ... softens the Bad Debt blow. It is very kind of you to send these [letters] along, and we really do appreciate the courtesy' (PJ to JSS, 18 October 1938). PJ knew it was important to tell JSS that it appreciated JSS's honesty and concern for how PJ would react to the size of bad debts.

When all details of the merger were complete, PJ wrote to JSS:

the writer would like to take this opportunity of expressing our appreciation of the very amicable manner in which the negotiations have been carried through, and we do feel that ... our trading prospects in the China Territory are as happy as could be expected.

(PJ to JSS, 5 November 1938)

Such courtesy was important at a juncture when the partners had aligned themselves on a new basis, and it helped to set a co-operative tone for future relations (see Chapter 6).

After the merger, inter-firm correspondence displayed a tone of growing trust that appears to have helped the participating companies to overcome differences more easily and more rapidly. In attempting to resolve a disagreement over how OP and PJ could share access to South Asian markets, for example, PJ wrote:

we think you will understand that the above ... suggestions are not put forward in any difficult or carping spirit, but are in order that we may all work on very clearly defined lines and avoid confusion, overlap, or unnecessary competition of any kind.

(PJ to OP, 15 December 1938)

The straightforward tone of the letter reinforced the logic of trying to find a mutually beneficial yet workable arrangement that would ensure smooth relations in the future.

Another issue requiring *ex post* adjustment concerned PJ's fee as technical adviser and B&S's management fee. Although entitled to $30,000 per annum each, neither firm had received any payment from OP since its inception. By August 1938, B&S found its management duties burdensome, and, although it recognised that some of its work involved safeguarding Swire interests, it felt that it spent much more time on OP's business than did PJ officials (JSS to PJ, 26 August 1938). B&S estimated the cost of management to be £4023 after deducting monitoring expenses. The firm sought to recover at least its out of pocket costs. PJ agreed to waive its fee for another year and possibly, as JSS staff said 'we hope for ever'. Although PJ would still earn profits by selling material to OP, its action signalled that it observed a long-term perspective and an attitude of forbearance.

Even though relations between the parent firms were friendly, B&S still mistrusted PJ. Shanghai staff remained sceptical about the prices PJ charged for inputs and its policy towards South Asian markets. JSS repeatedly had to keep B&S suspicions under control:

> the writer blames himself for not having realised what a mare's nest this question was and for not having given due weight to your incurable mistrust of PJ & Co's motives and sincerity. After carefully considering your letter in conjunction with the agreements and arrangements come to with PJ & Co, it became quite clear that you were banging on an open door, and we have now confirmed this with Mr Mackintosh.
>
> (JSS to B&S, 23 June 1939)

After JSS presented B&S with a clear set of options devised by both parent firms, B&S's suspicions began to wane.

By September 1938, OP had turned the corner. In addition to solving the riddle of how to make cheap paint, the destruction of competing factories and economies arising from the WH&C merger brought profitable results. It was ironic that success came just as tensions in the East mounted. The Japanese tried to force B&S to sell a controlling stake in OP and then commandeered the factory when the Pacific War broke out.

In August 1945, B&S resumed manufacturing, but within two years plans were being made to shift the base of operations to Hong Kong. By 1948, OP merged with Duro Paint 'not so much on account of their specific connections with paint and the existence of their factory, as on account of our belief that they will make durable partners with whom we can work in mutual trust and respect' (OP to JSS, 5 December 1947). On August 5, 1949, OP and Duro concluded a 'Gentleman's Agreement' as Swire and PJ had done back in 1933. In fact, the formal contract with Duro was identical to the one that the original partners had arranged except that OP was now technical adviser (JSSIX 2/9 2016 F). PJ was associated with the Duro scheme, but by 1949 OP had absorbed and created sufficient knowledge of Far Eastern paint-making and -selling operations that it could play this vital role itself. Moreover, the merger created a new opportunity to build a larger foundation for further growth. The Swire group's learning skills served it well since the new operation became the basis of the extensive paint business it runs today in conjunction with ICI.

Conclusion

JSS decided to use a joint venture framework instead of forming a new subsidiary, because this course offered a way to avoid potential competition and a way to remedy deficiencies in its technical capabilities. Having decided to employ a co-operative structure, Swires recognised that extensive interpersonal and inter-organisational learning would be required to transfer expertise and create new knowledge. It was also vital for OP staff to absorb, translate, and blend information in order to adapt expertise available from affiliates to suit conditions in China. In doing so, they developed learning capabilities and co-operative skills needed to build a bigger business in Asia after 1945.

The theoretical literature concerning international joint ventures focuses on *what* should be considered when selecting a partner, planning, and controlling a project, and building trust and a co-operative reputation. The OP case provides some guidelines about *how* participants may achieve these aims. The main finding is that – in the absence of the type of public good communicating infrastructure discussed in Chapter 2 – a purpose-built construct is needed to contain the relatively high cost of communicating to build trust within a voice relationship. The study also reveals that the partners manipulated the components of this framework in interdependent ways to support a considerable amount of *ex post* adjustment for which the original trust based contract left wide scope. In this regard, the partners accurately assessed each other's attributes. This determination in turn enabled them to achieve an important trade-off that all joint venture participants need to consider, that is striking an appropriate balance, in light of environmental and partner-specific characteristics, between the degree of trust and the scope for *ex post* modification. (Chapters 5, 6, and 8 describe other attempts to achieve such a balance.)

The ways in which interpersonal/inter-organisational learning, knowledge transfer, and the creation of project-specific knowledge unfolded shows that complementarity evolved over time as the partners forged a series of co-operative equilibria in response to internal and external shocks. This was vital because the initial basis of the venture appeared to be so poorly founded in the context of the criteria for success identified by Lorange (1988). As Casson (1990) suggests this form of project acted as an instrument for building co-operative relations, showing forbearance, and creating a reputation as a dependable partner. Finally, this case reveals a distinctive set of co-operative skills. Communicating in subtle ways, signalling that one has listened attentively and grasped a salient point, sensitivity to incentives, anticipating problems, crisis resolution, team building, observing recognised etiquette or courtesies, and knowing when to act or when to let the logic of one's position reveal itself to others were all important talents commanded by PJ and JSS staff. Above all, they knew how to act in ways that did not reflect enlightened self-interest, but which instead convincingly demonstrated concern for the other party's welfare. As in any relationship, how something is done is at least as important as what is done.

5 A purchasing co-operative

The Steel Manufacturers' Nickel Syndicate, 1901–39

This case examines the history of an unusual intermediate arrangement: a purchasing co-operative. This organisation used a distinct contractual mix that relied mainly on monitoring mechanisms. It also designed inter-firm communication lines to enhance transparency and yet to concentrate its market power. The success of the syndicate largely reflected how it used its power. As a complement to the formal model presented in Chapter 2, this case study measures the efficiency of the syndicate relative to the next best institutional alternative.

This chapter explores the history of the Steel Manufacturers' Nickel Syndicate, which operated successfully for nearly forty years. As a manufacturers' purchasing co-operative, the syndicate was a rare form of intermediate mode that has not attracted much attention.[1] It was established in 1901 by several British armament firms to combine their purchasing power and to support the arrangement of a preferential supply agreement with La Société de Nickel, then the world's leading producer of nickel. Although membership in the syndicate changed over time, new sources of demand for nickel arose, and additional suppliers emerged, the syndicate endured, alongside its contract with La Société and a global pricing agreement among the largest nickel producers, until at least 1939. These arrangements survived the wide shifts in demand and supply that characterise commodity markets and which were particularly severe in the inter-war period, when many supplier cartels were formed but later fell apart under the strain of acute price fluctuations (Rowe 1965).

The durability of the syndicate can be attributed to several factors. First, its structure suited the commercial aims it was designed to serve. The syndicate mobilised combined purchasing power initially against a large supplier and later against a tight oligopoly of nickel producers. Members would have paid higher prices had they conducted independent purchasing activities. No single participant required sufficient nickel to adopt a strategy of vertical integration. Although the syndicate controlled its own smelter in south Wales, using this facility as a basis for collective backward expansion into nickel mining would have left the syndicate exposed to severe cyclical swings. Combined demand was inadequate to ensure a consistently high level of capacity utilisation. Second, the syndicate endured because, in contrast to the OP case where PJ and JSS had fairly equal power, it occupied a strong bargaining position relative to La Société after new suppliers emerged, but it used this power in a restrained manner. Indeed, since participants in any type of co-operative endeavour must make what Richardson (1972) called a willing sacrifice of some of their sovereignty, how they exercise force or forbearance will have an important impact on long-term relations (see Langlois and Robertson 1995). Third, the syndicate's behaviour was shaped by strategic information about La Société's circumstances channelled through a communication system that included both internal and external constituents. Moreover, these inter-organisational links were designed to capture a wealth of purchasing and price data. Whereas, the HSS case analysed the operation of an inter-firm Decision-support system, this chapter examines a transaction-processing system that extended beyond a single organisational boundary. Finally, the syndicate survived because it was efficient. The price and purchasing information that the syndicate gathered will support comparative quantitative assessment of this institution's performance in relation to the market, which was the most likely alternative transacting framework. The results confirm that members derived growing benefits from association. Thus, in response to Williamson's (1975) call for more searching examination of information handling capabilities of intermediary modes, this chapter considers both the structure and the contents of the syndicate's communication channels and how it used them in practice.

The discussion analyses two interdependent contracts: one that bound syndicate members together and one between the purchasing co-operative and La Société. Both relied mainly upon monitoring mechanisms, in contrast to the previous cases where culture played a formidable role. (Data about the third contract, the global pricing and marketing agreement between International Nickel Company (INCO), Mond Nickel, and La Société, are too scarce to support detailed analysis, but its supporting role is described below.) To sustain co-operation among syndicate members, monitoring channels were designed to provide transparency so that participants could observe directly the financial advantages they secured. The contract between the syndicate and La Société gave both parties constitutional power that enhanced their monitoring capabilities. Together with links that served other communicating purposes, these monitoring channels supported sequential adjustment and inter-firm learning.

Historical background and the syndicate's formation

Nickel was used to harden armour and special steels. A strategic material, it was in strong demand during the naval race leading up to the First World War and during the conflict. As armament manufacturing declined in the 1920s, the American and European automobile industries provided a rapidly expanding alternative market. When re-armament began in the mid-1930s nickel output soared.

Before 1900, the vast majority of the world's nickel came from New Caledonia (Cohen 1956; Vickers 57/61 statement, 31 July 1935). In 1880, Australian entrepreneur John Higginson began to develop the ore bodies on this Pacific island. He soon overstretched his finances and sold a twenty-five per cent interest in his firm, La Société de Nickel, to the Rothschilds, who provided trade credits and marketing services (McKay 1986). Nickel deposits had been discovered near Sudbury, Ontario, in the 1880s and were exploited on a small scale during the 1890s. It was not until The Mond Nickel Co. and INCO were formed in 1900 and 1902, respectively, that Canada emerged as the world's principal producer.

Dr Ludwig Mond discovered a chemical process for separating nickel from the composite ore in which the metal was fixed. Unable to interest La Société or North American producers in his invention, Mond set out to exploit it on his own. He purchased mining property near Sudbury, where he built a smelter, and constructed a large-scale refinery at Clydach near Swansea, south Wales (Cohen 1956). By 1902, the Mond company was producing refined nickel.

Canadian copper companies became interested in nickel because both metals were entrained in the same ore. About the same time that Mond made his discovery, the Orford Nickel & Copper Co. invented an electrolytic separating process, which it introduced at its Canadian refinery. The firm also owned a smelter and a refinery in New Jersey as well as a mine in Quebec. By 1902, Orford's mine was nearing exhaustion and it merged with the Canadian Copper Company, which operated a refinery and mines in the Sudbury region. Together with a small American firm they combined to form INCO under the incorporation laws of New Jersey with capital of US$24 million (Wilkins 1970; Chandler 1990).

The threat that this combination posed to La Société's dominant position and its exclusive selling arrangement with the syndicate was removed some time before 1914, when it concluded a global market-sharing agreement with INCO which Mond Nickel joined later.[2] However, additional pressure for La Société, as a New Caledonian firm, to co-operate with Canadian producers came from the British Government. Official departments first encouraged the use of nickel produced within the dominions and later insisted that Admiralty orders be made from nickel from this source in order to promote imperial self-sufficiency in strategic commodities.[3] In 1929, the global market-sharing arrangement was strengthened when INCO acquired Mond Nickel and thereby came to control seventy-five per cent of the world's nickel production. The formation of the much smaller Falconbridge Nickel Mines in 1928 did not undermine what was effectively a global duopoly.

Upon its foundation in 1901, the syndicate's members included Vickers, John Brown & Co., William Beardmore & Co., Charles Cammel & Co., and Sir W. G. Armstrong, Whitworth & Co. With the exception of Armstrong, which obtained its nickel from INCO under the terms of the market-sharing agreement, the participants founded the Anglo-French Nickel Company, as a wholly owned subsidiary, to operate a nickel refinery in Swansea. Between 1901 and 1907, a total of seven German, French, and Italian armament firms, along with British special steelmaker Hadfields joined the syndicate and enhanced its purchasing power. (Although Hadfields continued to draw supplies from Mond, its inclusion within the syndicate accentuated the co-operative's leverage over all suppliers, and from Hadfields' perspective ensured that that firm would pay the same prices that INCO and La Société charged other members.) During World War I, the syndicate cancelled the shares of its Austrian and German members and expelled them from its ranks (SMNS DM, 8 March 1918). After this, membership in the co-operative did not change. (Figure 5.1 depicts the inter-organisational ties that enveloped the constituents.)

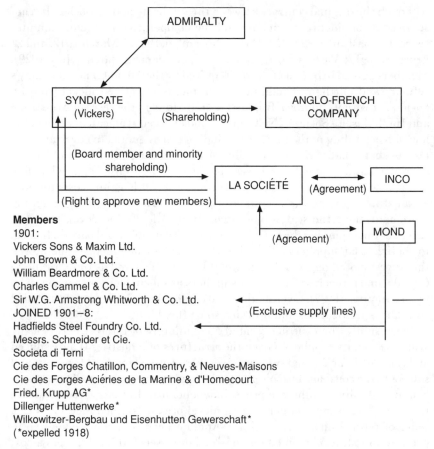

Figure 5.1 Strategic links and information flows, 1902

An estimate of the raw purchasing power that the syndicate wielded after its membership stabilised can be made by comparing the total output from Canada and New Caledonia with the syndicate members' annual purchases when these were noted in the syndicate's directors minutes from 1924 to 1934 (Table 5.1).

The calculation reveals that the co-operative absorbed just over 4.5 per cent of world output, just under 5.5 per cent of Canadian production, but 36.6 per cent of New Caledonia's output. For Canadian producers, the syndicate was a relatively unimportant customer, but to La Société it was a vital outlet. The co-operative could exert more pricing leverage on the relatively small New Caledonia producer than it could on the much larger Canadian firms, INCO and Mond.

The syndicate–La Société contract

Although the original contract between the syndicate and La Société has not survived, subsequent agreements and the co-operative's directors minutes reveal the basic terms (SMNS DM 31 November 1903, 6 March 1912, and 21 February 1917; Vickers 57/61 Appendix 7, Agreement dated 1 July 1929). Members agreed to buy all of the ore required by the Anglo-French company's refinery and all their remaining requirements of refined nickel from La Société, or with its approval from INCO and Mond in the cases of Armstrong and Hadfields. La Société, INCO, and Mond charged syndicate members the lowest price ruling in the market (excluding prices quoted to governments), less a rebate that varied on a sliding scale according to the size of the co-operative's total annual purchases. The use of the well-recognised sliding scale device provided legitimacy and reduced *ex post* haggling costs to those entailed in adjusting the overall scale (p. 90). Price changes representing movement along the scale would occur automatically. Moreover, the price variables underpinning the scale were readily observable to all parties. Indeed, to confirm that suppliers adhered to these terms, the syndicate monitored the prices quoted on the London Metal Exchange as well as those ruling in Canada, and it received from other suppliers unsolicited offers that conveyed price data (pp. 91–92). Overall, the legal component of the contract included verifiable specifications and provided some flexibility.

More subtly, the contract created a community of interest between the syndicate and its suppliers. Given the structures of industries that produced and consumed nickel, market prices were determined by supply and demand subject to the considerable power of large suppliers, whereas small purchasers had little ability to influence prices independently. In these circumstances, the syndicate, as a consumer of both nickel ore and refined metal and as a seller of refined nickel (through the Anglo-French company), benefited in two ways. First, its combined purchasing power secured its members a cost advantage (lowest world price less the rebate) on purchases of refined nickel. Second, because the Anglo-French firm sold some refined nickel to outside

Table 5.1 The syndicate's purchasing power

	Nickel output (tons)			Syndicate orders	Syndicate as percentage of		
Year	Canada	New Caledonia	World		Canada	New Caledonia	World
1924	31,500	3,700	35,400	1,780[a]	5.65	48.11	5.03
1925	33,400	3,400	37,000	1,780[a]	5.33	52.35	4.81
1926	29,900	3,800	34,000	1,780[a]	5.95	46.84	5.24
1927	33,000	3,400	37,500	1,780[a]	5.39	52.35	4.75
1928	43,900	5,900	51,400	1,780[a]	4.01	30.17	3.46
1929	50,000	5,400	58,000	1,800[b]	3.60	33.33	3.10
1930	47,100	8,900	60,000	1,900	4.03	21.35	3.17
1931	29,800	7,800	40,000	1,862	6.25	23.87	4.66
1932	13,800	5,000	22,000	1,660	12.03	33.20	7.55
1933	37,800	5,000	46,000	2,822[b]	7.47	56.44	6.14
1934	58,400	8,600	72,000	3,382	5.79	39.33	4.70
Total	408,600	60,900	493,300	22,326	5.464%	36.66%	4.53

Sources: Schmitz (1979); SMNS DM (Vickers 1198).

Notes

[a] SMNS DM 4 July 1929 reported that on average the annual tonnage purchased for the last five years was 1780 tons.

[b] Tonnage of members' requirements estimated by the syndicate.

customers, syndicate members benefited from the higher world price. In effect, the market-sharing agreement of the rebate suppliers 'bought off' the co-operative for supporting the quoted world price from which syndicate members gained as shareholders in the Anglo-French company. The suppliers were compelled to do so because the Anglo-French company's Swansea refinery, which could meet one-half of syndicate members' requirements for refined nickel, presented a latent threat to Mond, INCO, and La Société. In the event of a hold up in nickel ore supplies or opportunistic collusion by suppliers, the Anglo-French firm might acquire its own mine and expand the capacity of the facility. However, this policy would involve the investment of a considerable amount of capital and the commitment of resources to developing stable outlets for what was a commodity subject to pronounced cyclical swings in demand. (The impact of asymmetric information is unclear in this instance: had La Société recognised the disadvantages of vertical integration by the Anglo-French firm – and we have no evidence that it did – the credibility of the latent threat would have been diminished, but on at least one occasion the syndicate did investigate the potential of ore deposits. Whether La Société was aware of this is not known.) By using the refinery to supply some of its members' total requirements and drawing upon INCO, Mond, and La Société to 'top up' supplies, the syndicate was able to run the Swansea plant at a steady production rate and let its suppliers absorb the swings in demand for refined metal. [Indeed, Vickers' records indicate that the refinery generated large profits (Vickers 57/61 statement, 31 July 1935).] Moreover, the syndicate bought enough ore and refined nickel from each of the three mining firms to preserve relations with all of them. Thus, the overall arrangement created significant mutual interest between the syndicate and all of its suppliers, especially La Société.

For La Société, the agreement had two main attractions. First, it supported the world price for nickel, and, second, it assured the New Caledonian firm of a reliable outlet for a sizeable proportion of its total output. It was clearly in the interest of La Société to build and retain a long-term relationship with the syndicate. The size of the syndicate's demand relative to La Société's output gave the purchasing co-operative an initial advantage in bargaining power especially when Mond and INCO emerged as viable alternative suppliers by 1902 and raised the possibility that unrestrained price competition might break out. The conclusion of the global market-sharing agreement between the three nickel producers nullified some of the strength that the syndicate derived from its raw market power, but the agreement also meant that INCO and La Société would not collude to the disadvantage of the syndicate.[4] In any event, pursuing this alternative strategy of colluding with the Canadian producers might not have served La Société very well. It could have resulted in the syndicate dividing its orders more widely among all suppliers with the result that La Société might have secured a smaller and less consistent flow of orders. Worse, with no incentive to co-operate with the New Caledonian firm, the syndicate might have given preference to dominion enterprises in accordance with the Admiralty's priorities. Rather than risking the possibility that ordering patterns would take the form of a series of one-off market transactions or be influenced by strategic concerns, La Société was further ahead to make concessions in order to demonstrate good will and establish a long-term relationship with the syndicate. Indeed, the purchasing organisation reciprocated.

Regarding overall contract design, the parties arranged a legal component that was simple and had observable specifications. They could not rely on a common culture because the participants represented a multiplicity of national affiliations and did not share a common background. Indeed, the divisive effect of national allegiance is reflected by the Admiralty's policy, but in this instance the syndicate shrewdly used official preferences for deterrence. Despite the lack of a mutual affiliation through which cultural forces could be mobilised and trust founded, the two parties forged a co-operative tie based on mutual advantage, strategic factors, and market conditions. The real strength of the contract's design, however, lay in its monitoring mechanisms.

Communication lines and monitoring mechanisms

In 1902, the syndicate used its commercial strength to gain a measure of constitutional power over La Société, instead of wringing short-term concessions from its supplier. With this capacity, it could shape the content and configuration of inter-organisational communication lines in order to establish and sustain a long-term co-operative tie with the New Caledonian firm. Subsidiary channels between the syndicate and La Société on the one hand and the Admiralty, the Anglo-French Co., Mond, and INCO on the other hand strengthened the co-operative's position relative to the New Caledonian supplier (see Figure 5.1).

To ensure that it had access to strategic information, the syndicate – ever with an eye to minimising costs (pp. 93–95) – induced its members to pool enough funds to acquire the smallest number of shares needed to obtain a directorship in the widely owned La Société. [The amount required from its members proved to be £35,000, or less than £3,000 each (SMNS DM, 9 May and 30 October 1902).] The syndicate might have insisted that it should be given a seat on La Société's Board as a precondition for signing the original agreement. La Société did not have enough countervailing power to demand reciprocity and could not purchase shares in the open market to force its way into the directorate because the syndicate was a private company. Although information asymmetry existed at the strategic level, La Société had the benefit of the syndicate's signal of financial commitment to support the purchasing agreement. To secure access to the board and to reinforce the contract, the syndicate posted a redeemable bond that generated contingent returns in the form of dividends.

La Société did, however, have a measure of constitutional power over the composition of the syndicate. The New Caledonian firm had the right to approve or disapprove of any new firm joining the co-operative (SMNS DM, 9 December 1908). This provision enabled La Société to influence the size and purchasing strength of the syndicate and to prevent the entry of firms that were known to have opportunistic tendencies. Moreover, having the right to approve new members was vital for La Société in ensuring that the terms of the global market-sharing pact with Mond and INCO were respected since the three firms exclusively supplied specific members of the co-operative. The syndicate knew the details of the tripartite market-sharing agreement and could therefore protect its members' interests while avoiding taking any actions that might inadvertently impinge upon its provisions. From the perspective of both parties, La Société's right to approve new members meant that they recognised the interdependence between their contract and the market-sharing agreement.

At the operating level, Vickers handled all administrative functions, partly to simplify communicating procedures between syndicate members, suppliers, and outside constituents, including the Admiralty. However, as a result, these various parties became enmeshed in multilateral communication channels within which Vickers occupied a central, nodal position (see Figure 5.2).

For example, in response to a request made by the Admiralty in 1902,

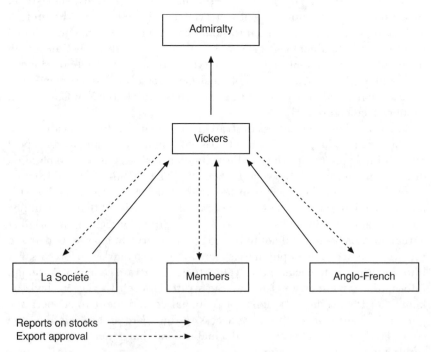

Figure 5.2   Flows of reports on stocks of nickel held in the UK and lines of authority for approving exports, 1902

arising from its concern over the security of the nation's supplies of the strategic metal, the syndicate instructed Vickers to obtain reports on the size of nickel stocks held by UK members, the Anglo-French company, and La Société (SMNS DM, 30 October 1902 and 30 July 1903). La Société also submitted monthly reports to Vickers about the size, location, and form of its stocks in the UK. The syndicate gained the right to verify this information and to approve exports subject to a reserve of 1,000 tons, requested by the Admiralty, being retained. La Société also conveyed details of expected deliveries from New Caledonia. The design of these reporting flows, which was established right after the syndicate was formed, placed the organisation, or more precisely Vickers, in a position from which it could monitor and influence the stock of all nickel in the UK.

During the First World War, arrangements for invoicing, making payments, and reporting on deliveries were streamlined – in response to a request made in 1915 by La Société – so that once again all the relevant data flowed through Vickers, as shown in Figure 5.3 (SMNS DM, 17 November 1915).

The Anglo-French company's refinery and La Société sent invoices and reports concerning the weight of metal delivered to individual members to Vickers, which in turn forwarded the invoices. Members sent payments to

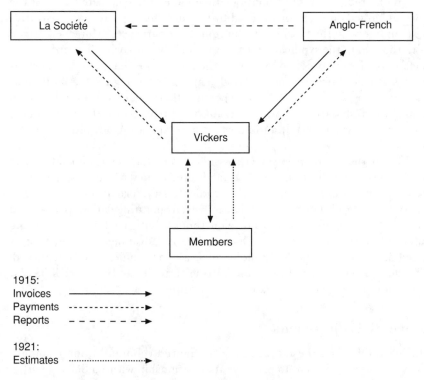

Figure 5.3 Flows of invoices, payments, reports on deliveries of nickel, and estimates of members' consumption during the next half-year, 1915–21

Vickers, which deposited the cheques in the accounts of the Anglo-French company or La Société. The arrangement implicitly made the syndicate responsible for making collections from its members. However, it also enabled Vickers to monitor members' consumption and the income that La Société generated from the co-operative.[5] Moreover, since the Anglo-French firm sold some refined nickel to outside customers (at market prices but with no rebate), the syndicate's communication channels ensured that it had an independent source of information about external demand conditions and the competitive advantages members secured by having the rebate. However, La Société was not excluded from information about the Anglo-French company's refining operations. The Swansea works forwarded to La Société reports of its deliveries to both members and outsiders so that the New Caledonian firm could determine whether or not market sharing quotas and uniform pricing practices were being observed.

To facilitate production scheduling and deliveries, members began in 1921 to send estimates of their requirements for the next six-month period to Vickers, which on behalf of the syndicate forwarded them on to La Société (SMNS DM, 14 January 1921). Thus, the syndicate could monitor the total volume of members' estimated orders and determine in advance the size of the annual rebate. This information also enabled the syndicate to adjust the levy it charged on each ton ordered by members to meet its administrative costs in line with fluctuations in the volume of purchases. Moreover, armed with these data the syndicate encouraged members to bring forward or hold back purchases in order to maximise the size of the rebate for the current year or the next twelve-month period. Thus, by ensuring itself a position at the centre of a series of related reporting flows that were established in cumulative fashion, the syndicate was able to gain progressively more detailed information, which gave it an important and increasing advantage over La Société.

Overall, the contract between the syndicate and La Société depended most heavily on communication lines that facilitated formal monitoring activities. Board level representation gave the syndicate an information advantage at the strategic level. The channels that conveyed operating data were designed in part to be reciprocating, but even though both parties shared some information the syndicate again had the overall advantage. Finally, Vickers acted as the central node through which all communication lines flowed. This design feature simplified transmitting activities and contained the cost of communicating across organisational frontiers.

Sequential adjustments

Having established these favourably configured communication channels, the syndicate used them to preserve its relationship with La Société with a view to enhancing the size of the rebate over the long term. Indeed, as Table 5.2 shows, from 1923 to 1935, when statistics are available, the syndicate

Table 5.2 Size of levy in relation to rebate

	Year	Price paid by syndicate (£)	Market price (£)	Rebate (%)	Rebate (£ per ton)	Levy (£ per ton)	Net savings won by the syndicate (£ per ton)	Total tonnage ordered	Total net savings to syndicate (£)	Net savings as % of market price
2/2[a]	1923	120	127.95	2.5	3.00	0.625	2.375			1.98
	1924	130	147.63	2.5	3.25	0.25	3.000	1780[b]		2.30
1/2[a]	1925	160	159.93	2.5	4.00	0.25	3.750	1780[b]		2.34
2/2[a]	1925	170	Average	2.5	4.20	0.25	3.750	Total	6,853	2.32
	1926	170	169.77	2.5	4.20	0.15	4.050	1780[b]	7,209	2.38
	1927	170	167.31	2.5	4.20	0.15	4.050	1780[b]	7,209	2.38
	1928	170	169.77	2.5	4.20	0.15	4.050	1780[b]	7,209	2.38
	1929	170	171.25	6.0	10.20	0.60	9.600	1800[c]	17,280	5.65
	1930	170	171.25[d]	6.0	10.20	0.60	9.600	1900	18,240	5.65
	1931	170	171.25[d]	8.0	13.60	0.375	13.225	1862	24,624	7.78
	1932	170	171.25[d]	10.0	17.00	0.35	16.650	1660	27,639	9.79
	1933	170	171.25[d]	11.0	18.70	0.50	18.200	2822[c]	51,360	10.71
	1934	151	171.25[d]	15.0	22.67	0.40	22.270	3382	75,317	14.79
	1935		171.25[d]	15.0	30.00	0.35	29.650	NA		

Sources: Schmit (1979); SMNS DM (Vickers 1198).

Notes

[a] SMNS DM record data for second half of 1923 only and data for first and second halves of 1925 separately. All other years are annual figures.

[b] SMNS DM 4/7/1929 reported that on average the annual tonnage purchased for the last five years was 1780 tons.

[c] Estimated tonnage of members' requirements.

[d] UK prices are not available. Market prices for these years are US prices converted to £ sterling.

NA, not available.

increased the size of the rebate from 2.5 per cent to fifteen per cent even though its purchasing power, as reflected by the size of its orders, remained static between 1923 and 1932. The key to the syndicate's success lay in its ability to recognise La Société's vulnerability, owing to its relatively small size and the Admiralty's import preferences, and to use the power of its position in a restrained manner. The syndicate's co-operative behaviour stemmed from the possession of superior intelligence as well as significant deterrence. The co-operative made and demanded concessions as conditions changed, but it did so on an informed basis. As inter-organisational learning unfolded, the syndicate established, in the eyes of its main supplier, a reputation as a reliable but powerful co-operator.

The process of making serial adjustments began during the War when the U-boat campaign caused La Société's shipping and insurance costs to rise dramatically. To ease this burden, and thereby ensure that members continued to receive supplies, the syndicate agreed to pay the New Caledonian firm a special allowance of £25 per ton in early 1917 (SMNS DM, 21 February 1917). At the same time, it used its link with the Admiralty to press for the return of shipping space requisitioned by the shipping controller to overcome supply problems that affected all parties: syndicate members, La Société, the Anglo-French company, and the Admiralty itself (SMNS DM, 28 March 1917). In May, and again in December 1917, the co-operative made further financial concessions in an effort to maintain supplies (SMNS DM, 15 May and 5 December 1917). The next year, rising costs and supply pressures created price confusion between suppliers and consumers of nickel, and the syndicate learned that the Admiralty enjoyed a price advantage of £15 per ton on its purchases from INCO (SMNS DM, 3 March 1918). In response, the co-operative tried to obtain similar terms by acquiring supplies from North America through the Admiralty. To prevent the situation from destabilising relations between the various suppliers and customers who were party to the world-wide pricing and market-sharing agreement, INCO applied to the Admiralty for a price increase so that all mining firms observed the same base price. The syndicate instructed Vickers to monitor closely prices paid by the government to prevent a recurrence of the problem. In July 1918, suppliers reduced the special allowance and included the remainder of this payment in the fixed invoice price (SMNS DM, 31 July 1918). Moreover, the syndicate gained a new concession when La Société agreed that if it quoted terms lower than the fixed invoice price to government agencies, the co-operative's members would receive the same terms.

It is possible that the syndicate was able to win some of these concessions from La Société because an offer from an unknown party who wished to sell a nickel mine enabled it to threaten the New Caledonian firm (SMNS DM, 10 May 1918). Although it is not certain that La Société was informed of the offer, and although the sale did not go through, this episode, along with the discovery of the Admiralty's price advantage, indicates that the syndicate had other contacts that enabled it to explore alternative sources of supply and to learn about 'side-deals'. Such private channels, as well as the central place it occupied within the reporting flows, gave the syndicate an intelligence advantage. This it used to make informed and justified concessions to La Société to preserve the relationship when the war threatened supplies, dislocated pricing levels, and caused costs to move against consumers.

After the First World War, the balance of supply and demand swung back to the syndicate's favour, and it became La Société's turn to accommodate its customers in order to retain their loyalty. For example, when the syndicate's purchases for 1919 fell just short of the tonnage needed to obtain the maximum rebate, La Société allowed the full reduction to preserve goodwill (SMNS DM, 14 January 1920). The New Caledonian firm also made concessions designed to develop operating links that would ensure that the Anglo-French company's Swansea refinery remained a focal point of co-operation between itself and the syndicate and to prevent this facility from being used as a competitive weapon. Thus, in 1918, the New Caledonian firm agreed to supply the Anglo-French company with oxide from INCO to keep the Swansea works in operation, and the two firms divided the profits arising from outside sales (SMNS DM, 30 December 1918). This arrangement may have also benefited La Société by helping it to evade UK import restrictions (Vickers 57/61 Statement dated 31 July 1935). Despite La Société's accommodating actions, however, the Anglo-French company was forced to cease operations at its Swansea works in 1926.

At first sight, the closure of the refinery appears to be a very curious development. It meant that the syndicate sacrificed the measure of its bargaining power which stemmed from the latent threat that it might buy its own mine and expand the capacity of the works to meet its members' total requirements. Moreover, it removed a facility that had been used to extend the basis of co-operation and to develop greater interdependence with La Société. The reason behind the closure was that the refinery was no longer efficient enough, relative to the prices charged by INCO and La Société, to pose a credible threat to the syndicate's suppliers, who had sufficient information about the Anglo-French company's costs to be aware of this fact. Yet, without the advantages conferred by having its own refinery the syndicate's close ties with La Société endured. It could be that the co-operative won vital concessions from the New Caledonian firm when the two companies concluded an agreement, the details of which have not survived, at the same time that the decision to close the works was taken (SMNS DM, 10 December 1926). However, it is evident that the syndicate no longer needed to exert a latent threat upon La Société. Learning effects generated over the previous twenty-five years of co-operation, the syndicate's intact information lines through which it could monitor outside prices, and its residual bargaining power and information advantages meant that it was able to win larger rebates when prices came under further pressure again in 1930.

Confirmation that the syndicate retained communication channels that provided outside price data can be found in the directors' minutes for 29

October 1930. This recorded the fact that Canadian producer Falconbridge and other unnamed firms could not match La Société's prices. By December, however, syndicate members had offers of lower prices (£158) and although La Société kept the same base rate it granted a supplementary rebate of two per cent (SMNS DM, 17 December 1930).

In 1931, the syndicate appealed again for a reduction and La Société introduced a more generous sliding scale of rebates based on the volume of members' purchases. Thus, even without the threat implicit in having its own refining capability, the syndicate was able to preserve most favoured pricing terms during the severe downturn of 1930–2, when world nickel production fell from 60,000 tons to 22,000 tons while the syndicate's orders slipped slightly from 1,900 tons to 1,660 tons. During the recovery of 1933–4, when world output rose to 72,000 tons and syndicate purchases increased to 3,382 tons, the co-operative was able to secure a fifty per cent higher rebate. Some of the increase in the rebate can be accounted for by the syndicate's heavier purchases (movement along the sliding scale). However, La Société also revised the scale itself to offer price parity when fluctuations in currency values made US prices lower than those prevailing in the UK. That the syndicate was able to win this concession at a time when the recovery in demand boosted world production by over 200 per cent attests to the effectiveness with which it exploited its information channels. What adjustments the two participants made after 1934 are not known because the following directors' minutes have not survived, but the relationship endured until war broke out in 1939.

The syndicate's contract with members: transparent costs

As we have seen, members agreed to allow the syndicate to co-ordinate their nickel purchases and agreed to pay a per ton levy to meet administrative costs. In return, they received a rebate from suppliers. The legal component was therefore simple and direct. It made no sense to mobilise cultural forces because members were to some extent competitors and because their national affiliations were diverse. The strength of the contract's design stemmed from the mutual interests of its members, recognition of which was reinforced by the transparency of the contract's monitoring component. Clear transmissions of operating data on which both the levy and the rebate were based encouraged members to participate.

Throughout its history, the organisation adopted an extremely lean approach to administration. Initially, it strove to avoid any form of fixed operating expense. For example, the syndicate did not allow fees for directors or emoluments and thus prevented any recriminations concerning the distribution of private gains from arising among members. The secretary was not paid a fixed salary, but rather an honorarium at the board's discretion (SMNS DM, 19 December 1901). As late as 1912, the secretary received only a paltry fee of £50 along with £50 for office expenses (SMNS DM, 6 March 1912). The next year, this parsimonious approach to minimising costs could no longer be sustained and the syndicate granted the secretary a salary of £300 rising by £50 per annum over the next three years. However, the extra cost was divided on a two-thirds to one-third basis between the Anglo-French company and the syndicate so that the latter's direct expenses were the same as the year before (SMNS DM, 1 October 1913).

The same spirit of mutual accommodation that tempered price adjustments between the syndicate and La Société also influenced the way in which they treated expenses. For example, in 1917 La Société requested new invoicing procedures that imposed additional costs upon the syndicate. In recognition of this, the New Caledonia firm contributed £200 per annum toward these extra expenses. Participants shared operating costs until 1923 when La Société declared that falling prices meant that it could no longer pay its £200 share (SMNS DM, 6 June 1923). In co-operative fashion, the syndicate did not press for payment and shouldered the expense itself.

By 1929, the Anglo-French company also ceased making contributions, and the syndicate had to meet all administrative costs itself. However, the total expenses at this time amounted to only £1060 per annum, a reflection of the tight cost control that the co-operative exercised in order to pass on to its members the largest possible proportion of the gross rebate recovered from suppliers. Thus, while cost sharing for a time reduced the burden of the levy placed on members, the ability of the organisation to contain its administrative expenses was of greater importance over the long term.[6]

Through the syndicate's inter-organisational reporting system, members knew the exact size of its running costs. Moreover, participants did not have to tie up their cash by making advances to the syndicate so that it could meet its commitments. Since many of the co-operative's expenses were payable yearly or half-yearly, it used rebates received to date or reserves to make payments. The syndicate automatically deducted the levy from the rebate received from suppliers so that members could observe directly the net benefit of association. The presentation of a cash 'bonus' in the form of a half-yearly net rebate payment served as an incentive for members to remain loyal. By such indirect communication the organisation showed its members the fruits of their combined strength. From surviving reports we can quantify the benefits participants gained over an eleven-year period.

Operating efficiency

The size of the advantage that members won can be calculated by comparing market prices with the amounts they actually paid between 1924 and 1934. With the exception of 1923 and 1924, the records confirm that – in accordance with the agreement with suppliers – the syndicate did pay market rates. Thus, the members' benefit was equal to the size of the rebate less the levy (Table 5.2).[7]

The total value of these savings for the syndicate rose more than tenfold, from £6,853 in 1924 to over £75,317 in 1934. In percentage terms, these figures represented a saving that rose almost as dramatically, from just under two per cent of the market price of a ton of nickel in 1923 to almost fifteen per cent in 1934. As time passed, members enjoyed steadily growing benefits from the arrangement.

Because the syndicate's records contain little information about how much nickel individual members ordered, it is impossible to calculate the benefits that each derived from the arrangement. However, for Vickers' subsidiary, the English Steel Corporation, appropriate data are available for 1931–4 (Table 5.3).

This company purchased a total of 1876 tons of nickel and secured a saving of almost £34,000 during these four years. The significance of these savings can be assessed by comparing them with reported net profits before depreciation (10.9 per cent). Clearly, this co-operative purchasing arrangement, which governed just one of this firm's inputs, generated important financial advantages, quite apart from the unquantifiable benefits of having a more secure supply and greater capacity to deter the global nickel duopoly from increasing prices in the future. The impressive size of the financial gains alone raises questions about how efficiently the syndicate ran its operations.

The syndicate's operating efficiency can be measured by calculating the ratio of the rebate's size to the levy (Table 5.4). This ratio was 1:0.21 in 1923 and fell dramatically until 1929, when a minor upturn occurred; it then declined to progressively lower levels to reach 1:0.01 in 1935. The overall trend indicates that the syndicate's administration absorbed less and less of the rebate it won for its members. Moreover, the organisation's increasing efficiency during the 1923–35 period, when expenses fell from twenty-one to one per cent of the rebate, must have strengthened the members'

Table 5.3 The English Steel Corporation's savings

Year	Saving (tonnage X amount saved per ton) (£)	Reported profit or loss before depreciation (£)
1931	6,626	46,011[a]
1932	5,495	225,323[a]
1933	8,554	113,550
1934	13,251	498,908
Total	33,926	311,124[b]

Source: Vickers 58/124.

Notes
[a]Loss.
[b]Net profit (10.9% before depreciation).

Table 5.4 The size of the rebate relative to the levy

	Year	Rebate (£)	Levy (£)	Levy as % of rebate	Ratio of rebate to levy expenses
2/2	1923	3.00	0.625	20.80	1:0.21
	1924	3.25	0.25	7.70	1:0.08
1/2	1925	4.00	0.25	6.25	1:0.06
2/2	1925	4.20	0.25	5.95	1:0.06
	1926	4.20	0.15	3.57	1:0.04
	1927	4.20	0.15	3.57	1:0.04
	1928	4.20	0.15	3.57	1:0.04
	1929	10.20	0.60	5.88	1:0.06
	1930	10.20	0.60	5.88	1:0.06
	1931	13.60	0.375	2.76	1:0.03
	1932	17.00	0.85	2.06	1:0.02
	1933	18.70	0.50	2.67	1:0.03
	1934	22.67	0.40	1.76	1:0.02
	1935	30.00	0.35	1.17	1:0.01

Source: Table 5.2.

Note
SMNS DM record data for second half of 1923 only and data for the first and second halves of 1925 separately. All other years are annual figures.

commitment. The resulting stability of membership in turn served to reinforce the syndicate's contract with La Société and the global market-sharing agreement.

Conclusion

In the context of existing industry structures and basic supply and demand conditions, the syndicate was an appropriate and efficient co-operative device. The design of its contracts suited the particular constituency and prevailing environmental circumstances. These agreements combined clearly specified provisions, little culture, and heavy reliance on highly transparent monitoring mechanisms. The mix of components reflected a lack of inter-organisational knowledge and trust stemming from multiple cultural affiliations; as a result, simplicity and clarity in communication was vital. The combination of contractual elements provides a poignant contrast to that used by the HSS network and at OP, where reputation, inter-firm knowledge and broad interdependence made it appropriate to rely upon a cultural foundation. The OP case also highlighted the adverse consequences of unavoidable delays in perfecting the accounting part of the monitoring mechanism and serves to emphasise the advantages that arise when circumstances permit the use of a simple and easily understood financial reporting framework. Again reflecting different levels of trust, the use of formal monitoring procedures by the syndicate, also contrasts with the informal methods used by the HSS network and by shipowners and their agents.

The simple design of the syndicate's information lines was also important. Vickers acted as a central node through which all data flowed. In comparison, the HSS network consisted of multiple nodes, with the result that communication flows were far more diverse and much more complicated. These features were appropriate given the high levels of trust among constituents and in light of their need to tap numerous sources of intelligence about diversification opportunities. The differences in HSS's system and the syndicate's system also stemmed from the distinct functions of DSS and TPS and differences in the breadth of their businesses. In Richardson's (1972) terms HSS affiliates sacrificed more of their sovereignty in a strategic sense than did syndicate members who delegated information-gathering functions concerning just one of their purchasing activities to a co-operative organisation. Nevertheless, in time the simplicity and clarity of the syndicate's channels helped to generate increasing levels of trust.

The way in which the syndicate aligned and used its communication channels was also important in building a stable relationship with La Société. Instead of mobilising its raw market power to extract short-term concessions from its supplier, the syndicate used its bargaining strength to place itself at the centre of interrelated communication lines, and then used its augmented power in a restrained manner. The organisation preserved co-operative relations and secured prices below levels set by the world market over the long term by possessing but never using in an overt manner its considerable bargaining power over La Société. Thus, the case alerts us to another type of balance which must be struck if successful co-operation is to unfold: that between exercising power and willingly sacrificing sovereignty. It also highlights how power can be retained for deterrent effect, in contrast to shipowners who sometimes overtly demonstrated their strength for signalling and reputation-building purposes. Power can be diminished with frequent use; it may be more effective when used sparingly and, in this case, proved to have maximum impact when held in reserve.

Finally, the history of the syndicate confirms that co-operative structures of any form can work only if they provide an efficient solution to co-ordinating problems. As a complement to the model of shipowner–agent relations presented above (p. 19), this case has measured the benefits and costs that arose from the use of an intermediate structure relative to those of market mechanisms. By ensuring that members could see that the syndicate's efficient administration prevented savings from being absorbed by operating expenses, it ensured that they did not lose sight of the long-term benefits of their inter-organisational relationships. The next case examines a different approach to initiating co-operative conduct.

6 A licensing pyramid
John Brown Company and International Curtis Marine Turbine Company, 1908–29

Charles Curtis formed a pyramidal licensing structure to promote his new technology. This chapter examines in detail the legal component of his contract, and it shows how he went about creating an inter-firm culture to encourage innovation by his licensees. In particular, the discussion focuses on how he sought to shape members' cognitive processes.

In 1897, Charles Parsons (later Sir Charles) shocked the world by running his revolutionary vessel, the *Turbinia*, almost literally in circles around the Grand Fleet assembled for the Spithead review. The principle of his new engine was simple: instead of injecting steam into cylinders that moved up and down to rotate a crank shaft, the turbine passed steam directly onto vanes mounted on a drum which revolved and turned the shaft. Generating faster speed and less vibration, the turbine was well suited for naval and passenger ships. Subsequently, Charles Curtis, an American engineer, patented a more efficient compound impulse turbine, which in 1908 he licensed in the US and Europe. Why did Curtis choose to license his invention instead of exploiting it himself?[1]

Economic theory provides few guidelines for this decision in so far as the domestic market is concerned, but deduction suggests that inadequate resources, a lack of local commercial contacts, and a desire to spread risk or to penetrate the market quickly are all relevant considerations. In contrast, the Caves–Hymer thesis (see Chapter 1) offers a strong foundation for answering the question of overseas exploitation. Caves (1982) and Hymer (1976) suggest that firms face higher costs when initially expanding overseas because they have to learn about different legal prescriptions, cultures, and markets. On the other hand, multinationals possess intangible assets, including skills, knowledge, brands, or technology, which generate a quasi-rent that more than offsets the extra cost of doing business overseas. When considering the form that this overseas venture should take, transaction cost theory posits that management will select the framework which offers the lowest cost for arranging a contract that in turn allows their firm to appropriate as much of the quasi-rent as possible.[2]

Curtis's licensing pyramid is difficult to explain purely in terms of transaction cost theory, which sees licensing primarily as a bilateral mechanism that has specific exchange attributes when used to transfer intangible assets abroad. Consideration of the licensor's capabilities in relation to those of sub-licensees leads to the alternative view that the arrangement can serve to aggregate all the participants' intangible assets. By so doing, the value of the total quasi-rent stream may increase. Indeed, Curtis's framework was designed to harness inter-organisational learning, innovation, and the intermediary capabilities of the chief licensees in order to penetrate a market dominated by Parsons.

How well did Curtis's pyramid perform? By the mid 1920's his turbine had reached a peak of about fifty per cent of the naval sector of the market (*Jane's Fighting Ships*).[3] Thereafter, problems with 'disc flutter' (vibrations which caused discs to shatter) (Jung 1982: 121–9) induced the Admiralty to rely upon Parsons' machinery exclusively. Although the difficulty was overcome in the US, Curtis could not regain his position in Britain. To explain the dramatic short-term success and long-term failure of Curtis's assault on the British market, it is necessary to examine the contracts and inter-firm communicating processes that supported his licensing pyramid.

The first section below describes the pyramid and the supporting contracts. The second part analyses the inter-firm communicating lines that underpinned the structure. In the third section we evaluate how these channels handled transfers of technical, commercial, and legal information to promote joint learning. Next, the discussion reveals how Curtis tried to create an inter-firm culture to encourage co-operation. The final section examines how Curtis adjusted communicating methods and shaped members' conceptions of the costs and benefits of inter-firm exchanges.

Structure of the licensing agreements and the pyramid

Curtis's blend of the three main contractual components differed from those used in the other co-operative frameworks examined so far. He relied most heavily on legal specifications that cleverly created incentives for participants to innovate. Curtis placed less emphasis on monitoring mechanisms that simply required licensees to report on orders and production and were subject to audit. He did however also stress the cultural component, but he could not mobilise recognised cultural forces in a comprehensive manner because pyramid members did not share a common affiliation. As a result, he was compelled to try to create a framework-specific cultural edifice. This section provides a detailed examination of the legal specifications.

The International Curtis Marine Turbine Company (ICMT) as patent holder and licensor rested at the top of the licensing pyramid (Figure 6.1). Chief licensees, including the John Brown Company (JB) in the UK, AEG in Germany, J. F. Monot in France, and Fore River Shipbuilding in the US, all occupied middle positions, and numerous sub-licensees in each national market made up the base. The contract binding licensor to chief licensee, in the case of John Brown the renowned Clyde shipbuilding firm, recognised

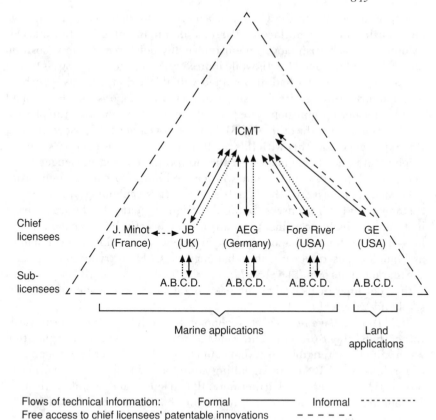

ICMT

Chief
licensees

J. Minot ◄--► JB   AEG   Fore River   GE
(France)   (UK)   (Germany)   (USA)   (USA)

Sub-
licensees

A.B.C.D.   A.B.C.D.   A.B.C.D.   A.B.C.D.

Marine applications   Land
                                                    applications

Flows of technical information: Formal ———— Informal ----------
Free access to chief licensees' patentable innovations – – – – –·
Free access to licensees' patentable innovations   ·················

Figure 6.1 Curtis's licensing pyramid

the latter's innovative capabilities, market connections, and reputation. The agreement that ICMT and JB signed in 1908 was structured to enable both parties to share in the rent stream, to expedite market penetration, and to encourage rapid innovation (John Brown records, UGD UCS, 1/11/6).

Regarding rent sharing, the agreement entitled JB, on paying a fee of £25,000, to participate in fees and royalties derived from sub-licences. It could sell to any UK engineering firm one of three classes of sub-licence for a lump-sum fee. In addition, sub-licensees also paid a royalty, according to ship type, for each engine they built. (On engines it produced JB paid ICMT one-half of these royalty rates.) ICMT and JB equally divided licensees' fees and royalties until the latter had recovered £12,500 and thereafter JB accepted a smaller proportion. The effect of the arrangement was to allow JB to participate in the long-term rent stream, albeit initially on a declining basis, but to recoup its licensing fee quickly and so confirm the benefit of association.

Curtis shared rents with JB and placed that firm in an intermediary position within the pyramid because it possessed advantages that could help his invention to penetrate the UK market more easily than ICMT could have done on its own in the face of Parsons' dominant place in the market. (Moreover, the British Government informally bolstered Parsons' position and thus disadvantaged Curtis while indirectly strengthening Brown's future bargaining power.) JB had also gained valuable experience as a turbine manufacturer through its licensing contract with Parsons, but Brown had licences for both propulsion systems, and this created room for it to play off one licensor against the other (UCS1/11/6, 14 November 1905). Nevertheless, this experience, together with JB's reputation as one of the country's leading shipbuilders and its contacts with the Admiralty, leading passenger lines, and other shipyards could help to win the vital initial 'break-through' order needed to demonstrate the benefits of Curtis's technology to potential customers and sub-licensees. Being a foreign company, ICMT would have had some difficulty securing Admiralty orders directly. In the civilian sector, long-standing financial and commercial links between shipping companies and builders posed a formidable challenge to ICMT in trying to break into the market on its own (Slaven 1977; Boyce 1995a). However, JB had close ties with major liner firms, and by sub-licensing it could take advantage of other shipbuilders' client bonds.

ICMT could have licensed its technology directly to all British shipyards rather than using Brown as an intermediary. Yet, Brown's national reputation was a valuable intangible asset that could be used to greater effect than that of foreign-owned ICMT in signalling confidence in the new invention to prospective sub-licensees. Furthermore, JB had long-standing links with other shipbuilders and could use the underlying bonds of trust, to reduce the expense of negotiating sub-licenses, which being based on knowledge were likely to generate high transaction costs. Indeed, Brown may have begun to use its connections before arranging its licence: the agreement named seven other builders whom it was to approach to take up sub-licences. The balance of Brown's intangible assets in terms of its local contracting capabilities relative to ICMT's patents and know-how encouraged Curtis to enlist JB as an intermediary in order to accelerate market penetration.

The licensing and sub-licensing agreements included monetary incentives designed to stimulate technical improvement. Clauses stipulated that the royalty paid by sub-licensees would begin to fall in 1912 until it reached zero in 1918 *unless* a member of the pyramid developed an innovation that was 'practically essential or ... of substantial value.'[4] For example, if Brown made a discovery, it had to assign the patent upward to ICMT, but the royalty payments it received from sub-licensees would not decline. (JB and ICMT would share these royalties.) If a sub-licensee innovated, it had to assign the patent to JB, which could use the improvement (as could ICMT). However, other sub-licensees could not take advantage of the improvement unless they paid to the innovating firm a royalty in which JB shared (GD 319/3/5/2 contract, 20 May 1915). Thus, the incentives operated somewhat like those in pyramid selling schemes, except that licensees rose to higher ranks by innovating rather than by recruiting new distributors (Japanese supplier chains have similar features, see Chapter 11). Curtis's provisions were intended to induce discoveries that preserved the rent stream and made his turbine superior to Parsons', whose contracts did not include similar terms.

Curtis's contracts also encouraged mutual learning and discovery by ICMT, Brown, and British sub-licensees. The clauses stated that Brown and ICMT were to share technical information and that ICMT was to assist Brown in devising improvements. In turn, Brown was to help sub-licensees. Yet, enforcing these types of provisions is notoriously difficult, but ICMT devised several ways to avoid compliance problems. First, including these provisions within a legally binding contract provided a basis for recourse in the event of dispute, even though proving non-compliance would be difficult. Second, ICMT relied upon the royalty-preserving clause above to create a monetary incentive for Brown and its sub-licensees to collaborate. Third, Curtis developed personal links to smooth the flow of information. Thus, he used a blend of formal and informal mechanisms to promote communication and mutual learning.

Despite the clever way in which Curtis's specifications mobilised incentives, his contractual provisions exhibited several serious weaknesses. The agreements did not contain sanctions that could be used to prevent a firm that held licences for both Parsons and Curtis turbines from playing off one licensor against the other. Nor did the ICMT–JB contract compel Curtis to defend his patent; later this became a point of contention. Finally, future events were to show that the agreement did not segment national markets sufficiently for licensees to exact rents from discrete territories. The contract did not take into account that ships are mobile assets purchased in an international market. Whether these contractual defects would have a serious impact depended on how well communication channels operated to build co-operative relations.

The design of the pyramid's communication lines

Within the licensing pyramid direct communication lines linked ICMT and the chief licensees. Another set of vertical channels connected the chief licensees and their sub-licensees. Curtis did not at the outset establish formal horizontal links between the chief licensees; rather, he encouraged their formation. This section examines how inter-organisational communication lines developed.

The conduits between ICMT and each of the chief licensees were not uniformly effective. Before the US entered World War I, Curtis developed a sound tie with AEG [UCS1/11/6–10 Curtis (C) to Pigott (P), 4 August 1914]. Initially, he had difficulty securing the co-operation of the chief US licensee, the Fore River Shipbuilding Co., but after a change in management at that firm more consultative relations arose (C–P, 27 August 1914). Curtis also formed a strong tie with J. F. Monot, the French licensee, and in this instance common cultural affiliation facilitated communication: Monot had grown up in the US (C–Bell, 18 June 1912). Bifurcated communication lines developed between ICMT and John Brown. Curtis wrote officially to Thomas Bell (later Sir Thomas), JB's managing director, to discuss royalties and confirm orders. However, on technical matters Curtis liased with Stephen Pigott (later Sir Stephen), a young American whom he suggested Brown hire to help design turbines. Although he was an autocratic figure, Bell, to whom Pigott reported, quite understandably felt that by using such an informal channel Curtis undermined his authority. Thus, Curtis made a basic error by attempting to use formal and informal channels to triangulate information flows and generate complementary monitoring capability. His suspicions aroused, Bell obstructed several co-operative initiatives (C–P, 13 May 1912 and C–P, 4 August 1914).

Nevertheless, Brown did provide designs and advice to British sub-licensees (P–C 26 March 1915; UCS1/1/1/1 DM, 20 June 1918). The firm also transmitted technical data from sub-licensees back to ICMT (Newton–P, 27 April 1912). JB sent designs to its Russian subsidiary and opened up markets in Chile and Japan (UCS1/1/1/1 DM, 24 June 1911, 24 February 1917). Thus, JB's contacts and renown enabled it to play the intermediary role envisaged in the licence agreement.

Overall, Curtis's inter-firm channels exhibited several defects. Bilateral links between ICMT and the chief licensees were not uniformly strong. Curtis did not initially install channels between all chief licensees, and he did not create a forum in which chief- and sub-licensees could meet and establish direct relations. Instead, the direct ties that did develop between chief licensees arose in an incidental manner as common affiliations revealed themselves or in response to problems that called for improved communication. As a result, informal conduits assumed great importance and their initial formation, at least in JB's case, hindered the creation of effective official channels.

Contents of inter-organisational communication channels

Through these diverse links pyramid members exchanged a variety of information. Curtis also conveyed indications of the reputation of participating firms in order to provide a foundation for co-operation. His aim was to build confidence in his technology and in the participants' capacities to innovate. This section examines the contents of the pyramid's communication lines by considering in turn transmissions of commercial, legal, and technical knowledge.

Commercial intelligence

The ICMT–JB correspondence, which also refers to other licensees' activities, included information about new orders and naval construction programmes developed by the US and UK governments. Details of naval plans, especially, helped to generate confidence within the pyramid by conveying to members some impression of future market prospects. Notifications of definite orders, particularly breakthrough contracts that incorporated new technical features, confirmed the value of a member's capabilities and reflected favourably on all participants. This collective reputation could help to win further orders and attract other firms to join the pyramid.

Participants also shared their knowledge of selling techniques. For example, Curtis told Pigott about the approach he used to get the US Navy to accept a new four-shaft arrangement. This

> ...was the result of our Company taking up the matter directly with the Navy Department in a studious and friendly way long before they were ready to issue the circular [laying out the specifications on which firms would tender]. Instead of endeavouring to thrust upon them one particular design, as the Fore River Company has always done heretofore, we have taken the designers of the Bureau right into our confidence, showed them everything that we had gotten up here, and asked them to co-operate with us in getting up the best thing that could be gotten.
>
> (C–P, 31 December 1912)

In the same way that PJ sought to instruct JSS, Curtis tried to teach Pigott to use a technical sales approach that relied on the advantages of his design to create the market and used consultations with the customer to promote joint learning and possibly shape contract specifications.

Curtis used a similar but more indirect approach in pursuing sales for geared turbines by consulting with the US Bureau of Steam Engineering (C–P, 17 September 1914). Curtis also wanted Pigott, who was developing similar designs, to assist him in making a joint approach, but Bell refused his request. In this instance, inter-organisational learning unfolded only as far as the transfer of knowledge about new sales methods. Bell's action meant that the experience obtained by applying such techniques was not imparted and reciprocal joint selling activities were obstructed.

Thus, transmissions of commercial intelligence took place, but they could have been more extensive if Curtis had not placed Bell in a position where he felt alienated.

Legal information

Exchanges of information regarding legal matters were important in assessing the commercial prospects of Curtis's technology and protecting the rent stream generated by his patents. The pyramid provided numerous listening posts which gathered information about developments that might affect members' reputations and the security of their intangible assets. Transfers of intelligence about legal aspects of the international business environment also contributed to joint learning and the co-ordination of development strategies. How well did the pyramid act as a mechanism both for harnessing distinct sets of legal expertise and for devising joint policy?

The Curtis–Pigott correspondence reveals how two constituents shared information about legal developments in their countries in order to reduce uncertainty and maintain confidence. For example, a particularly insidious development occurred in 1914, when Pigott reported that a Mr Edwards initiated a rumour that Curtis had infringed upon a Westinghouse patent. Recognising that this allegation could undermine both his personal reputation and the confidence of pyramid members, Curtis forcefully assured Pigott that there was 'not a scintilla of truth in [this] statement' (C–P, 2 October 1914). The rumour most directly affected General Electric (GE), ICMT's principal licensee for land turbines, and Curtis consulted with that firm's legal officer to give assurances and to seek advice. The incident reveals how the pyramid aggregated legal expertise.

Edwards' rumour also proved to be the catalyst that induced ICMT and JB to develop a joint policy for patenting their inventions and charting a future course for turbine development. The declining royalty schedule provided another incentive to adopt a systematic approach. As Curtis stated, 'to do justice to ... [the technology] requires constant thought and vigilance and continuously looking a long way ahead' (C–P, 6 October 1914). By developing a joint strategy, they could anticipate the direction of future work and thus be in a better position to pursue 'gateway patents' that foreclosed avenues of development to rivals.

Thus, Curtis and Pigott devised a comprehensive strategy straddling the interface between legal and technical developments. They did so belatedly, and in response to a specific event. Perhaps they should have anticipated the need for a methodical joint approach from the outset given the incentives in the contract. Yet, their capacity to develop a joint strategy so smoothly afterwards reflected a high level of trust that also supported transfers of proprietary knowledge.

Technical knowledge

Exchanges of sensitive technical data between ICMT and its licensees enabled pyramid members to solve performance problems, devise incremental improvements, and install feedback mechanisms. The Curtis–Pigott correspondence includes confidential working sketches, blueprints, and calculations. For example, Curtis sent Pigott plans for a gearing system that was not patented on the understanding that if he had an opportunity to use the design he would cable first so that Curtis could register the innovation (C–P, 14 November 1913). Curtis's assistant, Newton, gave Pigott the *only* copies that ICMT had of GE's latest designs (N–P, 16 June and 5 September 1913). To emphasise the importance of discretion, Curtis asked Pigott to keep them confidential only using them for your own purpose in developing machines for marine purposes; they must not be used or seen by anybody who could use them in land uses, because this would not be fair to the General Electric Company. I feel that we are entitled to use only such information as will enable us to design marine turbines as well as possible ... I am sure you will appreciate the importance of this.

(C–P, 5 September 1913)

Curtis knew that he had to be seen to act consistently and equitably towards all parties in order to encourage reciprocal exchanges. Based on trust and a shared sense of fairness, the private Curtis–Pigott conduit supported transfers of sensitive data from the land to the marine sectors.

The pyramid's channels were also used to conduct many-sided discourses directed towards solving specific performance problems (C–P ,17 June, 2 July, 18 July 1912, 3 October 1913; and N–P, 6 August 1912). These discussions confirmed the efficacy of technical principles, produced policies for developing standardised turbine designs for each class of ship, and helped the designers devise an integrated strategy to guide future work in light of rivals' activities (C–P, 28 November 1913; C–P, 17 September, 6 October, and 19 November 1914). They also helped generate confidence in a way that could not be done had the designers worked in isolation.

Nevertheless, these exchanges were unable to prevent a crisis from arising in 1914. The problem occurred in part because of defective communication and in part because Pigott's design ideas for a high-speed geared turbine went beyond the store of knowledge that could be drawn upon from within the pyramid. In the early stages of this work, Curtis was able to provide only some assistance; there were some matters about which he simply did not have any information (C–P, 3 and 20 October 1913). Pigott pressed on for about a year, and by late 1914 was ready to incorporate his new system in a passenger liner. Curtis offered to send Newton to John Brown's works, but, still suspicious of ICMT, Bell refused to permit the visit. Unable to give help directly, Curtis repeated an earlier warning that the incorporation of a third row of blades would seriously impair efficiency (C–P, 18 September and 28 December 1914). The fact that Curtis allowed Pigott to pursue his new design for so long without apparently confirming that Pigott had heeded his earlier warnings indicates that the feedback mechanisms within the pyramid's communicating systems were either defective or were not used effectively.

By mid-January 1915, Pigott realised that he had made 'a colossal blunder' (P–C, 15 January 1915). He had made a series of requests for calculations and advice, but Curtis

instead of realising the situation and giving such assistance as would be possible, ...ha[d] recommend[ed] such drastic modifications which only an entirely new design could satisfy ... I feel myself in the same boat with the heathen who has received a certain amount of instruction from a missionary in a new religion. I have lost faith in the principles upon which I have based my work and as yet have nothing to fill their place.

(P–C, 15 January 1915)

To overcome this crisis Curtis responded in a forthright manner. Recognising that Pigott felt isolated, Curtis encouraged frank communication (C–P, 29 January 1915). However, Curtis felt that Pigott's 'impressions of the situation are erroneous in some respects' and pointed these out to clarify the sequence of events leading up to the crisis. Of most importance, Curtis addressed the basic cause of the problem – defective communication techniques – in order to prevent problems in the future. Curtis's handling of the affair led to a resumption of their technical dialogue.

Having established a high level of trust at the outset so that they could transfer knowledge and discuss pioneering designs, Curtis and Pigott had to ensure that their communication methods remained effective. Feelings of isolation obstructed innovation. Although Curtis had not foreseen the source of the problem – aspects of it were impossible to predict – he had taken deliberate steps to build an inter-organisational culture that could facilitate the resolution of crises.

Inter-organisational culture

Curtis mediated over exchanges of inter-organisational knowledge within the pyramid. In so doing, he sought to furnish assurances of trust to licensees who had not previously come into contact with each other in order to facilitate direct communication. He also compiled an objective record of events, or a historical map, which he used to build an inter-organisational culture. Moreover, Curtis tried to shape both the cognitive and emotional aspects of culture so that they would reinforce each other (Smircich 1983; Cremer 1993). Thus, he used the map to condition members' cognitive processes by showing what kinds of action had produced beneficial results in the past and which had not. By focusing on the former, licensees would reduce the breadth of their decision trees and accelerate the pace of decision-making. Curtis also interpreted events so as to shape the emotional side of inter-firm relations to promote co-operation. Yet, his efforts were only partially successful; Thomas Bell remained aloof to Curtis's culture.

To open up new communication channels between pyramid members, Curtis wrote letters of introduction wherein he provided background information which revealed some commonality that might generate co-operation. For example, he told Pigott that J. F. Monot, the French licensee whom he wanted to meet JB staff, had grown up in the US and had secured the confidence of Thomas Edison, who 'placed the entire management of his large Storage Battery interests in France exclusively in his hands' (C–P, 17 June 1912). Acting as an intermediary, Curtis provided introductory services as well as information from which reputations could be deduced.

Curtis also transmitted assurances in order to prevent misunderstandings from dislocating established channels. In response to Pigott's inquiry why JB did not win a contract to design a turbine for a pyramid member, Delauncy–Belleville, Curtis stated that the fee was simply too high. To head off any misinterpretation, he assured Pigott 'This is why they did not deal with your firm ...They are exceedingly straight-forward and reliable people' (C–P, 3 December 1914). In this case, Curtis also imparted knowledge about incentives that governed inter-organisational transactions; licensees had to be price competitive to win business from within the pyramid.

Further, Curtis intended that his historical map would serve an incentive function by revealing the consequences of licensees' actions. For example, in 1912 the Fore River Co. designed a defective turbine for the Argentine Navy because the firm did not consult with Curtis, who would have recognised at once that the buckets were too weak. Curtis told Pigott that he 'should be glad to have you communicate the above to Mr, Bell, but of course I do not want to be understood as intending to do anything derogatory [sic] to the Fore River Company. I am simply letting you know the truth, which I think is always desirable from the point of view of everyone interested' (C–P, 8 September 1913). Thus, Curtis assured JB staff that he did not engage in malicious gossip but simply sought to state the bare facts. He also wanted to make it clear that the problem did not arise from any defect in his technology but rather from a failure of one participant to consult with him.

Despite Curtis's efforts, the episode did damage relations between two US licensees. New York Shipbuilding refused 'to take any designs from the Fore River Company because of the troubles they have had heretofore, even with the Fore River Company under new management' (C–P, 3 September 1914). Worse, Fore River's short-sightedness undermined confidence in Curtis's technology. New York Shipbuilding offered the US Navy separate tenders for Parsons' and Curtis's turbines, but artificially inflated the price of the latter because they wanted to proceed with 'something that was standard, like the Parsons, in which their responsibility would be much less'. However, to retain JB's confidence, Curtis told Pigott that Newport News Shipbuilding had used the same tactic but gave a price advantage to the Curtis turbine, 'which it regards as quite superior to the Parsons'. Curtis also believed that 'after the *Pennsylvania* is finished and tried with her Sister Ship, the Builders will be all the more anxious to bid with our Type'. Curtis would let events and facts speak for themselves. Indeed, without the means to prevent licensees from playing off his technology against that of Parsons, he had to let the advantages of his turbine reveal themselves and influence the pyramid members' actions.

While creating a historical record to guide members' behaviour, Curtis provided contrasting examples for instructive purposes. When news broke about Fore River's poor design, Curtis pointed to GE as an example of how things should be done. 'The latest designs of [GE] are all in accordance with our original ideas and designs, and I am not surprised that the results have turned out as well as they have' (C–P, 5 September 1913). The object lesson was that co-operation and consultation produced good results.

Curtis brought this point closer to home for JB officials by contrasting their behaviour with that of AEG. Concerning efforts to resolve a dispute between the two firms over their rights to accept foreign orders – a dispute that arose because his contract did not clearly demarcate licensees' national territories – he informed Pigott that 'while he [Bell] has written me nothing about the matter, the AEG has written me ... a very straightforward, fair minded letter and asked our approval, which we have given ... You might let him know, if you like, that this is the fact' (C–P, 4 August 1914). Such disclosures of 'facts' were intended to modify behaviour.

The way Curtis created a historical record of indisputable facts complemented approaches he used in other contexts. It was reflected in his marketing methods whereby he took navy staff into his confidence and objectively demonstrated the advantages of his technology (p. 103). It also lent greater credibility to the assurances he gave to Pigott during his crisis in 1914–15. Such consistency of behaviour enabled constituents to deduce Curtis's trustworthiness from his actions.

In order to use his map to shape the emotional side of the pyramid's culture, Curtis always congratulated JB when it attained notable achievements. For example, he was quick to comment on Brown's contract to build *Tiger*, which was the breakthrough order ICMT needed to establish its technology in Britain (C–P, 19 September 1913). Curtis also used comparative indicators to provide objective points of reference. Thus, when Brown won orders to build Curtis turbines for eleven of twenty-two ships called for in a new Admiralty construction programme he said it was 'a splendid showing' which indicated how well his technology performed against Parsons' (C–P, 2 October 1914). Curtis also congratulated Pigott when the JB reached the points at which it had built turbines totalling one million and then two million indicated horse power (IHP). Like anniversaries, these junctures enabled the two men to stand back from their day-to-day work and reflect upon the scale of their achievements.

In a sadder sense, Curtis and Pigott also noted milestones of a more personal nature. Though separated in age by twenty years, they lost parents at about the same time. Condolences offered opportunities to recognise shared experiences and strengthen personal bonds. Curtis told Pigott that before his mother passed away she had said that she always valued Pigott's 'judgement and character very highly' (C–P, 31 December 1912). Pigott's father died two years later and his passing contributed to the isolation he felt during the 1914–15 crisis. The pressure of work had prevented Pigott from seeing his father for several years. The realisation that he would never have a chance to do so bore heavily on Pigott, and his first reaction was to resign from JB and go home (P–C, 1 December 1914). Knowing this, Curtis communicated intensively and sensitively to ensure that the end result would be a closer bond, not a break in his relationship with Pigott.

Thus, by mobilising both the cognitive and emotional aspects of culture, Curtis sought to enhance communication, build confidence, facilitate transfers of knowledge, and promote joint learning and innovation. He understood that creating a culture for the pyramid was an essential leadership function, but he also knew that by itself culture could not sustain innovation. Pigott's crisis showed that these elements had to be supported by effective communication methods.

Communication methods and costs

To overcome the crisis, Curtis and Pigott had to reform their communicating procedures and establish shared conceptions of the costs and benefits of specific transmission methods. Five months before the crisis, there were signs that problems lay ahead. In August 1914 Pigott wrote:

> I am sorry to give you trouble in connection with my designs but I think that *at the early stages* … [of work on a new project] *criticism is a necessity* … *[I]t would greatly assist me and give confidence in undertaking new work which is now coming in an entirely altered form from the old practice*.
>
> (P–C, 14 August 1914, emphasis added)

Pigott knew that his inquiries posed time costs, but he needed feedback in the initial stages of the design to make sure he was using a suitable approach.

Curtis replied that the *way* in which Pigott framed his questions hindered the formulation of a timely and fully considered response in a cost-effective manner:

> I do not think you quite realise how difficult it is for us to criticise the propositions which you give us in the way in which you state them … It would be better if you would send us more complete information and make the inquiries as simply as possible. We are most anxious to assist you in every possible way, but we have found it quite laborious and time consuming to deal with the points in the way in which you have presented them in some cases. We want you to feel absolutely free to inquire of us and secure our co-operation in every possible way and write just as freely and as often as you like, but you will readily see that the vaguer the proposition is the more difficult it is for us to deal with and the more time is takes. If you do not quite understand what I mean … I wish you would so write me, because *I want to make the matter perfectly clear so that we can co-operate with you as effectively as possible*.
>
> (C–P, 3 September 1914, emphasis added)

Anxious not to discourage Pigott from writing often, Curtis repeatedly assured him of ICMT's desire to co-operate and closed with a personal invitation to reply added in his own hand at the end of the letter: 'Please write me anyway'.

Curtis raised the same point when the crisis hit four months later. He responded to Pigott's explosive letter of 15 January 1915 (see pp. 105–106) in a straightforward manner: 'one difficulty ... has been the difference between your point of view and ours, and your unwillingness or more probably your inability to put us in possession of the data and of your object as promptly as possible' (C–P, 29 January 1915a). The crisis arose in part from poor communication. Curtis did not blame Pigott but rather Bell and JB's policy. He criticised 'the custom of your company in the preventing or the delaying of furnishing us with sufficient information [sic] in the beginning to co-operate with and assist you' (C–P, 29 January 1915b). Curtis needed full disclosure of the context and direction of Pigott's work to achieve a common perspective and fuse their cognitive processes.

The speed of communication was also vital, and it was linked directly to the issues of complete transmission and cognitive integration. Curtis suggested that it was best

> to submit such facts promptly using the cable wherever necessary for promptness and *continuous consideration*, rather than leaving the matter to letter-writing which often means long periods of waiting and loss of interest or attention ... [I]t generally results in a loss of interest and a relaxing of effort to carry things through to completion, and the result is unsatisfactory. Besides this, you do not get our point of view ... and we do not get your point of view. Often neither party really appreciates what the other is driving at.
>
> (19 January 1915b, emphasis added)

Nor was Curtis unmindful of the expense involved, and he realised that Pigott required instruction in how to evaluate the relative costs and benefits of timely transmission if they were to develop a shared conception of the same and thereby enhance learning processes. '[W]hile the cost of cabling may seem to be an item of some consequence it really is a very small item considering the values involved and it often results in a saving of time or money infinitely greater than the cost of the cables' (19 January 1915b). To drive home the point, he cited past experience: 'after a number of years' experience ... we have found this to be true in dealing with our different licensees'. Once again, Curtis used his historical map to shape the cognitive dimension of the culture he sought to instil within the pyramid.

In the event, Pigott did communicate in a more timely and complete fashion, and he overcame his design problems and the crisis was resolved. [The John Brown Board recognised Pigott's success by awarding him a one per cent commission on the firm's annual total profits: the same bonus that the directors themselves received (UCS1/1/1, 13 June 1915).] The incident could have been avoided or its severity mitigated had he and Curtis responded to early warning signs. Yet, a crisis may have been required to focus attention. Once the crisis began, courtesy and culture were not enough to solve the underlying causes; the participants had to make fundamental changes in the mechanics of communication, and they had to arrive at a common understanding of cost and time considerations. All of these elements had to work in the same direction to promote effective co-operation. In the end, Curtis was only partially successful; he could not secure Bell's confidence.

Conclusion

The onset of 'disc flutter' in itself does not explain why Curtis's turbine lost its position in the UK market. The fact that Westinghouse and European manufacturers solved the problem while Brown did not take advantage of their findings suggests that some form of communicating problem was the fundamental cause of market share loss. We can only speculate about what actually happened, but the deterioration of the Bell–Curtis relationship must have impeded information exchange. In addition, after 1919 Pigott rose to more senior positions at Brown and may have lost touch with turbine development (*The Times*, 28 February 1955).

In this case failure manifested itself as the inability to sustain over the long term the advantages of aggregating the evolving mix of assets controlled by ICMT and John Brown in order to provide an ever-broadening foundation for collaborative learning. (A merger can also be seen as a sign of failure when the complementary nature of the attributes exhibited by formerly independent co-operators is diminished.) Maintaining links between units that tap distinct sources of information and generate autonomous learning helps to sustain creative tension. This was the very balancing act that HSS and JSS so actively sought to achieve.

Pigott's crisis and the disc flutter problem indicate that Curtis also failed to effect or maintain a knowledge advantage relative to his licensees. It was this superiority that enabled Scotts to exert a continuing attraction upon TD&E, and made OP a desirable partner for other Far Eastern paint makers after 1945. As the following case shows, however, if not handled effectively a knowledge advantage can create a legacy of dependence which, when it is ultimately overcome, can lead to strident assertion of independence.

Combining intangible assets in the form of the learning capabilities of pyramid members was certainly Curtis's objective. His construct is of theoretical interest because it exposes a link between the literatures devoted to multinational enterprise, intangible assets, and intermediation. More than simply a transfer mechanism, Curtis's unusual framework was designed to enable some participants to play intermediary roles in harnessing learning effects that enhanced quasi-rents across national borders. This insight suggests that transaction cost variables do not fully explain the internal processes that can determine the advantages of specific institutional alternatives.

Fundamentally, Curtis's failure to meet his overall aim stemmed from defects in the way he designed and used the three contractual components.

Weaknesses in each element reveal useful points for the consideration of participants in co-operative ventures. First, Curtis devised legal specifications that cleverly mobilised incentives intended to encourage innovation. However, the power of these inducements was undermined by asymmetric substitution possibilities available to pyramid members who were also Parsons' licensees. In the absence of a bonding device – perhaps interlocking contracts or a reputation-staking mechanism – problems undermined faith (to use Pigott's word) in Curtis's technology, and it was largely confidence that could activate the incentives he built. The fact that the licensing contract did not oblige Curtis to defend his own patent signalled that he himself did not attach significant value to his own invention. Finally, the failure to devise some way to assign distinct national markets from which quasi-rents could be extracted left scope for potentially damaging disagreement.

Second, the communication lines that provided monitoring functions within the pyramid also displayed weaknesses. Without devoting adequate attention to the layout of formal channels Curtis ended up relying too much on informal conduits. In turn, this reflected his inability to strike an appropriate balance between the degree of formality or informality of communication in relation to the level of trust between specific participants. In contrast, JSS knew that it could exploit the advantages of informal exchange with members of its network but recognised at once that it should avoid private communication entirely to gain PJ's trust. Curtis completely miscalculated the effect that informal 'side conversations' would have on Thomas Bell. He made an elementary error at the outset by not investing more time in assessing the differences in their personalities. The whole affair emphasises the importance – well recognised by JSS – of getting the right mix of people positioned at inter-firm interfaces and ensuring that the attributes of personnel and systems complement each other.

Further weaknesses in Curtis's communication system revealed themselves during Pigott's crisis. Feedback mechanisms within the inter-organisational channels failed to alert Curtis to an impending shock. To prevent a complete breakdown, Curtis first had to mobilise all the crisis management skills at his disposal and then belatedly adjust his basic communication methods. The crisis exposed deficiencies in the cognitive and conceptual foundations of his system.

The same episode also reveals another factor that is fundamental in shaping the performance of co-operative structures. The advantage of these voice-based relationships, relative to alternative institutional arrangements, depends on how effectively participants contain the cost of communication and enhance the benefits of collaborative learning. This, in turn, is contingent upon whether those involved can establish a shared conception of these costs and benefits. For example, the Nickel Syndicate relied on crystal clear indicators, whereas PJ and JSS took time to translate new ideas into familiar terms. In so doing, these organisations mobilised and manipulated patterns of cognition to support communication and co-operation.

Finally, Curtis's imaginative attempt to build an inter-organisational culture by conditioning both cognitive and emotional forces serves instructive purpose. Co-operators must address both of these dimensions of culture, especially when they have not shared similar experiences, but also when they have, as the example of Curtis and Pigott confirms. Curtis's historical map served as a device – and one which those who study the past cannot help but put forward as justification for their avocation – that provided a framework for structuring shared experience even as it unfolded. The case also draws attention to the amount of time it takes to create a customised cognitive instrument and the danger that unforeseen shocks may disrupt the process before it is complete.

The salient point that emerges here is that co-operation entails not only some degree of systemic synthesis, as the HSS and syndicate cases have revealed, but also a measure of strategic integration and cultural fusion. This is perhaps the essence of what Richardson meant when he said that co-operation involves a willing sacrifice of some sovereignty. True inter-dependence arises from sharing cognitive processes. This, in turn, reflects the capacity to communicate in imaginative ways, but also the ability to listen in an anticipatory manner.

The realisation that co-operation entails cultural integration undermines the conception of the corporate boundary as a distinct frontier. Not only does its permeability become manifest, but so too do the conditioning influences – as a consequence of communication – that pass through the pores of this membrane. Moreover, when this insight is combined with the observation that institutions consist of subcultures based on ethnic, occupational, or sub-unit affiliation, there emerges a picture of overlapping cultures within and beyond the corporate boundary. That culture may assume such manifold dimensions highlights both the complexity of relationship building and the broad scope available for such endeavour. The following case explores the significance of cultural differences.

7 A technology transfer agreement

Babcock & Wilcox, 1880–1970

This chapter examines a loosely specific co-operative agreement that was subsequently plagued by chronic *ex post* haggling between a parent firm and its subsidiary. The case exposes the limits of constitutional authority and the challenge involved in balancing autonomy and interdependence. The German and British Babcock companies simultaneously used combinations of institutional instruments – in contrast to theoretical literatures that see such devices as distinct alternatives – to transfer knowledge across boundaries. Yet, in the end they failed to establish a co-operative relationship.

The Babcock & Wilcox (B&W) group of companies has been renowned for its boiler technology since the late nineteenth century. Today, the firms are still world leaders in advanced engineering products. Originally an American firm, B&W established an international presence early. In 1881 it set up operations in Glasgow in league with the Singer Manufacturing Company and soon formed affiliates in France and Germany, as well as agencies in Europe, Australia, and the Far East.

By the early twentieth century, the B&W group as a whole was bound together by a complex mixture of inter-firm links that were used to transfer products and intangible assets, especially technical know-how, across national borders. Some affiliates were connected by licensing agreements, others by board level ties, and still others by minority ownership stakes. This structure was not unusual; other network structures developed variegated ties.

What did make the B&W group unusual was that a number of its internal links consisted of a *mixture* of different transactional frameworks. In contrast, the literature on institutional economics views individual contractual structures as distinct alternatives. An article that appeared in the 1971 issue of a staff publication, *Interfaces*, explained that the group chose one or a combination of three generic modes, direct exports, licensing, or foreign investment in plant or a firm's securities, according to market conditions (especially nationalistic biases in buyer preferences), tariff levels, and transport costs (UGD 309/2/24/1). It also indicated that one transacting mode often *reinforced* others, much like 'nested' contracts usually do:

> One of the drawbacks of a licensing agreement is that it's finite, eventually it expires. So long as your technology is ahead of your licensee's

technology, you'd get a return on the license and the licensee will be tied to you. But a direct investment, through stock ownership, gives you a relationship that continues indefinitely. Thus, the purchase of B&W Limited stock *gave us a long-term basis for working together* in technical fields and renewing the licensing agreement.

(UGD 309/2/24/1)

Thus, unless a licensor maintained a technological lead, as Curtis failed to do, a licensing arrangement by itself would not sustain a long-term collaborative relationship. But the article does not explain why, formal instruments, such as ownership ties and board links, would preserve inter-firm co-operation. Instead, it leaves readers to infer that constitutional power could modify a subsidiary's behaviour towards this end. The assumption was and is erroneous.

In the context of *intra-firm* relations, Barnard (1958) cautioned managers that authority resides at the bottom of an organisation, not at its apex. Authority is assented to. To be sure, subordinates who withhold their assent may suffer consequences if their resistance is detected, but there is usually wide scope for exercising surreptitious opportunism. Whether people will submit to the necessity of co-operative systems within the firm depends on how well managers communicate in formal and informal ways to condition subordinates' assent. Barnard's key insight is that authority is not inherent in a given position; ultimately, constitutional power is reflected in a leader's capacity to communicate (also see Mechanic, 1962).

This chapter explores the limitations of formal authority relations and the nature of institutional interdependence using as a case study the troubled relationship between B&W's British affiliate, B&W Limited (hereafter Limited) and its German subsidiary, Deutsche-Babcock & Wilcox (DB&W), from 1918 to 1975. A contract with inadequate *ex ante* specifications relative to the prevailing level of trust within the context of cross-cultural dealing created scope for endemic *ex post* haggling. Nor did DB&W executives engage in stealthy opportunism; they overtly resisted Limited's authority for fifty years. The case highlights the fact that it is impossible for any firm, even a parent company that employed a combination of contractual devices, to *force* another to co-operate.

The Limited–DB&W story contrasts other chapters in this book. It develops further the exploration of power initiated in the account of the Nickel Syndicate's history. The present discussion draws attention to the need for co-operators to maintain a blend of mutually attractive complementary capabilities as did members of the Holt–Swire–Scott network. The B&W case also brings to light several innovations in the design of a custom-made communicating infrastructure to consider alongside of those devised by the participants in the OP joint venture. The form of the contract arranged by B&W Limited and DB&W exposes contrasts to the agreements analysed in Chapters 2 and 4.

Historical background

In 1866, American engineers, George H. Babcock and Stephen Wilcox, patented a water tube boiler (Tweedale 1984; Heenan 1994; Bruland 1998). The innovation was more efficient than the so-called 'Scotch', or shell type, boiler in which a large quantity of water had to be heated before steam was produced. Babcock and Wilcox's invention incorporated firing chambers with exposed tubes that provided a larger heating surface and thus faster steam-raising capability. Water circulated through the tubes to the main boiler as a result of differences in the density of cold and hot liquid. Babcock and Wilcox's boiler was also safer than the older machinery, but it required that operators had more training and skill.

To exploit their invention, Babcock and Wilcox formed a partnership in 1867 with T. Manton, who produced the boiler at his Hope Iron Works (Bruland 1998: 223). However, Manton's factory had difficulty producing boiler parts to precise tolerances and overcoming a defect in the design of the headers. An engineer who worked for the Singer Manufacturing Co., a new customer of B&W, identified the source of the problem and devised a solution. In 1872, Singer began manufacturing B&W boilers under a subcontracting arrangement. When the B&W partnership was converted into a corporation in 1881, Singer executives and employees acting in a private capacity paid $225,000 for a fifty per cent interest in the new enterprise. The Singer Company continued making boilers for the Babcock & Wilcox Company under a formal subcontracting agreement.

When B&W took its first step overseas, just three months after its formation, it followed the Singer link. B&W initially founded a branch office in London and concluded a 50–50 joint venture wherein Singers manufactured the boilers at a factory it had earlier established at Bridgeton, near Glasgow. B&W staff handled design and marketing activities (UGD 309/1/11/6 Agreement, 30 March 1881).

As the leading industrial nation, Britain was a most attractive market for B&W. The use of wrought iron and later steel construction strengthened its boilers and made it possible to generate higher operating pressures. By the early 1880s, the resulting improvements in boiler performance paved the way for the adoption of the triple expansion engine by Britain's quickly expanding merchant fleet. The newly emerging market for electrical power, stimulated by the development of the turbine for generating purposes in the mid-1880s, offered another source of demand.

To exploit promising markets in the UK and Europe B&W had to offer high-quality products, quick delivery, and close customer service, but Singer proved to be incapable of providing the necessary support. Singer's manufacturing costs were high, and they were incapable of keeping up with demand (Bruland 1998: 231–5; 309/0/24/1–2 and 309/1/11/6). In 1895, B&W set up its own factory in Renfrew.

Meanwhile, in 1891 the US parent firm had sold a majority stake in its UK unit to the public. By that time, the subsidiary, now called Babcock &

Wilcox Limited, had become an important operation in its own right. Boiler sales had risen from just under 2,000 horse power (HP) equivalent in 1882 to over 46,000 HP in 1891 or about two-thirds that of its parent (309/1/9/12). The specific reason behind the partial divestment is unclear. One source indicates that the American owners wished to reduce their investment and secure a capital gain (*Interface*). Tweedale (1984) indicated that the parent firm could no longer provide sufficient funds to support the growth of the subsidiary and used the public issue to bring in fresh capital. Bruland (1998: 238) argued that managerial constraints or strategic considerations prompted the sale. The financial press suggested that the B&W patents would expire soon and that the US owners wished to sell before competition intensified (309/1/9/12). Company correspondence reveals that an argument broke out between George Babcock and brothers Charles and Henry Knight leading to the temporary resignation of Henry Knight. Whatever the reason, the Knights along with James H. Rosenthal (later Sir James Kemnal) ran the new firm.

The sale agreement assigned to Limited the rights to all the parent's licences throughout the world with the exception of the US and Cuba. At the time of its formation the new firm already had in place an international organisation to exploit its vast territory. By 1891, it had branch sales offices in Manchester, Paris, and Brussels, as well as a string of agencies in Lille, Sydney, Berlin, Egypt, and Austria–Hungary. Before 1914, new agents were appointed in Luxembourg, Mexico, Canada, and Russia, and branches were formed in Milan and Australia. Limited also set up subsidiaries in France and Germany and founded manufacturing plants in Japan, Italy, and Poland (Tweedale 1984: 579–80).

The formation of Deutsche-Babcock & Wilcox

Those considerations that governed Limited's choice of transacting mode – agent or branch office – were similar to those that shaped the selection of shipowners, as discussed in Chapter 2. Thus, the distribution of reputation, resources, and information (including knowledge and contacts) between the principal firm and available agents was a crucial factor (309/0/24/1 E. Frazar to N. Pratt, 24 March 1890; 309/0/24/2 Rosenthal to Knight, 18 August and 10 September 1890) The volume of business in the relevant territory, the average costs of the two parties, and the scope for future mutual growth were also important. However, the B&W case reveals additional factors that influenced its institutional choices: local legislation and prejudices against foreign companies shaped decision-making processes.

When Limited decided to enter the German market in order to avoid tariffs and protect its patents, it licensed the rights to manufacture and sell its boilers to a local firm, Schwartzkopffs. The licensee was a 'well-known concern and the fact that they have taken up our boiler is very much to our credit in that country' (309/1/11/6, 12 December 1887). Joining forces with such a company conferred reputation by association and provided customers with assurances regarding the quality of a new product and the confidence of having local repair facilities. However, Limited was concerned that Schwartzkopffs would not aggressively push its products because 'they have too much else to attend to' thus reducing the scope for mutual growth. By the mid-1890s, Limited had become disappointed with the volume of business won by Schwartzkopffs and set up its own German sales branch (309/1/1/1, 14 December 1895). In 1897, the board was informed that 'considerable difficulty is being experienced with the unfavourable attitude of the German people, generally, to us as a foreign concern' (309/1/1/1, 22 October 1897). This factor induced Limited to form a German manufacturing subsidiary in 1898.

The contract between Limited and the new company, Deutsche Babcock & Wilcox Dampfkessel Werke Aktion-Gesellschaft (DB&W), was partly embodied in the latter's articles of association (309/193/312). The parent firm's majority interest in DB&W secured for it board representation and commensurate constitutional authority. Local investors and DB&W's managers derived further assurance of Limited's commitment from its promise to guarantee DB&W's dividend for five years. DB&W was granted an exclusive licence to sell B&W boilers and ancillary equipment and to sub-license B&W patents within the German Empire and its colonies. In addition to the articles of association, a separate contract specified arrangements for information sharing and assigning new patents.

Under the capable management of Robert Jurenka and Alois Seidle, the new subsidiary flourished, and until at least 1939 it always paid an earned dividend. (309/193/24 memo, 13 October 1939). DB&W enlarged its capital base from 2 to 3.5 million marks in 1909, to 5 million marks during the Great War, and 8 million marks in 1939. The subsidiary opened a plant in Oberhausen, acquired another factory at Gleiwitz in 1909, and then built a larger facility at Friedrichfeld in 1921. Having started with just thirty employees in 1898, DB&W's workforce grew to 1,600 in 1927, over 3,000 by 1939, and 11,000 in 1960 (309/193/24/1; Heenan 1998).

Relations between B&W Limited and DB&W: the 1920 contract

Ironically, this impressive record of growth probably contributed to a deterioration in relations between Limited and its German subsidiary after World War I. The German managers were able to take an independent line in part because DB&W performed so well. In 1939 an official from Limited reported:

> This German Company has always been extremely well managed, the three leading members of the Management having been in charge of it since the formation of the Company ... Very strong reserves have been accumulated and the internal value of the Company as a going concern is very greatly in excess of its nominal capital.
>
> (309/193/24/1 statement, 13 October 1939)

Further irony arises from Tweedale's (1984) suggestion that Kemnal, Limited's manager from 1893 until the 1920s, was able to assert his autonomy from the board because Limited itself performed exceedingly well. Although it is possible that the German executives imitated Kemnal's behaviour, it is apparent that neither Kemnal nor Limited's board profited from their own experiences. Indeed, the memo above went on to describe a problem-ridden inter-firm relationship.

From the time DB&W was formed, but more so during the early 1920s and late 1930s, strong anti-British feelings in Germany deterred Limited from using its constitutional power overtly to bring into line the subsidiary's managers. DB&W executives seemed to have sensed the parent firm's vulnerability. And, they took advantage of the disruption of communications during the Great War to alter the basis of inter-firm relations as soon as peace was concluded.

Open conflict erupted in 1919 over DB&W's territorial rights. The issue centred on avoiding competition between parent and subsidiary by creating distinct monopolies from which they could extract quasi-rents. An opening for disagreement to arise was created in 1908 when the two firms concluded a ten-year contract. This document rescinded a clause in DB&W's articles of association governing territorial jurisdiction in order to 'cause an impression on the German public that the British hold on the concern [DB&W] had become lessened' (309/5/23 legal opinion 1919). There were two other matters at issue: first, whether the intention of avoiding competition embodied in the articles was overridden by the 1908 contract; and, second, whether the contract had expired or whether it had been suspended during the war and was therefore still in effect. However, what DB&W officials really wanted in 1919 was recognition of their firm as an autonomous contracting entity.

DB&W's Jurenka and Kemnal hammered out a provisional agreement to govern future relations sometime before October 1919. During the war, DB&W had conducted a considerable amount of business in Scandinavia, Holland, Luxembourg, Estonia, Lithuania, and Latvia (309/1/5/23 Jurenka to Kemnal, 4 September 1919). At their meeting, Jurenka and Kemnal agreed that the German subsidiary would withdraw from these markets in return for a free hand in Austria, Czechoslovakia, Hungary, Bulgaria, Yugoslavia, and Romania. They concluded that DB&W would pay Limited a five per cent fee on all wartime work and on future orders from this extended market and *ten* per cent on contracts from within Limited's territory if customers insisted on DB&W products. Limited would pay the German firm only *five* per cent on orders it received from within DB&W's territory when clients there demanded Limited's products.

DB&W's board of administration (*Aufsichtstrat*) did not approve this provisional arrangement, and Jurenka sent a revision incorporating suggestions from Herr Kirchhoff, the president. Jurenka asserted his firm's right to work in Luxembourg, the Baltic, and the newly formed Saar state along with the central European markets listed above, free of any commission, and he demanded equal commissions on work that DB&W and Limited did in each other's territories. In return, DB&W would renounce its rights to Holland and Scandinavia and release Limited from its promise to guarantee the German unit's dividend. (The parent firm had extended the duration of the guarantee included in DB&W's articles.) Jurenka proposed that the two parties meet to finalise the matter on this basis.

Kemnal's reply took a strong line that provoked a defiant response from Kirchhoff (5/23 Kirchhoff to Kemnal, 17 September 1919). Kirchhoff admitted that the contract of 1908 prevented his firm from exporting, but taking the line that this ten-year agreement had lapsed during the war, he proclaimed that 'we would now not again enter into [a similar agreement] so long as I am President of the Board of Administration'. He went on to dare Limited to use its constitutional power: 'I by no means fail to recognise that the English Company possess the power to obtain its own way if it is a question of coming up against each other "Hard against Hard" but then the English Company would have to take the German Business in hand itself and cannot expect *that we* do *its* business for it'. Kirchhoff knew that Limited, as an English firm, would have formidable problems conducting business in Germany.

Kemnal then took a more conciliatory tack (5/23 Kemnal to Jurenka, 23 September 1919). He conceded that DB&W could work in the Baltic region, Luxembourg (unless the Grand Duchy later came under French control), and central Europe, which before the war had been a more valuable market than Holland and Scandinavia. He went on to insist that DB&W pay Limited five per cent commission on orders from these territories as well as compensation for work it had done outside its allotted markets during the war. Kemnal asserted that the German firm had 'never had the right and have not now the right to sell outside Germany without our sanction', which had in the past been given to help it in developing an export trade with other German firms building plants abroad. He also reminded Jurenka that the German unit benefited from using the B&W name. Kemnal could not agree to the two firms paying equal commissions, and he stated that Kirchhoff's offer to renounce the dividend guarantee meant nothing 'because its acceptance would imply an admittance [sic] of poverty which is not justified'.

Kemnal wrote to Kirchhoff on the same day contending that the rights of the two firms were not based upon a contract but rather constituted part of the fundamental arrangements surrounding the formation of the German company. A central tenet of the inter-firm relationship was the avoidance of competition. Kemnal stated that two points separated he and Jurenka:

1   Jurenka felt that DB&W had the right to sell in Limited's territory during the war, and
2   he wanted territorial compensation for the loss of Alsace–Lorraine and the Saar district.

Kemnal then made a threat to counter Kirchhoff's dare regarding Limited working directly in Germany. To emphasise DB&W's subordination, Kemnal stated that if the two firms had an open confrontation 'it would mean the end of the German Company'. This would be less harmful to Limited than unrestricted competition.

Jurenka's next letter enunciated what he saw as the basic problem concerning inter-firm relations. He said that to reach a solution 'it will be necessary ... for the principal of equity to be given better expression and not for one party to be relegated to a position of subordinate dependence' (5/23 13 October 1919, Jurenka to Kemnal). DB&W's unequal status, which stemmed in part from Limited's technical superiority, meant that during the war 'the position of dependency into which we were forced by obtaining pressure parts from London might well have been fatal to us'. Moreover, affiliation with Limited during the War could have had dire personal consequences for DB&W's directors. Jurenka claimed that having just succeeded 'in proving the German character of our company in some degree' DB&W faced a competitive disadvantage because of its links with the American and British Babcock firms. 'The principle underlying our new contract must be that both firms remain independent companies, who are concluding a contract ... purely in order to avoid competition ...' He demanded that equal commissions should be paid when either firm took orders from the other's territory. He also stated that granting DB&W access to the nearly bankrupt middle European countries was inadequate compensation for the latter's withdrawal from Holland and Scandinavia, which 'are now among the richest countries'. Jurenka went on to claim the Saar and Luxembourg. He reminded Kemnal that since DB&W had eliminated provisions assigning territories from its articles in 1908, the relevant clause now 'has no legal importance in regard to our contractual relationship with you'. Thus, DB&W had freed itself of a constitutional constraint and was in a position – as an autonomous entity – to arrange any form of contract with its parent.

After conferring with DB&W's *Aufsichtsrat*, Jurenka wrote Kemnal a second letter wherein he stated that Limited was not entitled to compensation for orders the subsidiary had fulfilled during the war. Under German law, a party that had not met its contractual obligations, as Limited had failed to do by not supplying pressure parts, could not seek redress against the other party for non-compliance. Nor did Jurenka believe that Limited could claim compensation on the basis of DB&W's articles of association. As a compromise aimed at resolving the issue 'in a friendly way', the German manager offered to pay a five per cent commission on export orders received up to 5 November 1918. He did not mention commissions on DB&W's post-war export contracts even though these payments were the source of Limited's initial concern about inter-firm competition.

DB&W then received a legal opinion which found that the contract between parent and subsidiary was not interrupted by the war, nor had it been cancelled. Rather, it had lapsed through the passage of time and as a result

Limited was not entitled to compensation (18 October 1919, Giessing and Offszanka to DB&W). This cleared the way for DB&W to put additional pressure on Limited by competing more vigorously in the parent's territory (Kemnal to Jurenka, 21 October 1919).

As majority owner, Limited could change DB&W's articles and impose its will on the subsidiary. However, the managers of the parent firm did not pursue this option because they feared that overt demonstration of British control would harm DB&W's competitive position and reduce the value of Limited's investment (5/23 Legal Opinion, no date). Therefore, in early 1920, they acceded to an agreement that granted DB&W most of the points it sought (309/193/5/1, 1 February 1920).

The German firm secured rights to Austria, Czechoslovakia, Hungary, Bulgaria, Yugoslavia, Romania, the Saar, Luxembourg, and the Baltic states. However, it was excluded from doing business in Holland and Scandinavia except for specified equipment. The two companies would divide the Polish market, and they agreed to equal commissions and rules designed to eliminate competition. They also decided that each firm could install boilers free of commission in ships built by yards in their respective countries regardless of the vessel owner's nationality, thus avoiding one problem that arose within ICMT's pyramid. Limited and DB&W also agreed to share technical information, including data on unpatented products. The contract did not mention any commissions on DB&W's post-war export orders.

They left other issues loosely specified in order to accommodate future developments that could be foreseen. Scope was left for transferring rights from Luxembourg to the French subsidiary, if political conditions so required, with DB&W receiving compensation. Similarly, the Saar could be placed within the French firm's sphere of influence if the planned plebiscite resulted in a transfer of sovereignty, but in this instance the German firm would receive no compensation. Limited reserved the right to set up its own Polish subsidiary, and if it did so it would pay DB&W a five per cent commission on all orders from Polish customers. To avoid a recurrence of the problems caused by World War I, the contract also stated that in the event of another war the two firms would adhere to the agreement in so far as they could and return to its provisions as soon as possible after any conflict. Any period of hostilities would be treated as an interruption to the contract and the term of its duration would be extended by the equivalent amount of time. Parent and subsidiary also agreed that commissions on export orders could be modified by special arrangement in order to respond to market conditions.

To summarise this section, wartime dislocations in deliveries of crucial parts, but more especially in communications, created an opportunity for DB&W to act autonomously. Probably the first thing Limited should have done was to restore confidence by rebuilding inter-firm operating, communicating, and managerial links. Instead, negotiations focusing on legal matters were initiated and these were quickly soured by the use of brinkmanship tactics on both sides. In some ways, the attitudes of DB&W's

managers seem to have been shaped by the humiliation that the German nation felt as a result of its defeat. Perhaps this was why Jurenka was so strident in his claims. Limited responded forcefully at first but then signalled weakness in allowing so many concessions in the 1920 contract. Despite the flexibility built into that agreement, it could not accommodate the acutely adverse conditions that soon beset the German economy.

Inter-firm relations, 1920–39

Almost as soon as the contract of 1920 had been concluded, DB&W began exerting what was to become for the rest of the inter-war period continuous pressure on Limited to make further concessions. The British firm developed several new devices to promote co-operation, and these initiatives probably reduced tensions somewhat. However, the poor economic conditions faced by the German subsidiary, state regulations, and the achievement of technical superiority by DB&W compelled Limited to make a series of concessions. Throughout the period, the German managers pushed to see how far they could get, but inter-firm relations did not exhibit the acrimony that preceded the conclusion of the 1920 contract.

In the 1920s, Limited made minor concessions to help DB&W, but the subsidiary deliberately and consistently contravened the agreement of 1920. In particular, preventing inter-firm competition – the major aim of that contract – proved to be impossible. For example, DB&W supplied Dutch and Scandinavian customers with equipment that was not covered in the 1920 agreement. However, the German unit also exported powdered fuel plant 'more or less in competition' with its parent (5/23 memo, 28 May 1929). Competition also occurred in Poland. Limited permitted DB&W to export to Russia, which lay within the British firm's territory, at a commission of just 0.5 per cent and acceded to DB&W's request that it finance these orders. Then, having extracted these concessions, DB&W did not pay Limited the small commission it had agreed to (Greenly to Jurneka, 26 February 1931; 309/1/7/1, 28 July 1931; 309/5/23, 14 March 1934). DB&W seems to have sensed Limited's weakness and pushed for any advantage it thought it could win.

Finally, in early 1932, Jurenka felt that the moment was right to propose an entirely new contract 'intended to settle the commercial intercourse between us and you' (5/23 Jurenka to Limited, 18 February 1932). With the exception of equipment supplied by either firm in the other's territory (which remained the same except that DB&W claimed Danzig and Memel) in response to customers' requests, the German manager suggested 'the abolition of any commission or royalties.' As justification, he stated that the original B&W patents had lapsed and rival firms had copied the designs. Moreover, 'license fees most certainly could not be paid at the present juncture nor in the future that presents such a gloomy aspect as far as this country is concerned'. The agreement defined 'very distinctly the sphere of activity of the English and German Company and provide[d] ... for the mutual exchange of patents and experience.' Limited did not agree to relinquish at least its rights to commissions some of which DB&W did not pay anyway.

The expiration of B&W's original patents induced Limited to promote closer inter-firm collaboration. Starting in the early 1930s, staff from the British, German, French, Spanish, Italian, and American units met annually to discuss technical and sales matters. Limited's A. Mckinstry enunciated the purpose of these conferences:

> ... no concern can rest forever on one fundamental discovery. Patents vanish by affluxion of time and unless other technical advances take the place of the first basic invention, a period arrives when others are able to enter into competition and put forward schemes which ... may contain everything except the experience which has been gained by the older concern.

> There is a sense in which this position has arrived in the history of the Water-tube Boiler. We have no longer a monopoly ... We have, however, still the name and the prestige which belong to nearly half a century of successful, and until the recent slump, ever increasing business.

> The problem in front of us is how to hold that position ... [O]ur technique must always remain first among all our competitors, as well as the service we give ...

> It is for this reason that I want to stress ... the fundamental necessity of Research and Development work ... [W]e might with advantage study ... ways and means for closer technical co-operation between the different Companies bearing the name.
>
> 'Babcock' (309/1/7/1, 8 June 1933)

Somewhat like Charles Curtis, Mckinstry tried to mobilise history to condition patterns of thought. He drew attention to the group's long-term record of success at a time when intangible assets – accumulated expertise, tacit knowledge, learning capabilities, and shared reputation – reinforced by collaborative research and development (R&D) would increasingly act as substitutes for the expired patents as the basis of the B&W companies' competitive advantage. Like the annual sales conferences that began about the same time, the technical meetings provided fora where delegates could build interpersonal knowledge and a group-wide culture both of which could help to facilitate *ex post* adjustments, transfers of knowledge, and future collaboration.

These initiatives had little impact on relations between DB&W and its parent, however, because the German firm's growing technical superiority and new government regulations gave it an opportunity to assert its autonomy.

By 1939, government controls over exports and foreign exchange had forced the two firms to ignore 'for many years' competition-preventing clauses in the 1920 contract (Jurenka to Limited, 20 June 1939). Limited recognised that the Reichswertschafts-Ministerium would not sanction any arrangement which gave a foreign company authority to approve export orders by DB&W. However, Limited did not want to create any precedent that might give other affiliates grounds for departing from the terms of their agreements. Nor would Limited 'officially admit that the German Company is entitled to any special consideration in regard to export business because the present situation will not remain permanently' (*aide-mémoire*, 22 June 1939). They agreed that DB&W would not have to notify Limited when it received inquiries for orders that no other affiliate could fulfil. The German firm would, however, inform London when it heard of new business that other B&W firms could perform. Limited agreed to accommodate DB&W when it received an order that, in the event of another subsidiary declining to quote, would probably be placed with a German rival. Finally, Limited confirmed that 'the German Company today has to a very great extent departed from the original Babcock boiler design and the English Company's own engineering practice'. However, London asserted that this did not provide justification for DB&W to export outside its assigned territory (5/23 Franklin to Jurenka, 3 July 1939). The arrangement was a temporary one arising from abnormal circumstances.

Thus, after the 1920 contract, inter-firm relations were characterised by chronic *ex post* haggling. Limited had no option but to fight a rearguard action by making as few concessions as it could in light of environmental conditions and the growing technical prowess of DB&W. Limited's attempts to improve group-wide communication and collaboration made little impression on its German subsidiary.

Inter-firm relations, 1945–75

During World War II, the previous arrangements between DB&W and Limited were deemed to have 'ceased to have legal validity' under the agreement of 1920 (Limited to J. C. P. Brunyate, 22 January 1953). By 1953, London told its legal advisors that 'the control by us of the German Company is at present satisfactorily exercised by virtue of our majority shareholding and our Representation on the Board' (ibid.). Yet, Limited felt that it would be wise to have a formal agreement that clearly defined the two parties' duties and rights in case conditions changed.

In 1954, the two firms concluded an agreement that granted DB&W rights to Austria, Czechoslovakia, Yugoslavia, Hungary, Bulgaria, Rumania, as well as both West and East Germany. To accommodate future developments, it explicitly stated that DB&W would have jurisdiction in any future united Germany. The contract, which covered twenty-five years, provided for exchanges of patents and technical information. The two firms avoided the problems that preceded the conclusion of the 1920 contract by agreeing to equal commissions on work done in each other's territories. One issue left out of the arrangement was how a party that developed new technology was to be compensated if the other firm used it.

To close this gap comprehensively, in 1956 Limited, DB&W, and the French and Spanish affiliates agreed that if one of them incurred heavy research expenses any other company that made use of the knowledge 'would make an appropriate contribution'. However, the arrangement did not specify the actual terms. Acting on behalf of all the European affiliates, Limited concluded with the US Babcock Company a Technical Interchange Agreement (TIA) in 1958 to link all constituents' innovative capabilities. Limited agreed to pay the US firm $500,000 per annum, and would collect contributions towards this payment from each of the European B&W companies. Again, the amount each firm would pay was not specified.

These arrangements were part of a move to rebuild the intra-group links created in the 1930s. In 1954, the four European companies established an annual production conference for works managers (DM 309/1/1/12, 5 October 1954). Annual sales conferences resumed, and a management conference was founded to examine policy matters (DM, 14 May 1957). In 1961, the European firms formed the B&W Engineering Group to act as a centre for collaboration in engineering, sales, research, product development, and production cost systems design.[1]

This inter-firm construct, impressive though it was, could not contain tensions within the B&W Group. The annual conferences became fora where dissatisfaction with the TIA surfaced and a Europe-versus-America division emerged. This rift arose because the Americans had 'violated the spirit of the agreement' by invading the European market for atomic power stations. (309/1/18/33 notes by Jurenka, 31 July 1959). Similarly, the US company's acquisition of a British firm that specialised in diamond soot-blowing equipment, a move aimed at entering the Common Market, was 'a direct challenge' to the European firms (309/1/18/33 minutes for 1961). The Europeans also believed that the Americans had not rewarded them at all for their assistance with suspended fuel Benson boilers. Nor did the Americans share information fully. Even within the European branch of the group, divisions between DB&W and other members arose.

The Germans adopted a particularly strong stance against the TIA because they believed that their technology, and that of the European firms, was superior to what the Americans had to offer, especially small power stations (309/1/18/33, 1960). DB&W also developed a superior sectional fabrication and installation system that reduced the complexity of making oversize boilers. Thus, the elaborate inter-firm structure was undermined as changes in affiliates' knowledge sets reduced the mutual gains that could arise from co-operation. Moreover, the European firms, especially DB&W, felt that the Americans did not acknowledge their achievements and did not recognise the principle of reciprocity.

In late 1971, negotiations for the renewal of the TIA of 1954 (due to expire on 31 January 1972) got under way, with Limited negotiating on behalf of the European firms. The British expected to raise the $500,000 annual fee paid to the Americans by charging the French company $150,000, DB&W about the same, and the Spanish a comparatively small amount. Limited would make up the balance (309/1/5/22 P. H. Dunn to P. de Buyer, 2 November 1971). DB&W executives refused to accept the schedule of payments and objected to the fundamental basis of the TIA.

Limited had to go ahead and renew the TIA without securing agreement with DB&W on the size of its contribution. When discussions on the matter resumed, DB&W informed Limited that 'we cannot see what general technical information provided by the American Company would be of assistance in our daily business … to justify an expense of $150,000 per year'. The German directors suggested that payments and information exchanges should be made directly between DB&W and the US B&W Company – without Limited acting as an intermediary – on a case-by-case basis. Reminiscent of the assertion of contractual autonomy that created problems in 1919, they argued that this practice 'should apply in both directions' (309/1/5/26 27 DB&W to P. H. Dunn, 27 April 1972).

P. Dunn of Limited was 'very surprised' by DB&W's proposal since 'the basic principle that we would negotiate on behalf or ourselves and of our Associates … has never been questioned' (309/1/1/5/26 Dunn to A. Dreher, 16 May 1972). He argued that the arrangement was fundamental to European technical collaboration. This was especially true since constant exposure to US designs would shape the approaches used by DB&W, while intermittent exchanges would not sustain cumulative learning. DB&W replied that 'German technology, if not comparable, is even better than that of the Americans' and demanded a direct, two-way flow of information (309/1/5/26 A. Dreher to Dunn, 30 August 1972).

In an internal memo, J. S. Picton of Limited reviewed the aims of technical exchanges between the two firms (1/5/26, 28 November 1972). First, joint work 'must benefit both parties, particularly where products are complimentary and operating experience is different'. Second, he indicated that a break would damage the market standing of all parties since international customers expected the B&W firms to co-operate. Finally, Picton feared that without a comprehensive agreement, the various parties would 'arbitrarily hoard' technology leading to complicated cross-licensing arrangements. He cited DB&W's refusal to pay Limited £100,000 owed for work done on marine boilers as evidence that the Germans played an opportunistic game of obtaining information without reciprocating.

An indication that Limited's attitude had hardened towards inter-firm technical exchanges came in February 1973 when it pressed for payments on marine work. Picton informed Dreher that Limited wanted a definite agreement on remuneration *in advance* of it doing any more work for DB&W (309/1/5/26 Picton to Dreher, 1 February 1973). The lever was partially effective: the Germans agreed to a two-year arrangement (instead of the fourteen-year renewal agreement Limited wanted) whereby they paid $75,000 per annum for 1973 and 1974 as their contribution toward Limited's TIA fee (1/5/26, 6 December, Dreher to Taylor).

To exert more pressure, the British informed DB&W that its half-hearted compliance put at risk a proposal to conduct joint exports outside the European Community (1/24/8, 12 March 1973, Taylor to Dreher). Because this project would use American technology, only those affiliates that had signed the TIA could participate. This ploy was designed to allow DB&W time to reconsider its decision before the arrangement lapsed on 31 January 1974. DB&W assured Limited that it would pay the $75,000 owed for each of the two years 1973 and 1974 'to help *you* … because … the agreement with the American Company had [already] been signed' (5/26 28 September 1973, Dreher to Taylor). Despite its undertaking, DB&W did not forward any payment (1/5/26 2 October 1973, Taylor to Dreher). Limited told DB&W that its attitude threatened relations with the American and French firms over the joint export programme (309/1/24/8 9 October 1973 Taylor to Dreher).

The Germans then informed the American company that they intended to quit the TIA and to seek advice as needed in return for payments. They offered to sell the B&W Company information about DGS firing systems [5/26 29 October 1973 Dreher to Tendler (B&W Company)]. Limited asked for confirmation that this step had been taken and stated that if it was true, it would reassess its shareholding in DB&W, the joint export project, collaboration on marine boilers, and the status of its representatives on the German unit's board (1/5/26 30 October 1973 Taylor to Dreher). Limited was threatening a complete rupture.

The two parties met on 4 December 1973 when Limited explained to DB&W the consequences of its withdrawal from the TIA (5/26 memo, 4 December 1973, by Taylor). Taylor pointed out that 'free ranging technical discussion' with affiliates would cease. Commercial relations with other B&W firms would have to be of an 'arm's-length nature', and German participation in the joint export project would not be possible. DB&W officials would not be allowed to attend the various group conferences. Taylor concluded his memo by saying that 'there was no alternative' to these steps being taken. During the meeting, DB&W managers reiterated their position and stated that any change would have to be approved by their board.

Matters dragged on until mid-January (the agreement was to expire at the end of that month) when Limited sent DB&W a draft letter that it would circulate to affiliates outlining the types of exchanges that would not take place if the Germans failed to ratify the agreement (5/26, 17 January 1974, Taylor to H. Wiehn). At the last moment – 29 January – DB&W offered to re-open negotiations and finally paid the $150,000 owed for its share of the TIA fees for 1973 and 1974. By May 1975, Limited and DB&W agreed that the latter would pay $75,000 per annum made up of a base rate of $40,000 plus an additional $35,000 fee contingent upon it receiving at least one order as a result of references provided by the British firm.

Conclusion

The dysfunctional relationship between Limited and DB&W can be explained largely by the lack of effective strategic, structural, systemic, or cultural linkages between the two firms. The failure to create such ties from the start meant that there was no buffer, like the cultural one Curtis tried to create, that could absorb unforeseeable shocks such as those that occurred in World War I. Indeed, it was especially important to build an inter-firm culture that could provide a countervailing influence to offset the effect of the antagonistic national culture that existed before 1914 and intensified later. The negotiations of 1919 confirm that Jurenka and Kemnal did not share the same conception of courtesy or the same protocols for making adjustments. There was no suitable fit between those who occupied positions at the interface between parent and subsidiary. Without those parts of the communicating infrastructure that could support informal exchanges across national and cultural frontiers, there was no mechanism that could be used to condition an assent to authority.

The initial contract and those that followed were defective in that specifications were too loose in relation to the level of prevailing trust. Having failed to build a foundation of mutual confidence, Limited had to rely on the legal provisions in DB&W's articles and licensing contract. Subsequently, Limited signalled weakness in 1908 when it tried to obscure its influence and, in light of the confusion between it these two contractual devices, paved the way for chronic *ex post* haggling. Sensing Limited's vulnerability, Jurenka continuously pushed for advantages. While Limited learned from and attempted to remedy oversights in its previous contracts, DB&W always found other points to object to. The fact that the subsidiary won most of the concessions it sought encouraged further haggling. It appears that this type of behaviour was learned by succeeding DB&W executives. This historical trajectory characterised by overt sub-goal pursuit provides a vivid counterpoint to the way Curtis creatively attempted to manipulate conceptions of the past and cognitive processes. Events matter, and how interpretations of them are conditioned shape their legacy for better or worse.

The contrast with B&W France is also poignant. The contract between this unit and Limited was also loosely specified, but the two firms established a momentum of smooth adjustment involving very little discussion. The Germans did not recognise a *spirit* embodied in their agreement and focused instead on matters of detail. The result was costly and time-consuming debate.

Other imbalances are apparent in the Limited–DB&W relationship. Firm-specific technical capabilities were chronically mismatched. That DB&W was initially dependent upon Limited for crucial components and then superior in new technical fields confirms that too little and too much prowess can cause problems in co-operative relationships. In this instance, perhaps the humiliation of dependency created a desire to achieve superiority and exact revenge. Scotts and OP handled imbalances *and* shifts in capabilities more effectively.

Nor did Limited find a fulcrum on which to juxtapose autonomy and interdependence. JSS was far more adept at exercising guidance while allowing affiliates scope to use their discretion. The B&W case shows that sacrificing sovereignty, to use Richardson's telling phrase, requires careful management. Allowing another party to feel enthralled or creating scope for them to proclaim autonomy as stridently as DB&W did is a grave mistake.

Although Limited did not successfully condition an assent to its authority, it also failed to use its raw constitutional power effectively. It lacked the creativity that the Nickel Syndicate exhibited when it used its position to design advantageous communication lines without alarming its suppliers. Nor did Limited use its power overtly as did some of the shipowners examined in Chapter 2 in order to forge reputations. Although some forms of power are sometimes enhanced when used sparingly, other types, especially legitimised power, are augmented by demonstration. Because Limited vacillated it became constrained – rather than empowered – by its affiliation with DB&W. It was trapped by its investment and could not devise an exit strategy that would allow it to make a gracious departure. Without viable substitution possibilities, Limited had no option but to haggle, minimise its concessions, and endure. In effect, real power rested with DB&W, but that firm did not use its position to advantage either.

What gave DB&W its power was public opinion and government policy. These forces not only represented additional considerations to those that, as Chapter 2 showed, influence mode selection but they highlight an another contracting problem. How do participants in a bilateral contract accommodate what was in effect a third party? The Nickel Syndicate used the power conferred by Admiralty preferences in a restrained manner, and members of the HSS network used additional contractual links to constrain partners they were unsure of. Perhaps DB&W could have gained more by using its power in a judicious manner.

Finally, this case alerts us to the fact that, in contrast to theories that view specific contractual devices as distinct alternatives, transacting frameworks can be made to overlap. This may be done for various reasons. Limited used licensing, investment ties, and board links to transfer knowledge, gain enhanced access to quasi-rents, and to exercise and monitor influence. However, these devices did not serve the 'nesting purpose' it intended because they were not symmetrically aligned. Indeed, what created scope for trouble to arise initially was the loophole left when the contract of 1908 superseded the territorial provisions of DB&W's articles of association. The next case shows how knowledge exchange can be achieved using less formal, interrelated instruments.

8 Learning within an inter-organisational group

The Union Steamship Co. and oil propulsion, 1912–39

This case shows how a network can provide a context for inter-organisational learning and for capturing learning by using effects. Extending the analysis of networks in Chapter 3, it also shows how information gathering, processing, and storing activities supported technological adaptation. Further, it highlights the importance of staff capabilities and the value of establishing inter-firm links at many organisational levels.

In contrast to the B&W and Curtis cases, which showed how communicating and institutional processes influenced the effectiveness of arrangements designed to facilitate technological *transfers*, this chapter explores in detail how similar variables shaped technological *adaptation*. Here, we examine the link between information gathering and processing, decision-making, and institutional structure by investigating how the Union Steamship Co. of New Zealand (USS) responded to the opportunity to adopt diesel and oil-fired propulsion systems. USS was formed in 1873 by James Mills (later Sir James) and had developed services around the New Zealand coast, over the Tasman Sea, and across the Pacific by 1917, when it was acquired by the P&O group (McLean 1990).

As we saw in Chapter 3, relative to hierarchical structures, inter-organisational networks, like the P&O group, have extensive lateral links, afford wide scope for informal communication, allow sub-units considerable contracting autonomy, and rely upon interdependence to deter opportunism. These frameworks have highly permeable boundaries and manifold external communication channels that offer affiliates access to diverse information sets. The group structure can provide considerable flexibility as long as it achieves an appropriate balance between interdependence and sub-unit autonomy and does not distend its finances. For a single firm within these constructs, successful innovation depends upon how effectively it gathers information and sustains learning effects across its own corporate frontier.

This chapter represents, therefore, another response to Powell's call for further investigation into the information-handling and learning activities that occur within networks. Although it examines how one firm within a larger group discovered new knowledge, the case goes beyond the consideration of a single 'learning organisation' to examine how the P&O

group provided a *context* for inter-organisational learning. However, in contrast to Chapter 3, which analysed high-level, strategic learning processes within the HSS network, this case presents a bottom-up perspective on knowledge-creating activities that – for about thirty-five years – were focused more narrowly on technical matters.

The discussion describes how USS used existing channels and created new communication lines through which it gathered data from within and beyond the P&O group regarding the sources of uncertainty associated with the adoption of new propulsion systems. We also explore how USS used and adapted its existing analytical skills, relating to market analysis, cost accounting, and engineering, and developed new expertise to confront this technological challenge. Finally, the case shows how the firm mobilised *across organisational boundaries* what Rosenberg (1982) called learning-by-using effects (the capacity to devise incremental improvements by using a new technology and thereby realise its full commercial potential). Moreover, staff codified such tacit knowledge and embedded it within USS's organisational memory.

Historical context

Following the development of viable prototypes before 1914, subsequent investment in motor ships was influenced by higher capital costs, the availability of oil supplies, the price of oil relative to coal, and the promise of operating advantages (lower labour requirements, fast refuelling, greater earning power derived from storing fuel in spaces where cargo could not be stowed). However, during the inter-war period, shipowners from Denmark, Norway, Sweden, and Holland were much quicker to adopt the diesel engine than their British competitors. To explain the slow pace of innovation in Britain some historians examined the information-gathering and processing methods used to assess the suitability of the new technology on specific routes, whereas others took a broader perspective and questioned the efficiency of the institutional structures employed in the British shipping industry.

First, some commentators wondered whether British entrepreneurs had sufficient information to reduce uncertainty to acceptable levels. In their assessment of the motor ship's competitiveness in the Europe–Australia trade, Henning and Trace (1975: 354, 375) argued that British operators underinvested in diesel engines, especially during the crucial years of 1920–25, because turbine manufacturers' made misleading claims for their products, future oil supplies and prices were uncertain, the reliability of the motor ship was still doubtful, there may have been a shortage of competent engineering staff, and pro-coal sentiments prevailed. Citing poor bunkering facilities and unsatisfactory experiences with prototypes, Orbell (1978: 87–8) found that Lyle Shipping achieved good financial results using mainly coal-fired ships in tramping trades. Fletcher (1975: 5–6) argued that uncertainty about oil distribution and monopolistic oil companies was considerable, but it had dissipated by the early 1920s.

Second, regarding data-processing methods, Henning and Trace (1975) based their findings on discounted cash flow (DCF) analysis. Robertson (1988: 109–7) questioned the appropriateness of using this methodology because it was not widely employed by shipowners in the inter-war era. However, he cited T & J Harrison & Co., which *did* use a rudimentary form of DCF analysis to determine that the diesel was not superior to coal fired systems on all their trades. Overall, these findings suggest that British shipowners faced considerable uncertainty, especially until about 1925. Information was far from complete, the sophistication of decision-makers' analytical methods varied, and route-specific conditions were important in shaping technical choices.

Adopting an institutional approach to analyse British performance, Sturmey (1962: 397) blamed the group structure, which he argued engendered a conservative attitude towards innovation. With financial structures burdened by debt and imprecise decision-making processes, most British groups were slow to adopt the diesel engine. However, Sturmey (1962)and Davies (1972) both recognised that the Royal Mail Group was for a time an exception because it had a close link with shipbuilder Harland & Wolff, which had licensed one of the best diesel designs, the Burmeister & Wain. However, the group's collapse in 1932 dissipated this source of innovative energy. These findings hint that inter-organisational ties were important in determining performance.

USS's records support an analysis of its decision-making in the context of both route-specific conditions and institutional processes. Having secured sound information from a variety of sources, USS accurately judged the degrees of risk and irreducible uncertainty it faced in relation to the skills of its staff. This determination justified an initial course of innovation that was cautious and designed to preserve flexibility, but subsequent learning led to reassessment and a more decisive policy. There is little evidence that P&O made poor decisions regarding technology; indeed, affiliation with the group was an advantage to USS, especially in the early stages of fleet conversion. In terms of this sub-unit's technical policy, P&O struck an appropriate balance between allowing management sufficient autonomy and harnessing the benefits of interdependence.

USS's technical choices and innovative performance

The technical options facing any shipping firm in the inter-war era were diverse and subject to considerable uncertainty (Henning and Trace 1975: 383–8). The only technology that was completely reliable was the conventional reciprocating steam engine, which derived increased efficiency from higher boiler pressures and the addition of exhaust steam turbines. In the turbine sector, direct coupling was suitable for fast passenger vessels, and to extend the market to include cargo ships manufacturers developed double reduction gearing, but technical problems hindered wider adoption during the 1920s.

Diesels promised greater efficiency (they used only about forty per cent of the fuel consumed by oil-fired ships of equal power), but early varieties, especially the four stroke, suffered from metallurgical and design defects. It was not until 1930 that the influential publication *Brassey's Naval and Shipping Annual* stated that the two-stroke diesel was almost as reliable as steam machinery (cited in Henning and Trace 1975:367).

Eventually, individual engine types came to be recognised as being most suitable for specific applications. Fast passenger and mail ships relied on oil-fired steam turbines. Large cargo liners used the diesel, and slower tramp steamers continued to use steam-reciprocating machinery fuelled by coal. Although this pattern of diffusion provides a bench-mark for assessing the accuracy of decision-making, subject to route-specific conditions, it was not readily obvious to shipowners until the late 1930s.

How innovative was USS? Table 8.1 shows that in 1922–3 the composition of the firm's fleet mirrored that of the British Empire. Although USS lagged slightly in adopting the motor ship, by 1938–9 it had a larger proportion of oil-fired steamers, which represented an 'intermediate' innovatory step since these ships were costlier to run than diesels, but cheaper than coal burners. Overall, the firm was more reliant upon oil than the rest of the imperial fleet, but the higher percentage of oil-fired tonnage suggests that it adopted a flexible approach. In fact, USS designed its oil-fired ships so that they could be easily converted back to coal in case oil supplies failed.

Although we lack complete information about fleet deployment, the directors' minutes indicate that conditions on USS's various routes influenced technical choices. For example, in 1913 USS built *Niagara*, the first passenger ship licensed by the British Board of Trade to burn oil as well as coal. After wartime disruptions, USS converted its remaining fast trans-Pacific mail steamers to oil-fired turbines by 1922. Its fast ferry services were also converted to oil-firing in the 1920s, as were coastal ships that needed a reserve of power to cope with strong tides. USS employed large motor ships in its trans-Pacific cargo lines and for its refrigerated services. Finally, the firm's New Zealand–Australia coal-carrying operations were served by conventional coal burners, including some ordered in the late 1930s. (USS also owned coal mines, but its records do not indicate that this influenced decision-making.) By 1939, the fleet was deployed broadly in line with what came to be the widely recognised pattern described above.

As recorded in USS's directors' minutes, the sequence of decisions to order new ships or convert existing vessels from coal to oil reveals two important trends. First, the firm experimented widely with many propulsion systems, including several types of diesel and an advanced turboelectric drive. It usually tried out a single ship equipped with new technology, and if results confirmed expectations all vessels in the same trade were converted. For example, the results achieved by *Niagara* induced USS to switch its other trans-Pacific mail and passenger ships to oil-firing. The same pattern of experimentation followed by wholesale change unfolded in USS's trans-Pacific cargo trade and its ferry services.

Table 8.1 Percentages of USS and British Empire fleets propelled by diesel, oil-fired, and coal-burning engines in 1922–3 and 1938–9 (by tonnage)

	1922–3			*1938–9*		
	Diesel	*Oil-fired*	*Coal-fired*	*Diesel*	*Oil-fired*	*Coal-fired*
USS	3	16	81	19	38	43
Empire	2	15	83	21	29	50

Source: Lloyd's Register of Shipping, 1922–3 and 1938–9.

Second, the directors' minutes also confirm that an important shift in policy occurred in 1931–2. From 1918 to 1932, USS built many coal-fired ships and concentrated on expanding the oil-fired component of its fleet, by converting eight existing ships that were relatively new (including three fast mail steamers) and by purchasing six new oil burners (four of which were ferries). In the same period it ordered just three new motor vessels (including two cargo liners). In contrast, from 1933 to 1938, the firm switched its emphasis by purchasing eight new diesel ships and three used ones, mostly for its refrigerated and inter-colonial cargo lines. After 1933, USS ordered only three new oil burners and just four coal-fired ships. The overall pattern suggests that from 1918 to 1932 USS innovated cautiously in order to preserve its flexibility in light of constraints imposed by its routes, uncertainty over oil supplies, and the age of its fleet. After 1932, the company adopted the motor ship more decisively, but trade-specific conditions, which sustained the viability of coal-fired colliers and fast oil-fired steamers, also influenced decision-making. These two broad trends were shaped respectively by:

1   improved access to wider information channels after USS's affiliation with P&O, and
2   cumulative learning, which, according to a report written in 1933, indicated that the diesel had finally become mechanically reliable, but was not superior to steam technology in all applications.

Initial uncertainties

An illustration of the types of uncertainties that induced USS's management to adopt a prudent approach between 1918 and 1932 is to be found in those factors that shaped their decision to convert all ships on one route for the first time. The results achieved by *Niagara* on the trans-Pacific mail run revealed that higher speed and faster refuelling would make it possible to operate the line with two instead of three ships (USS Letters 'Fuel Oil' (hereafter 'Oil') memo, 13 May 1916). Table 8.2 reveals that the Directors anticipated that by investing £185,000 they would save £34,532 per annum (a return of eighteen per cent). These data show that extra revenue derived

Table 8.2 Financial gains and losses arising from converting USS's trans-Pacific steamers to oil-firing (per annum)

	Gain (£)	Loss (£)
Extra cost of oil		11,461
Cost of converting engines (amortised over six years; 12.5% of £60,000)		7,500
Insurance and depreciation on relieving ship for eight weeks		2,000
Depreciation on withdrawn ship	18,375	
Savings in crew costs	32,388	
Extra earning power *Makura* *Tahiti*	3,412 1,498	
Total	55,673	21,141
Net gain	£34,532	

Source: C. MacDonald memo, 13 March 1916.

Note
Some increase in fuel consumption arose when operating speed was raised from 13.5 to 15 knots after converting the ships to oil.

from freeing cargo space by storing oil in non-earning parts of the ship provided a minor gain, less than £5,000. Moreover, most of the savings came not from using cheaper fuel but from the depreciation recovered on the withdrawn steamer and reduced crew costs. Indeed, although a higher operating speed increased consumption, oil was more expensive than coal, a fact that reveals the danger of getting locked into exclusively using this fuel by adopting diesels instead of flexible oil-firing equipment.

The return on investment was attractive, but it could have been much more so had the firm not been compelled to invest in oil storage tanks and a tanker for carrying oil. Of the total £185,000 investment, only £60,000 was needed to convert the ships. Building storage tanks would absorb at least £5,000, whereas the amortised cost of a tanker amounted to £120,000 per annum. These figures show the clear disadvantages faced by firms that had to set up distribution facilities themselves to compensate for the lack of an established infrastructure on a specific route. Unable to proceed with the plan under wartime conditions, the directors decided to wait until hostilities had ceased.

By December 1918, the board felt that USS had to upgrade its trans-Pacific mail ships to meet competition from American operators. However, the directors realised that booming conditions in the shipping and shipbuilding industries would make it impossible to buy or build geared turbine or diesel vessels in the foreseeable future (DM, 11 December 1918). Consequently, they decided to convert the existing ships to oil-firing, but reflecting supply uncertainties they ordered that this be done in such a way that the ships could be changed back to coal 'if the oil position becomes impossible' ('Oil' general manager to C. Holdsworth, 31 May 1920). The scheme also gave rise to a variety of problems concerning technology, storage, and distribution.

Illustrating the advantages of affiliation with a group, USS relied on the wider ties of the P&O Group in addition to its own contacts with non-affiliated firms to mobilise the information needed to reduce uncertainty arising from these sources and to assemble the required assets. Sir James Mills, then resident in Britain, sent officials in New Zealand technical data that he had gathered from UK sources (Mills Papers, hereafter MP). The board supplemented this intelligence with information and cost estimates obtained from USS's regular shipbuilders, Denny and Fairfield, and from the P&O's affiliated shipyards, Stephen and Caird (DM, 5 February and 8 June 1919, 4 February 1920). The New Zealand managers secured advice about the design and installation of storage tanks that they proposed to build in Sydney and Tahiti from the Asiatic Petroleum Co., which was both a customer and a supplier of the firm, and from Standard Oil, which had close ties with P&O's bunkering subsidiary William Cory & Co. (DM, 12 February 1919; 'Oil' Holdsworth to Cowan, 15 May 1919; and Johnson to Holdsworth, 17 March 1920). To win related advantages, the firm planned to run the two oil storage facilities as joint ventures. In Sydney, USS would co-operate with P&O subsidiary Federal S/N to aggregate purchasing power (DM, 13 September 1916). After its own previously established operating ties in Tahiti, USS intended to join forces with a French phosphate mining firm that had a monopoly in the bunkering trade of the island. The deal would enable USS to participate in the bunkering business and to secure more phosphate-carrying business (DM, 8 January 1919). To transport oil from its chief source of supply in California to Sydney and Tahiti, USS modified some of its coal-fired cargo steamers so they could carry oil in their double bottoms. The firm obtained other ships that could be used for this purpose from P&O unit Frank Strick & Co. Using its parent company's ties to break through the shipbuilding backlog, USS bought a similarly suited diesel ship under construction at Denny's yard for another group affiliate, British India S/N. These acquisitions made it possible to avoid the desperate alternative of towing oil barges across the Pacific (DM, 2 July 1919 and 5 May 1920; 'Oil' Holdsworth to Cowan, 23 April 1920).

USS attempted to overcome oil shortages in California arising from a dearth of tankers and steel castings for oil wells by using another networking arrangement, this time involving the Union Oil Co. which was an established supplier and a customer, but was not otherwise linked to the P&O group. USS used the P&O's link with Cory & Co. to acquire a tanker, which Union Oil was unable to obtain or afford, to bring crude from Tampico to Union Oil's refinery in San Francisco. The oil company would then have sufficient supplies to provide refined fuel to USS's mail steamers calling at Vancouver and San Francisco and would do so at preferential prices. Confirming just how tight oil supplies were on the west coast of North America, USS learned from the CPR, its partner in the jointly run Sydney–Vancouver service, that that firm could not arrange a similar scheme with Standard Oil and had to convert its ships back to coal firing (DM, 10 and 17 November 1920). In the event, the USS–Union Oil venture worked for only a short time because the oil company could not provide sufficient Mexican crude, but it continued to supply USS with bunkers from other sources at concessionary rates. This left USS with a £550,000 tanker on its hands but, illustrating the flexibility that could arise from affiliation with a major group, the firm was able to charter the vessel through Cory.

USS's first comprehensive move to oil firing illustrates the many sources of uncertainty that justified cautious innovation despite the promise of substantial savings after allowing for the cost of building a distribution infrastructure. The episode also reveals the importance of ties with both P&O units and outside firms in providing the required information and assets.

Extending USS's information sources

Intra-group links, contacts with non-affiliated forms, and channels permeating various levels of USS's organisation also supported the subsequent expansion of the oil-fired and diesel components of its fleet. From these sources, managers learned about technology, other firms' strategies, the oil market, and government policy. This section examines how they collected data about each of these areas of concern.

Chairman Sir James Mills, then resident in England, acted as USS's chief contact with British engineering firms, shipbuilders, and P&O officials. He provided USS staff with reports that compared the efficiency of different engine types along with opinions circulating among P&O officials (MP *passim*). From USS's builders and those of the P&O group, he secured information about the competence of specific engine manufacturers and the reliability of their products. Mills visited shipyards and engine works to gather data and observe tests. However, in opposition to the view that groups tended to have constrained communication lines, Mills actively encouraged information sharing across firm boundaries at lower executive levels. For example, he introduced Mr Tucker, a USS engineer, to staff at Fairfields, one of USS's regular builders, who had been in 'very close and friendly collaboration' with Sulzer Brothers 'who [in turn] are considered to be the leading authorities on Diesel construction' (MP Mills to Holdsworth, 29 November 1922; and

DM 9 August 1922). These exchanges enabled USS to make very quickly the sound decision to adopt the Sulzer engine.

USS's superintendents had their own contacts from whom they gathered technical data. Much of what they obtained consisted of detailed operating information that supported incremental innovation. For example, Superintendent J. Smith drew upon personnel from Federal S/N (a P&O unit) and Union Ironworks (no affiliation) for data about new burner designs and oil separators, and suggested that USS's Vancouver engineer ask CPR's Marine Department for similar information ('Oil' Smith to Holdsworth, 18 February 1924, 30 March and 1 April 1927). USS's seagoing staff also collected data through their own informal channels; for example, the chief engineer on the *Makura* sought information about burners from a friend who worked for the CPR ('Oil' Howarth to Smith, 10 December 1923). Thus, many levels of the organisation gathered technical data and transmitted it to decision-makers.

Similarly, staff in various positions within USS continuously monitored conditions in the oil market to assess the security of supply. Moreover, because the firm had to build essential parts of an oil distribution system, it had to learn almost as much about the oil industry as it already knew about its core shipping business. Mills, senior officials in New Zealand, and branch managers applied market-analysing skills that they had developed in monitoring trends in the sea-borne trade to this new task.

At the most senior level, Sir James provided an overview of the oil market based largely on P&O Group sources. He conveyed to USS managers press reports voicing concern about the sustainability of world oil supplies, but indicated that Lord Inchcape, P&O's chairman, had signalled his faith in the new fuel by announcing that all of P&O's new mail steamers would be oil-fired. Inchcape 'was quite satisfied to rely upon the Anglo-Persian Company [of which he is a Director] to meet the demand at all points' (MP Mills to Holdsworth, 8 December 1919).

To obtain an alternative, inferential assessment, USS's general manager, Charles Holdsworth, asked F. P. Evans, the firm's UK superintendent, to find out whether those shipping firms that were designing oil-fired liners were devising flexible arrangements that allowed for reversion to coal. Unable to secure the required information directly from the firms themselves, Evans relied on a private contact with a consultant, Sir John Esplen, from whom he learned that all companies, except those building diesels, were retaining the capacity to shift 'more or less readily' back to coal ('Oil' Evans to Holdsworth, 2 September 1919). This applied to the Royal Mail S/P, Cunard, CPR, Furness–Houlder, and Federal S/N. Other companies, including White Star, British India, and even P&O, were in Evans's view, more conservative; at this time these firms were only considering the question. He concluded that 'the cause for such natural hesitation ... of course, is the impossibility of forecasting for any reasonable period the future price of oil'. Whether this reflected unreliable supplies or simply volatile, short-term market conditions is unclear, but the result produced significant uncertainty for many firms. The episode shows how Holdsworth used private conduits to gather more accurate information than that conveyed by public pronouncements which may have been designed to support Inchcape's oil interests but which could have unintentionally misled shipping executives within the group. In this instance, USS's informal channels played a valuable role in 'filtering' public information.

USS's sources of oil were much different from and probably less dependable than those of P&O and the other firms mentioned by Evans. Although USS could draw supplies from Borneo or the Middle East, Mexican and Californian sources were more important in aggregate. With roughly three-quarters of its annual requirements (100,000 tons in 1919) coming from California and Mexico, USS had to monitor closely the local oil industry in these areas. The task fell to Reginald Back, who was a USS man seconded to the firm's San Francisco agents. Mr Irons, manager of USS's Vancouver office, watched conditions at his port. C. Hughes, USS's branch manager in Sydney, and Val Johnson, the Melbourne manager, monitored the situation in Australia, where the government took an active role in promoting exploration. A source of wide-ranging intelligence and technical and pricing advice was P&O's bunkering unit, William Cory & Sons. Together, Back, Irons, Hughes, Johnson, and Cory officials represented a comprehensive and complementary set of listening posts.

The intelligence gathered from these sources enabled senior USS staff to assess the degree of uncertainty that arose from the two key sources identified by Henning and Trace: oil prices and security of supply. USS officials sought to ensure that they could protect the firm from supply disruptions and take advantage of price falls. These considerations determined the timing of their contract negotiations and the form of the resulting agreements. Information from the branches and Cory shaped their perceptions of the underlying supply and demand conditions of the oil industry.

Johnson and Hughes provided a stream of intelligence about the development of oil distribution in Australia, information about government activities (sometimes drawn from inside sources), and market data indicating that oil supplies might soon be exhausted ('Oil' Johnson to Holdsworth, 17 March 1920; Hughes to Holdsworth, 11 January 1921). They reported that oil companies rigged the Australian market, and passed along corroborating price information obtained from a non-allied firm, Royal Packet Navigation. Indeed, the local price of oil was three times that ruling in the US in the mid-1920s ('Oil' Hughes to Aiken, 9 November 1921, 21 July 1922, and 15 December 1924). By the 1930s, however, USS was able to secure lower prices than its Australian rivals by purchasing through Cory, which contracted on behalf of the P&O Group as a whole with Anglo-Persian ('Oil' Metcalfe to Falla, 5 November 1935). This arrangement concentrated Cory's purchasing power and kept custom within the sphere of Inchcape's contacts. Thus, in addition to the concerns of shipowners over the relative price of oil and security of supply, concerns identified by Henning and Trace (1975), the USS records reveal that a further source of uncertainty which Fletcher recognised but was not, as he contended, comprehensively eliminated by the early 1920s. USS staff in Australia believed that the oil companies had a significant measure of monopoly power. They sought to exert a degree of countervailing power using USS's affiliation with P&O. North American managers also suspected that the oil firms colluded in their local market ('Oil' Back to Falla, 14 May 1936).

In response, Reginald Back, who had gained an understanding of the positions of the various oil producers in California in the course of monitoring price trends, consumption rates, production flows, and stocks, decided to use USS's large purchasing power against the relatively small Union Oil Co. ('Oil' Back to Holdsworth, 25 June 1920 to 20 November 1924). After the abortive attempt to network supplies by purchasing the tanker *Orowaiti*, Union Oil had supplied USS on an *ad hoc* basis, and USS staff were plainly nervous about the exposure this entailed. However, armed with superior information Back arranged a contract that reduced price uncertainty for USS when the market broke and prices tumbled in 1922. That year, the two firms negotiated a twelve-month deal whereby USS paid market prices less $0.10 per barrel up to a maximum price set for each port of call. [Reflecting the importance of fuel costs, USS stood to save £67,776 per annum, or about three-quarters of the firm's profit for 1921, at the *maximum* prices set out in the contract (contract 30 July 1922).] The maximum limits also provided a temporary measure of insulation from price spikes. In addition, the contract did not bind USS to take the full quantity stipulated (400,000 barrels per annum), but Union Oil had to provide this amount or more on receiving notice from USS. This one-sided contract gave USS temporary security of supply and considerable flexibility, but indicative of senior manager's lingering fears, they asked engineering staff to draw up estimates for how long it would take to convert five oil burners back to coal ('Oil' memo 1923, no exact date). USS staff had been traumatised by the events of 1921–2 when the *Orowaiti* deal fell through and the CPR switched back to coal, and they remained fearful for years.

This outlook also shaped the way in which they arranged the contract for Union Oil to supply oil for the Wellington storage depot. USS needed security of supplies for at least three years before entering into this deal. Reflecting its concerns over prices and collusion by the oil firms, it again secured preferential rates and a price ceiling. This contract enabled USS to supply its coastal ships and to build up a wider bunkering business serving outside shipowners ('Oil' Holdsworth to Back, 25 May and 24 June 1923; and Back to Holdsworth, 26 June 1923).

Supply at Vancouver was a special problem for many years because USS had to tie itself to Union Oil at San Francisco and Honolulu in order to obtain bunkers at its Canadian terminus. In 1926, Back reported that this arrangement cost USS £8,000 per annum ('Oil' Back to Holdsworth, 6 September 1926). There was no alternative: other oil firms, including Imperial

Oil, were unable to provide supplies. However, by 1929, when Standard Oil had built tanks at Vancouver, USS was able to switch suppliers without damaging its relations with Union Oil. Acting on USS's behalf, Cory negotiated a three-year contract with Standard Oil and won an agency to sell that firm's products in Europe. When USS and CPR merged their Sydney–Vancouver services to form the Canadian Australian Line, they combined their buying activities through Cory to obtain lower prices and more freight from Standard Oil ['Oil' Standard Oil to USS, 7 September 1929; Leathers (Cory) to USS, 12 March 1932].

Closer association with Cory posed a trade-off for the New Zealand firm. Through this P&O unit, USS secured outside business for its Wellington bunkering operation and won advantages in chartering tankers. Although USS gained enhanced purchasing power because Cory concentrated the P&O Group's buying, Falla, USS's new general manager, regretted that the firm had lost 'the advantage of the simple contract we had in the old days with California [Union Oil]'. However, he resigned himself to association with Cory 'realising the magnitude of [their] business and taking comfort in the fact that it is well managed' ('Oil' Falla to Back, 4 May 1934). Back agreed that 'the direct arrangements' which USS had with Union Oil were beneficial in a weak market, but if 'the pendulum ... swing[s] the other way some day, we will probably find Cory can help us'. In the meantime, USS, Cory and the P&O Group all benefited from the deal ('Oil' Back to Falla, 27 May 1934).

Showing how P&O provided a context for joint learning, USS and Cory established an ongoing dialogue about the oil industry. Moreover, Back's expertise was a valuable asset to USS in two ways. First, his knowledge demonstrated to Cory staff the value of a close relationship with USS. Indeed, Falla arranged for he and Back to meet with Mr Metcalfe of Cory to discuss oil matters face to face in order to establish the personal contact from which a freer flow of information might develop ('Oil' Falla to Metcalfe, 2 February 1935). This objective was realised, as Metcalfe wrote to Back on 28 April 1936 'the frank statement of your views regarding the Oil business in California has been one of the most helpful and pleasant features of my work during the past few years, and I sincerely hope that we shall continue in the same manner'. Back replied '[a]s you mention, the continual fluctuations of oil prices and the worldwide ramifications of the people we deal with calls for frank exchanges between us' ('Oil', 14 May 1936). Second, with this direct communication line established, Back could let Cory officials know that he possessed the information needed to protect USS's interests, and thus present a deterrent to opportunism. As Back told Falla on 14 May 1936, his objective was to ensure 'that they should not be too complacent'. Falla agreed 'I think your correspondence serves useful purpose in that while he [Metcalfe] is being informed of the Californian situation he can see that you are also watchful of our own interests' ('Oil Falla to Back, 24 June 1936). Joint learning exposed knowledge parities that shaped the type of hard internal bargaining which, although tempered by a spirit of give and take needed to preserve long-term relations, preserved the efficiency of large shipping networks (Boyce 1995a: 176–97).

USS's links beyond the P&O Group played a conspicuous role in providing the high-quality information it needed to contend with uncertainty arising from regulations governing oil storage facilities. The New Zealand government had not enacted such legislation by the time USS began planning to build oil tanks in Wellington, and the firm's officials feared that overly restrictive rules might be imposed. To inform the regulatory process, they asked branch managers to gather data about Canadian, American, and Australian legislation, and sent a superintendent to inspect storage depots on the west coast of North America ('Oil' secretary to Back, 12 April 1920, Wheeler to Hughes, 21 July 1920, and MacDonald to Dunedin, 13 September 1920). Through its contacts in the Ministry of Defense, USS gained the right to appoint a representative to the Committee that drew up recommendations for New Zealand regulations. Armed with superior information about overseas legislation, USS successfully shaped this part of the regulatory environment ['Oil' T. Williams (naval advisor) to USS, 4 June 1920; Kennedy to Dunedin, 24 December 1920].

Thus, to inform policy, the management mobilised a variety of information channels that linked many organisational levels within USS, other P&O units, and outside companies. Decision-makers possessed sufficient information to reduce directly uncertainty that arose from some sources or to assess more precisely the degree of risk associated with other conditions. However, to support innovation, USS staff also had to acquire and apply new forms of knowledge.

Developing and using new knowledge

USS's existing knowledge provided a foundation to support technological change. Yet, the adoption of oil-fired engines and motor ships also required the absorption and application of expertise on new commercial and technical subjects as well as the properties of oil itself. The firm's intra- and inter-organisational links played a key role in facilitating the 'blending' of new and existing knowledge.

The use of oil profoundly affected ship operations and commercial practice. Superintendent C. MacDonald carried out an extensive planning exercise in 1916, when USS began considering switching its trans-Pacific passenger liners to oil ('Oil' MacDonald to Holdsworth, 24 February, 1 and 13 March 1916). He analysed the required storage capacity and the effect on cargo- and passenger-carrying space in four ships under four different sets of conditions as determined by operating speed and variations in the ports at which the vessels could refuel. Although MacDonald also drew up a preliminary scheme for shipboard oil storage, recognising the limits of his own expertise he suggested that USS's builders devise detailed plans and requested feedback so he could learn more about the matter. Fairfield identified no fewer than thirty-one alterations that the *Manganui* alone would require. When conversion was authorised, USS's UK superintendent, Evans, developed flexible plans that allowed for using oil alone and for converting back to coal ('Oil' Evans to Cowan, 12 September 1919). He drew attention to the fact that coal bunkers occupied areas that were the most convenient places to store cargo and that using oil would reduce structural stresses that occurred when coal bunkers were gradually used up during voyages. Irons, the Vancouver manager, urged Holdsworth not to reduce the ships' water-carrying capacity to increase oil bunkers for fear of inconveniencing passengers ('Oil' Iron to Holdsworth, 16 December 1919). Thus, while drawing on existing skills acquired in adapting vessels to shifts in cargo flows to assess the impact of oil propulsion, USS staff also assembled new technical, commercial, and operating knowledge from external sources to promote learning.

USS continued to evaluate these variables in an ongoing manner as operating conditions changed and as the firm converted more vessels. In 1926, the managing director considered enlarging *Niagara*'s bunkers to take on more oil at Vancouver and avoid paying the higher prices ruling at Honolulu. The idea was abandoned, however, because the firm would lose more money by diminishing the ship's freight-carrying capacity than it would recover from lower fuel expenses and because the master stated that the oil taken aboard in Hawaii helped to stiffen the vessel ('Oil' memo, 13 February 1926). When USS considered converting its trans-Pacific cargo vessels, Superintendent Foster recommended they use only part of the double bottom for oil storage because the ships tended to have a light condition even with full ballast ('Oil' Foster to General Manager, 20 August 1927). Thus, USS had to draw ship design and operating information from many organisational levels in an ongoing manner in order to expand its oil-burning fleet and to respond to changing cost and trading conditions.

USS executives collected operating data from a variety of external sources to inform its conversion plans. For example, they monitored the public domain for data about other firms' experiences. The Sydney manager sent a cutting from the *Herald* (17 April 1914) reporting on a paper delivered to the Engineering Association about the reduction in labour achieved by the *Lusitania*, the *Murex*, and the *Clam*. To complement public information Superintendent J. Smith obtained actual operating data from a private contact, the superintendent of the Morgan Line ('Oil' Smith to D. A. Aiken, 22 February 1917). This report, which compared the results achieved by the *El Norte* on ten voyages using coal and ten trips burning oil, indicated that higher engine revolutions and average IHP were achieved using oil. P&O ties provided private information; USS compared its manning levels and engine arrangements with those of group subsidiary New Zealand Steam Shipping Company (NZS/S) ('Oil' R. L. Gillies memo, 14 May 1923).

USS officials also generated their own data about operating performance from their initial experiment with the *Niagara* and from vessels that were converted later. Indeed, the *Niagara*'s results provided a bench-mark against which to measure those of other newly converted ships (Smith to Aiken, 22 February 1917). USS compiled statistics showing all ships' consumption rates over time and comparing the rate of oil and coal consumption per 100 miles ('Oil' Gillies to Sydney, 18 October 1920; Smith to general manager, 20 October 1922). In this way, USS staff ensured that performance figures were retained within the organisation's memory.

Comparing the actual cost of burning oil to the historic cost of coal (adjusted for subsequent price changes) enabled officials to calculate the relative value of the two fuels as a ratio. In 1924, USS management discovered that for the ferry services this standard measure had moved slightly in favour of coal, and expecting oil prices to rise further they carried out sensitivity analysis to determine the break-even point and the impact of possible price movements ('Oil' memo, 23 June 1924). Although USS did not use DCF methods, like Harrisons, it did use a range of fairly sophisticated analytical techniques to process and standardise cost data. Its staff applied sensitivity analysis, break-even calculations, bench-marking, and forecasting methods initially developed in its core shipping business to questions that arose from the use of oil.

USS's statistical expertise supported its development of a bunkering business to serve P&O firms and outside clients. In response to questions posed by customers, whom it attracted by offering cost-plus contracts, USS staff could account for price fluctuations caused by changes in exchange rates, oil prices, and tanker charges ('Oil' memo, 6 December 1937). Using precise costing techniques to sustain a preferential form of contract, USS was able to enter a new business and aggregate buying power.

To build up its outside bunkering activities and ensure that its own services operated efficiently, USS staff had to familiarise themselves with the properties of different kinds of oil and learn how variations in chemical composition affected safety, combustion processes, and engines. Cory officials, outside consultants, Lloyd's Register of Shipping, oil companies, and engine makers provided USS with guidance. In addition, the firm's personnel gradually acquired knowledge from operations and learned how to test oil. With this new expertise, they could apply their analytical skills to determine how the use of different types of oil would affect costs.

One of the most crucial variables affecting safety at sea was the flammability of oil. Lloyd's issued different certificates for ships that burned oil with various flash points, a practice that influenced insurance costs, and advised USS to use oil with a flash point above 150 °F. From consulting engineers and chemists, the company learned that American refining techniques created higher flash points. Irons got samples of American oil tested ('Oil' F. Stow to USS ,22 April 1914; Irons to general manager, 3 August 1914). To obtain more detailed first-hand knowledge when USS began converting its trans-Pacific mail ships, Superintendent MacDonald collected flash point data on thirty-seven types of oil and visited refineries and storage facilities to learn about safety practices ('Oil' MacDonald to general manager,

13 September 1920). In the process, MacDonald found that the viscosity of oil was another important variable that should be specified in USS's supply contracts.

Viscosity determined the temperature to which oil had to be heated to ensure a satisfactory pumping rate so that USS could achieve one of the potential advantages of using oil: quick turnaround time ('Oil' Gillies to Sydney, 6 August and 18 October 1920). The master of a tanker chartered by USS provided heating guidelines ('Oil' Back to A. Wheeler, 29 August 1927). To its repertoire of statistics, USS added data concerning the different temperatures to which various oils had to be heated and the discharge rate achieved. To develop an independent capability for ensuring that the composition of fuels matched that specified on suppliers' certificates, USS trained its Wellington staff to use devices for testing flash points, specific gravity, and viscosity ('Oil' Smith to general manager, 15 May 1923). This new capability helped USS to provide its own ships as well as its outside customers with the right kinds of oil.

Motor ships required fuel of even more exacting specifications. When negotiating a contract with Union Oil in 1921, Back had to ensure that the diesel oil met the qualities called for by the engine manufacturers ('Oil' Back to Holdsworth, 8 October 1921). Demonstrating another advantage of aggregating purchasing through group ties, Cory secured compensation on USS's behalf for poor-quality oil supplied by the Anglo-Mexican Petroleum Co. because Cory had 'the special relations' with this supplier who did not wish 'to lose [their] goodwill' ('Oil' Cory to USS, 16 November 1923). Totally unexpected problems arose when USS switched suppliers in 1931. Dirt blocked oil heater tubes making it necessary to clean the storage chambers of tankers more frequently and to reward the crew with bonuses and up to five bottles of whisky 'instead of the usual 1 to 2' ('Oil' Captain Harris memos, 22 December 1930 and 22 April 1931). Thinking far beyond his sphere of responsibility the master of the affected ship alerted management to the effect of dirty oil on the firm's storage tanks.

USS also learned that the specific gravity of diesel oil affected combustion and that blended fuel could cause pistons to crack. To reduce the risk of encountering poor-quality oil, it based purchasing decisions on intra-group knowledge and interdependence. Thus, when USS introduced diesels to its Australian ferry service it felt that it could 'rely upon the usual good marketable quality of oil which is supplied generally by Anglo-Persian' ('Oil' Assistant Manager to Cory, 8 June 1934).

Not content to use inter-organisational links simply to deter opportunism, USS used these channels to learn more about the relationship between the properties of oil and the engine performance by gaining direct access to knowledge embedded in other firms' corporate memories. W. T. Tucker, USS's Glasgow superintendent, gathered data from the actual records of Fairfield the shipbuilder, Sulzer the diesel engine maker, and several oil companies ('Oil' Tucker to Smith, 12 April 1924). He assessed the impact of variations in flash point, specific gravity, viscosity, calorific value, as well as ash, sulphur, and water content on two- and four-cycle engines. He reached the overall conclusion that a rich oil burned slower, gave smoother running, and generated less smoke. Tucker then transferred the supporting data directly to USS's New Zealand superintendent, R. Smith, who in turn disseminated the findings to ship's engineers. In terms of how USS acquired and transmitted new knowledge, what is remarkable about this episode is how technical staff used inter-organisational channels to tap other firms' memories and then transferred information laterally to avoid risking delays caused by referral through vertical hierarchical channels.

A contrasting incident shows how the operating knowledge that was needed to inform purchasing policy was synthesised and analysed as it moved up the organisational pyramid ('Oil' memos, 25 March 1936 and 29 January and 18 February 1938). Having learned about relationships between oil composition and engine performance, USS staff could compare the overall value of fuels as new sources of supply were developed. Thus, in 1936 superintendent Gillies collected performance data generated from shipboard trials using California oil and newly available Oeban oil from Borneo. Having higher calorific value and viscosity, the Oeban product was cleaner firing and did not require heating to pump, but it burned more quickly than Californian oil. To compliment Gillies's technical study, M. B. Miller, an assistant manager, compiled a report that adjusted costs to reflect the varying voyage lengths for tankers, different consumption rates, and the distinct properties of Oeban oil. J. N. Greenland, general manager, then integrated the information contained in the two reports and concluded that Oeban oil had an overall advantage. The episode shows how USS generated knowledge independently and applied existing cost-analysing skills to newly acquired expertise in chemistry in order to evaluate an opportunity created by a new oil field.

To conclude this section, the adoption of oil-fired engines and the diesel engine was a most complex endeavour. At the firm level, technical innovation required a blending of new and existing knowledge sets and the harnessing of expertise from diverse internal and external sources. These activities were not discrete in duration but rather unfolded in an ongoing manner as business conditions and sources of supply changed, and they reflected varying degrees of tacit knowledge.

Learning-by-using effects

USS's capacity to obtain the full potential from the new technology depended on how quickly staff learned by using it and corrected problems. These tasks involved passing information between levels of the organisation and collecting procedural knowledge from other firms. Learning-by-using effects were thus transferred across organisational boundaries. Moreover, to ensure that learning unfolded cumulatively in order to prevent the recurrence of mistakes or the repetition of a problem-solving effort, the firm embedded newly acquired information into its corporate memory.

The board received reports on the first voyage of each newly converted oil steamer and new motor ship. For example, after *Niagara*'s maiden trip superintendents reported a number of defects, assessed staff levels, and criticised crew performance ('Oil' W. Smart to A. Lewis, 1 July 1913). Excessive consumption suggested that there was a fault in measuring fuel bunkering, and procedures were changed. A follow-up report confirmed that the recommended modification resulted in improvements, and the board noted the results (DM, 21 August 1913). Thus, information about initial performance and the results of learning were transmitted upwards and preserved.

When USS began the wholesale conversion of its Pacific fleet, Superintendent MacDonald ensured that operating knowledge was transferred to shipboard staff so that it could be applied uniformly. In a report on his visit to American oil firms in 1920, he stated that 'a good deal of knowledge is necessary to burn [the] oil fuel ... available in the United States ..., and in this connection I have every reason to believe that a good deal, if not too much, has been taken for granted' ('Oil' ,13 September 1920). He learned that the US Navy consumed 160 million barrels of oil in 1917 and that experts estimated that one-quarter of this quantity might have been saved 'by more intelligent operation of plant and boilers'. To minimise wastage, which on such a scale as that committed by the US Navy would have severely affected the relative cost advantages of the new fuel, MacDonald suggested that 'expert knowledge should be maintained on the ship until such time as economical results are obtained'. Once favourable performance was achieved consistently, he planned to put 'technical particulars ... on board [all] our ships ... for the guidance of engineers generally'. The superintendent clearly appreciated how the results of learning processes should be compiled and codified to improve operating techniques.

Apart from efficiency considerations, safety concerns demanded the systematic treatment of knowledge. USS gathered statutory data from official publications and procedural guidelines through inter-organisational channels. Cory provided USS with the Board of Trade's *Instructions to Surveyors*, which outlined cleaning, bunkering, and inspection practices intended to prevent fire ('Oil' USS London to Wellington, 16 January 1923). Union Oil supplied information regarding cleaning procedures and precautions ('Oil' H. Mirrisby to Aiken, 4 November 1913). From P&O affiliates, USS obtained booklets outlining shipboard rules in order to absorb the results of other organisations' learning processes ('Oil' Circular, 9 January 1913).

Not content to blindly follow official regulations or other firms' guidelines, however, USS staff inspected the ships of other companies to observe actual practice. Superintendent Smith visited New Zealand S/S's *Remuera* and 'was surprised at the condition of things' and assured USS's general manager 'that our four Oil Burning steamers would compare more than favourably with any ... afloat' ('Oil', 27 September 1923). USS directors monitored the incidence of fire on board all ships at sea and demanded detailed reports on the causes of outbreaks and the methods used to extinguish the relatively few fires that occurred on the company's own vessels. Given its large passenger business, refining safety procedures was a prime concern for USS.

Shipboard practices that ensured passenger comfort were another concern for the company. Experience revealed that if bad weather was expected ships should be topped up with oil to prevent excessive rolling, which might inconvenience passengers ('Oil' Aiken to Kennedy, 6 October 1924). Complaints of fumes entering cabins on board the *Taroona* invoked a comprehensive response ('Oil' Greenland to Gray, 9 June 1936). USS's local superintendents, the chief superintendent, the Melbourne manager, the *Taroona's* chief engineer, and officials from Cory and the Commonwealth Oil Co. all investigated the matter together until they discovered that the position of the intake fans was the cause of the problem. In this instance, consultative procedures enabled USS to capture learning-by-using effects by drawing upon experience that resided within and beyond its own organisational boundary.

USS relied upon personnel secondments to gather and transfer internally the operating experience of other firms. For example, ensuring the efficient operation of diesel engines demanded greater skill in adjusting machinery than oil-burning equipment did. To absorb such tacit knowledge, USS sent a former ship's engineer, Mr McCaig, to study diesels being built and tested in the US. He then joined the firm's new vessel the *Hauraki* and other motor ships in sequence to help engineers improve efficiency ('Oil' Back to Holdsworth, 16 August 1923). Acting in the capacity of a training instructor, McCaig accumulated and transferred tacit learning effects throughout the fleet.

In 1933, Superintendent R. Smith drew up a comprehensive memorandum that summarised all that USS had learned since it adopted diesel technology and provided a definitive basis for implementing a more decisive policy ('Oil' memo, 17 January 1933). Smith compared the differences in capital cost, weight per IHP, consumption rates per diem and per IHP, of five distinct propulsion systems. The results showed that diesels were significantly more expensive to buy, but more economical to run, than any other system. In Smith's opinion, however, the suitability of the motor ship depended upon 'a great number of conditions, length of voyage, prices of various fuels [diesel fuel cost much more than boiler oil], ...the amount of freight she will ... carry ..., the weight of machinery ..., and also weight of fuel and fresh water, boilers, etc.' He concluded that 'with a large freight on a long voyage undoubtedly the Diesel shows up to great advantage'. Smith emphasised reliability as a salient factor. He cited the 'vastly improved' diesels made from better steels available in 1933, particularly the *O. A. Knudson's* engines, which 'has been practically free from repair bills'. He contrasted this ship with USS's *Aorangi* (delivered in 1924), the engine of which was poorly designed and built of inferior metal. Referring to the newly completed *Wanganeela*, Smith also drew attention to 'vast improvements' that promised to reduce repairs. In summary, the fundamental conclusion of the memo was that the motor ship had only recently become mechanically reliable, and USS could innovate with greater confidence. Yet, important constraints to wholesale adoption remained: as late as 1933, it was not possible to state categorically that the diesel was superior in all trades to other technology. Finally, his report reflects the breadth of knowledge and experience that a senior technical official had had to accumulate over ten years before a more decisive course of technical innovation could be implemented.

Conclusion

This firm level study indicates that the adoption of oil-burning technology was a far more complex endeavour and required a wider range of information and skills than the literature suggests. In light of the composition of the Imperial Fleet in 1938–9, USS had a rather middling record as an innovator. Yet, the firm had to resolve unusual problems arising from its particular trades, the absence a bunkering infrastructure, and the market power of the oil companies it had to deal with. This study reveals that for USS the degree of attendant uncertainty remained at a higher level and for much longer than other scholars have suspected was generally the case. From an institutional perspective, the study highlights the importance of inter-organisational channels in collecting data, transferring knowledge, and generating wide-ranging learning-by-using effects. The findings also suggest that there was nothing inherently defective with the group structure: indeed in this instance P&O exhibited considerable flexibility and sensitivity to external stimuli. It could be argued that USS innovated cautiously before 1933 and more confidently afterwards because it possessed such good information, which it analysed with such effectiveness that its decision-makers could very accurately assess the degree of prevailing risk.

In terms of our other chapters, the USS story provides a number of additional insights. First, it shows in more detail than Chapter 2 how branch offices and, in a fashion, agents (recall that Back was seconded to the San Francisco agent) contributed to data gathering and learning processes. Second, the USS case, like others (Chapters 3 and 4) highlights the value of staff capabilities. The firm's external channels were not confined to senior managers; instead they radiated outwards from positions at the lower and middle levels of the USS organisation. Moreover, these were mainly private conduits that provided very high-quality information and enhanced USS's sensitivity to external conditions. The instance in which Evans used Esplen to 'filter' Inchcape's public statement on future oil supplies confirms the value of having – and allowing lower-level staff unstructured time in which to develop – overlapping channels as the HSS network also did. However, the incident alerts us to a potential defect in network structures: the danger is that given the private nature of these links many of them may not survive personnel changes. Not only should a balance between informal and formal transmissions be struck (see Chapters 3, 4, and 6), but management succession plans should ensure that private channels are preserved.

Third, the USS story reveals in greater detail than our other cases information-processing and systematising processes in operation. It shows how analytical skills developed to assess freight markets were adapted to evaluate conditions in the oil industry in order to assess the reliability of supplies and to set up an oil distribution operation. USS officials had previously devised costing procedures that were not as advanced as DCF methods but with modification enabled them to evaluate the commercial implications of the new technology. Over the years, the company's superintendents and engineers had accumulated learning-by-using skills while working with a variety of new ship designs and applied these capabilities to the new propulsion systems. Developing such adaptive capability at many levels in the firm and in so many different functional areas represents something of an ultimate goal for 'learning organisations'. Moreover, at USS staff demonstrated their 'empowered' status by independently adapting their skills and by taking the initiative in ensuring that the fruits of learning were not only shared but also codified and embedded in the firm's organisational memory to facilitate transfers and replication. Again, unstructured time must be provided to develop these attributes.

Fourth, like the HSS network, P&O developed extensive lateral links at all managerial levels. What this case highlights, however, is how these channels supported learning-by-using effects that are so vital in the creation of new technical – as opposed to strategic – knowledge. Here, it was not only the P&O group that provided the context for joint learning. Non-affiliated enterprises were also included, again often by means of the private contacts of USS's middle managers. Moreover, on occasion these officials were able to tap into other firms' organisational memories.

Fifth, the USS case shows how little a firm may initially know of the territory that it needs to search to find the information required to support technical innovation. Thus, staff were surprised when they discovered new things, such as the many properties of oil, that they had to learn about. Although this is a common problem for firms seeking to extend their knowledge base, the speed with which they 'find out what they *don't* know' and focus their learning activities is important. In highly competitive industries, it poses a crucial trade-off between the rate of environmental change on the one hand, and the pace with which companies chart out the territory they need to search, concentrate their inquiry, and then effect actual learning on the other hand. The next case exposes a similar type of trade-off.

9 A joint exploration venture
Western Mining Corporation and Hanna/Homestake, 1960–72

Western Mining Corporation and Hanna/Homestake agreed to form a joint venture to develop iron ore deposits in Australia. However, they failed to establish an enduring relationship because they did not set up a communicating infrastructure needed to build trust. The case explores cultural differences, considerations that affect exit strategies, and a variety of trade-offs posed by the passage of time.

Between 1963 and 1975 Australian iron ore exports rose from a negligible quantity to 80.3 million tons per annum and accounted for nearly one-half the tonnage imported by the Japanese steel industry (Trengove 1976: 208–9). The rapid growth of the iron industry was sparked off when the Australian government relaxed and then completely removed the iron ore export embargo that it had imposed in 1938. Growing evidence indicating that the Commonwealth's ore reserves exceeded by a large margin the size of future domestic requirements made rigid restrictions unnecessary, whereas increasing demand generated by the expanding Japanese steel industry, together with improvements in bulk transport technology, exposed a promising opportunity to earn revenue from exports. These new conditions and changes in government policy created powerful incentives for local firms to find, test, and develop iron deposits in Western Australia. However, exploration risks, huge development costs, and the need to learn about overseas markets and new processes for concentrating and pelletising ore encouraged domestic companies to co-operate with foreign operators.

This chapter examines the history of one of the earliest of these joint ventures, which in the end met with mixed results. A comparatively small Australian-owned company, Western Mining Corporation (WMC), and two much larger American firms, the Hanna Mining Company and the Homestake Mining Company (H/H), successfully developed one deposit in the Koolanooka Hills and made the first shipment of iron ore from Western Australia to Japan in March 1966.[1] Yet, the partners failed to undertake, as they intended, a series of ventures. Koolanooka provided them with substantial net profits – over A$3 million for WMC alone – but did not represent more than a one-off success.

WMC and H/H did not forge an enduring relationship primarily because they devised an initial agreement that was, in terms of the three basic elements of contractual design, utterly defective. A provisional memorandum of understanding laid out in a very general manner the basis of the partners' financial and operating association. In fact, the participants never succeeded in devising a formal, comprehensive agreement that specified the structural details of the venture. Effective monitoring mechanisms were not installed nor, as events would show, could the partners agree upon a reporting framework. Finally, WMC and H/H could not establish a common culture to condition inter-firm relations. The memorandum of understanding, therefore, did not achieve a workable balance between two critical variables. It left too much scope for *ex post* adjustment in relation to what was a low degree of trust

Deficient mutual confidence stemmed from the partners' failure to install an effective, venture-specific communicating infrastructure. None of the elements identified above was satisfactorily constructed. WMC and H/H could not devise an agreement that assigned them acceptable roles. They did not create inter-firm communication lines. Neither did they establish rules governing transmissions nor a workable accounting system. Finally, Hanna, in particular, did not deploy a suitable person at its boundary.

The WMC and H/H venture, therefore, provides a stark contrast to the Orient Paint case, but one which illuminates the operation of different variables that may shape the outcome of co-operative initiatives. Unlike JSS and PJ, who successfully modified their relationship to accommodate shocks, WMC and H/H repeatedly failed to make adjustments, revealing how differences in culture, approaches to business, accepted precedents, and behavioural patterns can undermine collaboration. Although the OP partners and the mining firms were all experienced joint venturers, the present case highlights the importance of acquiring wide experience in working with other firms and the value of having staff with highly developed co-operative skills. The WMC–H/H story also emphasises the difficulty of determining what constitutes failure in the context of inter-firm relations. Indeed, the partners themselves had different conceptions of success. Moreover, in several ways achieving an appropriate balance between the passage of time and the process of relationship adjustment stands out as an important consideration for firms that engage in co-operative endeavours. Finally, another trade-off – that between the degree to which an initial agreement leaves room for subsequent adjustment and the extent of prevailing trust – should also command attention.

The initial understanding

WMC, Hanna, and Homestake were all experienced co-operative venturers. Hanna and Homestake had worked together before, WMC and Homestake had explored successfully for gold in the 1930s, and WMC had co-operated extensively with other Australian and American mining firms. In fact, the three firms joined forces in 1962 on the suggestion of an official from the Aluminum Co. of America (ALCOA), with whom WMC was jointly developing a large aluminium business (Clark 1983: 12, 20, 174). After the relaxation of government restrictions in the early 1960s, WMC acquired prospecting rights for iron ore and manganese, but being heavily committed to copper and bauxite ventures with other firms, it lacked the resources to carry out an iron ore exploration programme on its own. Moreover, WMC was not familiar with new beneficiation and pelletising processes used to enhance the quality of iron ore. This knowledge, along with large resources and experience in marketing iron ore, the two American firms possessed (WMC 5/1/1 Box 77 L. Clark to Broken Hill South, 17 October 1961). Overall, the participants brought highly complementary knowledge sets and skills to the joint venture.[2]

In early 1962, Hanna officials visited WMC's iron properties and thought that two, Koolanooka and Tallering, looked particularly promising, whereas a third, Yilgarn, was not as favourable because the required transport infrastructure was not in place. (While three firms were involved, the venture was conducted in practice as a two-sided affair with WMC and Hanna setting the terms and Homestake following Hanna's lead.) Though the Americans were concerned about the small size of the reserves at Koolanooka and Tallering, they offered to help WMC carry out further testing. If the results proved satisfactory, they would support the development of the ore fields [WMC 9/31 Box 137 all references cite this box unless indicated otherwise W. M. Morgan (WMC) to F. M. Chace (Hanna), 9 May 1963].

In October, the three firms signed a memorandum of understanding, wherein H/H agreed to finance further testing and to participate with WMC in a jointly owned Australian company. WMC kept a fifty per cent stake in Tallering, Koolanooka, and other deposits in Western Australia south of the 26th parallel, whereas Hanna and Homestake each accepted a twenty-five per cent interest. Yilgarn was not included in the deal. Each venturer was to take a one-third interest in iron ore and manganese properties found elsewhere in Australia. WMC would manage work at the sites and report to its partners. Finally, WMC agreed to obtain complete control of Great Western Consolidated NL (GWC) and H/H would buy this firm's power plant at Geraldton. H/H also agreed to pay WMC £150,000 to participate in GWC's tax losses.

What might have been viewed as a telling development occurred the following April, when H/H asked for larger stakes in the Tallering and Koolanooka deposits. WMC's chairman, Lindesay Clark (later Sir Lindesay), agreed to raise the Americans' interests in these projects if they would participate in the Yilgarn venture and allow WMC credits for work already done at Yilgarn and for the value of the property (see p. 156). H/H agreed in principle, and to accommodate them Clark had to adjust WMC's relations with other local firms.

WMC was part of an extensive web that included other Australian mining companies. For example, not only was WMC working with Broken Hill

Proprietary (BHP) on the Yilgarn deposit, it was also participating with Broken Hill South (BHS) and North Broken Hill (NBH) in bauxite and copper exploration ventures [W. M. Morgan (WMC) to F. M. Chace (Hanna), 9 May 1963; Clark to Morgan, 15 May 1962]. Although WMC did not want 'to cut [itself] off from these associations and [would] join in other projects with them', its officials recognised that should their iron ore and manganese exploration programmes result in the discovery of other minerals, this development might complicate WMC's relations with the Broken Hill companies. Similarly, if in the course of prospecting for non-ferrous metals with the Australian firms, WMC found iron ore, H/H would have to be accommodated under the terms of the memorandum of understanding (5/1/ 1 Box 77 Clark to NBH, 17 October 1962).

In light of its links with the Broken Hill companies, WMC agreed to work with H/H on a venture-by-venture basis, according to the merits of each project, but without making a binding comprehensive undertaking. This approach did not, in itself, preclude the development of a long-term relationship between WMC and H/H, but it did raise the possibility that heavy negotiating costs might be incurred in arranging a sequence of individual, project-based deals. In the event, the agreement to include H/H in the WMC–BHP project at Yilgarn, Hanna and Homestake's acceptance of twenty-five per cent interests each in the Koolanooka venture, and the NBH– WMC understanding that H/H would be accommodated if ferromanganese was found in the Moonta copper field all indicated that achieving an initial co-operative stance was likely (Morgan, to Weber, 23 March 1964; Chace to Morgan, 15 May 1963; and 5/1/1 Box 77 Clark to NBH, 17 October 1962). Moreover, there was wide scope for sequential adjustments that could be undertaken successfully and without prohibitive haggling costs provided the parties communicated to build mutual confidence.

However, delays in finalising a definite agreement reflected low levels of trust and left the partners exposed to protracted and potentially damaging negotiation. In January 1964 the Americans unexpectedly informed WMC that for tax reasons they could not invest in a jointly owned Australian firm but would have to form their own local subsidiaries which would participate in the joint exploration venture. This meant that WMC would have to release H/H from their obligation to buy Great Western's plant valued at £450,000 and forgo payments for that firm's tax losses. This development was costly to WMC and took the Australian firm completely by surprise because it had believed that H/H had investigated US tax laws before it had agreed to the acquisition of Great Western.

Officials from the three firms met in Melbourne in February 1964 to settle all issues surrounding the iron ore business as a whole (Morgan to Weber, 23 March 1963; and memo, 31 March 1965). At these talks WMC agreed to include Yilgarn in the deal and to allow Hanna a thirty-six per cent stake and Homestake a twenty-seven per cent interest, while retaining thirty-seven per cent for itself. When the first sales contract for iron ore was concluded with the Japanese, the partners would participate in the profits from that deposit in proportion to their holdings. WMC and H/H accepted the same stakes in all future projects, in effect raising H/H's combined holding from fifty to sixty-three per cent. In return for these concessions and for releasing them from the obligation to buy GWC's equipment and pay to share in its tax losses, H/H agreed to allow WMC to treat its expenditure to date at Yilgarn as part of its thirty-seven per cent stake. The Americans also allowed WMC credits against the value of the Yilgarn deposit, credits that they would match with exploration spending to maintain their allotted shares in the various projects.

Having secured the Americans' consent to this cumulative investment programme, the first stage of which was required to fulfil a preliminary sales contract concluded with Japanese steel mills in December 1963, WMC drew up a draft agreement that embodied these terms (9 March 1964). The Yilgarn deposit was valued at £500,000, and in addition to the £150,000 it had already spent an exploration work, WMC was to be allowed a credit of £150,000 on the property's value. This meant that H/H had to spend a further £500,000 on deposits outside of Koolanooka – but not exclusively on Yilgarn – to retain their shares in the various projects:

WMC	37%	£300,000	(£150,000 spent to date and £150,000
Hanna	36%	£285,700	credit for Yilgarn property)
Homestake	27%	£214,300	Joint commitment to spend a total of
			£500,000
Total		£800,000	

If the Yilgarn field proved to be economically viable, WMC would receive a further credit of £350,000, representing the balance of the property's value, and H/H would spend a further £595,900 to maintain their thirty-six and twenty-seven per cent stakes:

			Total investment/credits
WMC	37%	£ 350,000	£650,000
Hanna	36%	£ 340,500	£626,200
Homestake	27%	£ 255,400	£469,700
Total		£ 945,900	£1,545,900

The draft agreement also stipulated that H/H had to make their additional investment at a minimum rate of £100,000 per annum unless WMC agreed to a lower figure.

The draft agreement would set in motion a phased process wherein the discovery of one promising deposit initiated further expenditure aimed at assessing viability, which once established triggered further spending on development. WMC would reinvest its profits in further exploration. Thus, one successful venture would support subsequent projects. The overall process could be sustained *only if* deposits were discovered and then proved viable (this was not defined). The programme could break down at either of these two points. However, the risk of failure was reduced by simultaneous exploration of several prospects and targeting the most promising for intensive testing.

The initial risk of prospecting was borne by WMC in each case. If it failed to find deposits it incurred costs without compensation. When WMC did discover ore fields it would be remunerated only if viability was established. Then, the burden of all future testing expenditure fell on H/H, and WMC's stake became, in effect, self-financing since the value of the property would be realised in the form of that firm's percentage interest in the project. The immediate £150,000 credit for Yilgarn was an exception granted by H/H in recognition for the concessions WMC made in February 1964.

This distribution of risk and commitment to invest reflected the partners' complementary resources. WMC had local geological knowledge but had limited funds, whereas H/H lacked the former but possessed larger financial means. However, the underlying relationships between the rewards for risk taking and investment could prove to be a source of discontent. To capture mutual benefits from their synergy, the partners had to accept their own and each other's roles and the potential returns they might gain from acting in their different capacities. Otherwise, resentment could arise over WMC's losses or rewards from taking exploration risks and from H/H shouldering a disproportionate share of future spending.

The draft agreement settled the size of each member's total commitment stemming from the Yilgarn venture (other agreements would lay down similar parameters for subsequent projects). Subject to WMC's approval of a minimum below £100,000 per annum, the rate of expenditure was treated in a flexible way to enable the partners to accelerate investment in response to favourable market conditions or to slow spending as their own financial constraints and the availability of promising deposits dictated. How well this flexibility was exploited in practice depended upon whether the partners could reach a consensus concerning the pace and direction of spending.

Overall, this agreement left considerable scope for *ex post* sequential adjustment. Although the arrangement provided a broad framework for inter-firm responsibilities, it implied serial, venture-by-venture negotiation concerning a number of important details. These included accepting WMC's exploration costs as bona fide, confirming the viability of a deposit, establishing the value of ore bodies, allowing credits to WMC, and agreeing to a suitable pace for testing and development expenditure. The structure of the contract as a whole was complex, and making it work in a cost-effective manner depended on how well the venturers communicated to build trust. Getting over the first hurdle would be an important test of their resolve. The prospects did not look favourable in early 1964 because H/H did not signal their trust by signing the draft agreement.

Divergent role expectations

Indeed, almost as soon as they returned home from Melbourne in February, H/H officials began to raise objections (Weber to Morgan, 9 March 1964). H/H did not agree that WMC should receive an immediate credit of £150,000 for Yilgarn until the size of the reserve had been established, a satisfactory sales agreement concluded, and arrangements completed with the government of Western Australia for developing the required infrastructure. H/H had no objection to WMC taking the full £500,000 credit when these matters were settled.

For WMC this represented a second unwelcome surprise. W. M. Morgan, the managing director, replied that his firm was alarmed that H/H wanted to re-open one of the major points agreed to at the Melbourne meetings when the partners had reached 'an overall agreement satisfactory to all ... so that we could develop the iron ore business rapidly' (Morgan to Weber, 23 March 1964). Morgan listed the points in the memorandum of understanding and the terms reached at the February meeting to show that WMC had made substantial concessions to H/H's advantage. He stated further that WMC was not prepared to renegotiate individual items within the agreement, which should be accepted as a whole, since his firm had adjusted each point in relation to concessions made on other details at the February meeting. WMC wanted H/H to accept the contract so that the partners could press ahead without discussion which went beyond sequential adjustment to threaten the very basis of the agreement.

Moreover, H/H's refusal to grant WMC the initial £150,000 credit on Yilgarn vitiated a vital principle in the agreement, that concerning the functional roles of the partners and the assignment of risk. Morgan wrote to Hanna's Weber:

> your proposal seems to presume that we [WMC] are to take all the material risk in establishing the Enterprise, that is exploration, sales contract, and government agreement, and that you should come in on the same terms ... as if you had been with us from the beginning. This is quite contrary to the *normal course of mining exploration*.
>
> (23 March 1964, emphasis added)

To illustrate recognised conventions within the industry, as WMC understood them, Morgan cited the example of a prospector who, having taken the initial exploration risk and found a deposit, sold shares at a higher price to investors when he needed outside funds to exploit the discovery. In this case, the prospector received a reward whether or not the venture succeeded commercially, whereas WMC would only obtain a premium if the project proved to be viable in the view of all partners. Morgan inferred that H/H were in a better position than the outside investor in his example because, armed with WMC's drilling results, the Americans had much better information on which to assess the level of risk. His comments suggest that the partners recognised different conventions or precedents and this threatened to undermine their ability to harness synergies to mutual benefit.

At this point, Weber was replaced as H/H's chief negotiator by J. W. Buford. Why is not clear. However, changing the key person at the interface between the firms, especially at such a critical juncture, was a very risky step to take. Moreover, Buford was an inappropriate person for the role and from the start he had a disruptive effect. Buford sought to present the points raised by Weber as differences in the way the partners interpreted the agreement, rather than questions about the basis of the overall arrangement. Having consulted with Homestake, Buford agreed that WMC's initial risks should be recognised, but he believed that this had been done adequately. Buford conceded the £150,000 credit for Yilgarn, but did not think that H/H should be compelled to spend a minimum of £100,000 a year for five years without regard to the final results of the venture. If, for example, within a year the partners had deemed Yilgarn to be unworthy of exploitation, H/H should not be expected to spend money on other projects in recognition of what would be in effect a £150,000 credit on a 'dead venture', since H/H would be paying a premium for something that had no value.

Then Buford proposed a formal approach to govern future spending: all parties should

> take a *very close* look at all exploration budgets and ... H/H must be *thoroughly convinced* that the budgets are *completely in line* with the possibilities rather than designed to simply spend a certain minimum, amount per year.
>
> (Buford to Morgan, 17 April 1964, emphasis added)

Buford's domineering tone was completely inappropriate and well outside the etiquette of co-operation. Moreover, his desire to scrutinise financial data and the suggestion that WMC might act opportunistically were extremely damaging. However, Buford went further by asking Morgan to discuss the various points raised with WMC's chairman Lindesay Clark, as if Morgan might have been acting without full authority, 'so that we can come to the final agreement on the discussions we had in Melbourne'. Thus, while attempting a very transparent and potentially damaging manoeuvre designed to undermine or intimidate Morgan, Buford placed the onus of making accommodations on WMC. In so doing, Buford played a concession-wringing game; perhaps WMC's previous willingness to give ground signalled that it was in a weak position and needed H/H more than H/H needed it. Or possibly, WMC's smaller size and the relatively greater importance it attached to the ore properties encouraged Buford to press his perceived advantage. Indeed, at this point he sought two more concessions: H/H would recognise WMC's £150,000 credit, only if the venture proved viable (contrary to what had been agreed to in Melbourne) and would commit to a slower pace of spending (only £58,000 in the current year).

WMC had been playing a different game. It had been earnestly seeking a workable arrangement and had made what it viewed as reasonable accommodations to that end. It sought to drive the relationship along a co-operative trajectory and did not wish to start trying to wring counter-concessions from H/H. Confronted with a third surprise – that H/H now wished to modify two central features of the understanding – WMC staff concluded that Hanna was opportunistic and stood their ground.

Showing forbearance, Morgan made one last appeal to logic: the slow pace of spending proposed by H/H would threaten commercial prospects since Japanese customers wanted to see signs of real progress before they negotiated for Yilgarn ore. Revealing an appreciation of the trade-off between risk, monitoring, and time constraints, he wrote 'We do not think any close examination of estimates can remove much of the inevitable risks of such exploration ..., but rather that minute scrutiny is likely to absorb so much time that ... a chance might be lost'. His message was clear: without sufficient trust, negotiating and transaction costs would be prohibitive. Then digging in his heels and stating that he had the full authority of his board, as a rebuff to Buford's poorly conceived stratagem, Morgan laid out three courses of action, any one of which was acceptable to WMC:

1   Adhere to Melbourne agreement, but lower expenditure on Yilgarn. Of course, WMC did not intend that money should be spent unless the prospects seemed favourable.
2   Amend Melbourne agreement to limit H/H spending in recognition of the initial £500,000 credit to a minimum of £120,000 per annum for two years 'if WMC so direct'.
3   H/H withdraw from Yilgarn and the partners revert to the conditions of the memorandums of understanding. In this event, H/H should not assume that any of the concessions made at the Melbourne meeting of February 1964 would apply (Morgan to Buford, 1 May 1964).

Thus, WMC presented H/H with a set of options ranging from moderate accommodation to a return to the original starting point. WMC might have been indicating that it was unclear how H/H wanted to proceed and gave the Americans a chance to pull out of Yilgarn (while at the same time signalling WMC's confidence in the venture). However, the Australians were clearly intimating that a point of crisis had been reached and it was up to H/H to demonstrate their trust or end the association. Either course was acceptable to WMC. The time had come for a face-to-face encounter, and the Americans returned to Melbourne in August 1964.

At the meeting, the partners determined how testing work on the various deposits would proceed, but they did not finalise the overall agreement and a management contract both of which WMC had sent to H/H in July (memo about meetings, 10–12 August 1964; and memo, 31 March 1965). The tone of the notes taken during the meeting indicates that Buford initially took an aggressive negotiating position. Although H/H subsequently made conciliatory suggestions, WMC's attitude definitely hardened.

At the outset, Buford was 'upset and alarmed' that WMC had not informed H/H that design changes to the ore loading plant might drive up costs by $200,000 (in terms of the project's total costs this represented a very small amount). Buford's complaint was designed to deflect attention away from the unpleasant surprises H/H had sprung on WMC and to justify the strong line H/H was to take on the need to improve reporting flows. Accepting the criticism at face value, WMC staff replied that final plant costs could not be established until tenders had been received. The partners agreed to cut expenses and re-estimate the total cost. In a conciliatory manner intended to prevent a recurrence of this type of problem, H/H stated that they 'wished to use Alan Blatchford to the fullest in *improving communication* between WMC and the American partners, and proposed that there should be *maximum co-operation*, assisted by a clear definition of Mr Blatchford's duties and means of liaison' (emphasis added). WMC responded positively: Blatchford should visit Australia frequently. H/H then went on to propose that, in addition to the monthly geological, operating, and financial reports that WMC had already sent to them, WMC should also submit a comprehensive review of operations each quarter.

For the Yilgarn deposit, H/H requested estimates that would enable them to determine potential profitability and thus the project's viability. Morgan replied that WMC was reluctant to supply these figures because, whether they proved too high or too low, H/H would criticise WMC! Indicative of how WMC's attitude had hardened and the extent to which its officials felt they were not trusted or treated fairly by the Americans, Morgan's response indicates that he considered H/H's request as simply a negotiating tactic. Adjusting his stance, Buford suggested that WMC compile a series of figures based on various output levels without allowing for cost escalation so as to avoid after-the-fact recrimination.

Discussions of other matters regarding the Yilgarn and Koolanooka projects showed similar patterns of inconsistent behaviour on the part of H/H. While suggesting ways of making reporting procedures more flexible and building 'maximum co-operation', H/H requested additional submissions from WMC. WMC officials were not convinced that H/H sought a mutually acceptable understanding about reporting; they probably felt that H/H was attempting to impose ever more costly and time-consuming procedures upon them.

Concerning the management of the projects, Buford adopted a reasonable posture by assuring WMC that it had 'full responsibility for estimating, planning, and operational decisions'. All that the US partners expected were progress reports. He recognised that WMC had no obligation to refer matters within its jurisdiction to H/H, but both American firms were ready to assist WMC if called upon. Morgan reminded Buford that H/H were entitled to appoint an official to the board of management, but Buford replied that this was not necessary since H/H 'were satisfied that WMC acted on behalf of all partners'. These statements were undoubtedly designed to meet objections from WMC concerning the number of reports H/H requested and to signal trust. In light of the volume and variety of submissions H/H wanted it is doubtful whether WMC officials were reassured.

Buford did not help matters when he suggested that WMC staff and Blatchford should develop a system for compiling intelligence on all iron ore projects in Australia. Hanna had an organisation that monitored the cost of rival mining ventures to assess its own competitiveness and suggested that WMC set up a similar unit. WMC's Lawrence Brodie-Hall (later Sir Lawrence) replied that his firm could not justify the cost of doing so until the US partners had made their long-term intentions clear. In a gesture of goodwill, Buford then offered to share data about a scheme in Tasmania involving heavy media plants. His attempt to demonstrate the benefits of association was probably interpreted by WMC staff as a means to emphasise H/H's greater size or as a condescending gesture.

Overall, the meeting failed to resolve the fundamental communicating and contractual issues that separated the partners. Although they clarified some reporting procedures, progress on this matter was limited given the level of concern shown by Buford's numerous references to cost data, intelligence gathering, and submissions concerning operations. Regarding inter-organisational transmissions, Blatchford subsequently did act as a conduit for liaison concerning operational matters, but this might have been more effective had he resided in Australia. At a more senior level, H/H did not appoint staff to the board of management, with the result that interaction continued to consist of arm's length correspondence and infrequent meetings. Therefore, the partners did not install, even at this late date, a comprehensive communicating infrastructure that could help to generate trust. Nor did WMC and H/H settle their contractual differences, although they did revise estimates and determined the sequence of exploration work on the various deposits. With neither a definite agreement nor a communicating infrastructure, these accomplishments were largely chimerical.

Worse, from the notes on the meeting, one gets the impression that the partners failed even to establish a common outlook. WMC viewed the Americans' actions as inconsistent, their signals conflicting, and their overall performance unconvincing. Buford did not realise that adjusting peripheral matters signalled obfuscation; as far as WMC was concerned the time had come for H/H to address the core concerns. From H/H's perspective, WMC's abrupt change from being accommodating to being a tough negotiator must have come as a shock. H/H probably thought WCM's behaviour was also inconsistent. After the meetings of 10–12 August 1964, the partnership was dead in all but word.

The break-up

In fact, in November WMC staff drew up a memo weighing the merits of ending or preserving the association (20 November 1964). The document also outlined how, if WMC were to break with H/H, this course might be navigated, and then it sketched out the terms on which WMC would admit a new partner. The memo is remarkable because it reveals the extent of the cultural divide between WMC and H/H.

The cultural divide had both corporate and national dimensions. WMC staff wanted a partner who would give them more authority as managers and one who had 'an Australian outlook'. By this they seemed to mean a partner who demonstrably observed co-operative conventions and did not attempt to extract concessions for their own exclusive benefit. WMC objected to what it considered to be Hanna's unnecessarily detailed reports and interference in affairs that were WMC's responsibility. Not only did Hanna's stance reflect mistrust, it undermined WMC's status as an equal and valued partner. Each venture was treated 'virtually as a division of Hanna'. The failure to resolve differences in how the partners valued deposits reflected their distinct modes of conduct. WMC felt that it was co-operative by making concessions to accommodate the Americans, but H/H exploited WMC's goodwill by competing hard to make gains at each step. Other factors, such as the complexity of the agreement, made it hard to reach a broad understanding, but fundamentally cultural distinctions and variations in management style prevented the partners from establishing the basis of trust that was a prerequisite to settling outstanding issues.

The reasons why WMC should not terminate the association also reflected its co-operative culture and its perception that the opportunity cost of defection was very high. Although WMC felt that Hanna's operating experience and its knowledge of pelletising ore would be valuable for future projects, it was more concerned about the adverse signals a break might convey. WMC feared that Hanna's withdrawal would raise doubts in the minds of Japanese buyers and the Australian public concerning the soundness of the project. Dissolution might 'create an unfavourable climate for Joint Ventures with other overseas companies' which might think 'that we have used Hanna to "pick their brains" and then dumped them'. WMC feared that rupture might also create practical contracting problems – for example obtaining funds might prove difficult unless a new partner accepted the same terms offered to H/H – but reputation loss was a prime concern. Fearing for its local reputation and future contracting options, WMC wished, at the least, to retain relations with Homestake.

Concerning how it might induce Hanna to withdraw, WMC could revert to the terms of the memorandum of understanding since the joint venture and management agreements had not been finalised. This course would exclude Yilgarn from the deal, and it would leave Hanna with interests in several properties that were unlikely to prove viable as well as a twenty-five per cent stake in Koolanooka that was suitable for development. Hanna might consider these assets to be too small to be worthwhile and withdraw.

If Hanna did so, WMC devised terms that would make the break graceful and so preserve its co-operative reputation in the eyes of other constituents. WMC considered reimbursing Hanna for its share of the expenditure incurred only on those deposits (Koolanooka and Yilgarn) that WMC considered to be viable, with interest if necessary. The firm also considered paying Hanna for the knowledge it had provided and for its executives' time to counter suspicions that WMC staff had 'picked the brains' of the Americans.

With regard to adjusting membership in the venture, the Australian firm wanted to give Homestake, whom it felt was co-operative, first option on Hanna's interest in order to retain continuity and minimise adverse signals. If both American firms departed, WMC believed that it had wide substitution possibilities. It planned to offer a new partner only a forty-nine per cent stake so that it could retain control. The new participant would allow WMC a £500,000 credit for Yilgarn, and the cost of additional expenditure would be met in proportion to both partners' shares. Further, the new venturer would have to commit itself to spending a minimum of £50,000 per annum for five years on exploration and research. From a co-operative perspective, these terms represented a retrograde course. WMC sought absolute control, a full credit, and a definite base expenditure. Although these terms would resolve the issues over which conflict with Hanna had occurred, they did not reflect any consideration of how to build trust. WMC learned only obvious lessons from its experience.

From this point on, the partnership drifted. H/H made two half-hearted attempts to extend the association to include other projects and other minerals [J. K. Gustafson (Homestake) to Morgan, 12 January 1965; Buford to Morgan, 9 August 1965]. WMC claimed that it could not participate because its resources were fully stretched by other ventures and because its agreements with the Broken Hill firms prevented it from exploring jointly with H/H for non-ferrous minerals (Morgan to Gustafson, 20 January 1965; memo, 27 August 1965). By this time the price Japanese paid for ore had fallen significantly as firms developing the huge Pilbara deposits entered the market. As WMC had feared, delays in pushing forward projects had jeopardised commercial prospects [Morgan to R. W. Boswell (secretary, Department of National Development, Canberra), 16 February 1965]. Meanwhile, H/H made no concessions to resolve the basic differences between the partners concerning their existing interests and refused to ratify yet another draft agreement presented by WMC in February (memo 1 March 1965). Indeed, Buford aggravated matters further by demanding a larger share of the successful Koolanooka project as compensation for the Yilgarn deposit which he considered uneconomic to exploit [memo D. McIntyre (WMC), 3 March 1965].

At the end of March, Morgan drew up a memorandum analysing the factors that had created the impasse (memo, 31 March 1965). Hanna's minority equity stake in the relatively small project undertaken by the partners was not large enough to attract strong support from within such a large firm and probably lowered the opportunity cost of not co-operating. WMC had a much less exacting approach to reports, budgets, and financial estimates than Hanna; in general, the Americans took a short-term 'accounting attitude' towards estimates, whereas WMC used them as 'statistical' tools. In part, these viewpoints reflected the partners' different risk tolerances and divergent conceptions of their activities. WMC saw itself as a mineral exploration company taking high initial risks. H/H saw themselves as mineral developers who sought to minimise risk but were unwilling to reward WMC for the chances it took looking for new deposits. As manager of other projects, WMC was accustomed to having considerable freedom of action, whereas its American partners wanted to exercise close control, in keeping with their 'accounting attitude'. Relations had also been strained by differences concerning how to organise the project as a company or joint venture in light of the partners' differing exposures to taxation. WMC and H/H had never been able to agree on the value of the Yilgarn deposit. Finally, WMC felt that it had made significant concessions to H/H, who, far from reciprocating, had been continuously 'chipping away in an endeavour to improve their position at WMC's expense'.

The final point confirms that cultural differences caused the partners to observe distinct rules of conduct. WMC and H/H had failed to learn about each other and devise ways of accommodating their differences. From this perspective their distinct views of their activities – as explorer and developer – could have been complementary and generated considerable mutual advantages. Similarly, the exacting reporting approaches and risk averseness of the Americans might have been used to *balance* WMC's informal procedures and high risk tolerance. Ultimately, inter-firm learning did unfold, but the partners merely learned that they could not trust each other.

A memo written in November 1967 confirms precisely when WMC and H/H made this realisation (memo, 28 November 1967). The document suggested that the inclusion of Yilgarn in the arrangement 'created virtually all of the disputes'. It seems unlikely that the inclusion of this deposit made the agreement too complicated. Rather, the Yilgarn deposit stood out in the writer's mind because it brought to the fore, especially during the meetings of 10–12 August 1964, fundamental differences which convinced WMC officials that Hanna behaved opportunistically. It is significant that this was the point where WMC sought to move beyond the first venture within the envisioned series of projects.

To confirm the Japanese sales contract formally, the partners did finally conclude a joint venture agreement in March 1967 (retrospective to 1965). However, it was a mere formality that did not provide a basis for future co-operation and further exploration. Only Koolanooka was developed, Yilgarn was not exploited. Worse, WMC's legal officer, J. O. James, noted several years later that the partners had not included a deadlock-breaking mechanism in the 1967 agreement (memo, 26 March 1971). As a result, the partners remained gridlocked until they concluded a further agreement wherein each party allowed the other to explore independently for iron ore throughout Australia.

Conclusion

The WMC and H/H joint venture proved to be a one-off encounter instead of an enduring relationship. The main reason for this outcome can be traced to the partners' inability to establish a workable balance between the degree of prevailing trust and scope of sequential adjustment. The lesson that emerges from this case is that while every contract must leave room for future modification, the extent to which this feature is manageable in practice depends very much upon the effectiveness of inter-organisational communication and the resulting level of trust. Determining a suitable balance at the outset required intensive communication. WMC and H/H communicated only intermittently at infrequent meetings, usually in response to a crisis. (Nor were the crisis resolution skills of their staff as highly developed as those of Curtis and JSS personnel.) They failed to install a communicating infrastructure, which was all the more vital because of the physical distance that separated the partners. By supporting an ongoing dialogue, such a construct could have helped them to learn about each other's cultures and to adjust gradually to differences in outlook. They did not devise communicating procedures and an accounting system acceptable to all parties. Nor did the partners accept each other's spheres of responsibility. H/H took a tremendous gamble by changing the personnel at the inter-organisational interface at a crucial point and made what proved to be a critical error in selecting Buford as their chief negotiator. (Recall how reluctant JSS was to replace Radford and how carefully they adjusted the team at OP.) In the minds of WMC staff Buford's aggressive behaviour embodied what they saw as a typically American concession-wringing approach. Nor could his actions have possibly led WMC to understand him as being 'tough but fair'; he was abrasively self-interested. His conduct also made it utterly impossible to create a distinct joint venture culture.

The WMC–H/H example reveals insights regarding the importance of having past experience in joint venturing. Indeed, if limited to a certain constituency, prior experience can create expectations, routines, and behavioural patterns that are inappropriate when dealing with a partner from a different background. (Chapter 2 confirmed that similar behavioural conditioning and wide acceptance of specific models and precedents lubricated adjustment processes and contained the cost of making transactions between shipowners.). Although WMC, Hanna, and Homestake had all worked with other firms, only WMC and Homestake had collaborated together in the past, albeit over twenty years earlier. WMC's dealings with ALCOA and the Broken Hill companies had made it accustomed to working with considerable independence within a fairly informal structure with the result that H/H's insistence on minute reporting and close control took its officials aback. (It was probably unfortunate that Homestake did not play a more active role because WMC's internal memos confirm that the Australians felt that Homestake was a co-operative player.) Thus, having extensive experience in joint venturing is advantageous, but it is in itself no guarantee of success.

Variety of experience may be more important than the volume of experience. Staff who have wide exposure to different partners and situations can develop an enhanced capacity to recognise distinct games, protocols, conventions, and rules and adapt to them. All of this highlights the importance of developing suitable personnel resources to support successful joint venturing. (Members of the HSS network devoted considerable effort to giving their staff a thorough grounding in co-operative processes.) This type of business requires a distinct skill set: the ability to listen, learn quickly, and adjust.

Regarding criteria for assessing joint venture outcomes, WMC and H/H failed to achieve a dynamic juxtaposition of capabilities that could serve as a basis for future learning and growth. In fact, the partners observed distinct business approaches and conceptions of success. And they failed to recognise these differences at the outset. WMC wished to co-operate and was clearly disappointed that a long-term relationship did not materialise. H/H observed a short-term view that, given its 'accounting perspective', may have led it to consider the association to be a success because Koolanooka generated large profits. Reflecting the differences in the two firms' approaches, its officials probably could not understand why WMC hardened its attitude in May 1964. H/H's concern for reports and precise accounting showed the limited type of learning it was concerned with. [This case provides a poignant contrast to the depth of learning pursued by the HSS network, the J. Walter Thompson Company (Chapter 10), Curtis, and USS.] Worst of all, H/H displayed no real interest in learning about its partner: this should have been its first objective. Learning can change one's outlook or a particular outlook can shape one's learning; the outcome depends on whether joint venturers can step outside themselves and their own cultures and co-operate on terms that are meaningful to their partners, as JSS did with the Chinese investors in OP.

The WMC–H/H story suggests some refinements to our consideration of those other variables that affect co-operative endeavour. First, it shows how differences in local presence can influence how participants respond to threats of exclusion and the attractiveness of harnessing the complementary attributes of other prospective partners. As we saw in Chapter 2, such concerns were vital to shipowners who were so deeply embedded in highly localised and occupation-specific contracting arenas. In contrast, it was important to DB&W to conceal its British affiliations and to project a German image to constituents within its business environment. For Australian-based WMC, reputation loss was a serious concern, whereas the attitude of Hanna staff indicates that for them a breakdown was not a serious matter as far as local credibility was concerned. Second, disparities in the importance that participants attach to a specific venture will influence the degree of commitment they have to it. For Hanna, the benefit of involvement in such small deposits was not particularly significant, but for WMC the Koolanooka venture represented what potentially could have been an important stepping-stone towards greater participation in the iron mining industry. Hence, the Australian firm demonstrated a greater willingness to try and preserve the joint venture. Third, differences in the partner's substitution possibilities affected their behaviour. In this regard WMC and Hanna both had other opportunities they could pursue. However, WMC had more limited resources and it may have felt greater pressure to redeploy its relatively scarce financial means. Moreover, the Australian firm had a wide range of ties with other more familiar domestic firms who could help it find more attractive exploration opportunities. Fourth, differences in the size of players may influence their behaviour. As a large multinational, Hanna might have expected that it could intimidate its much smaller Australian partner. Finally, ensuring that each partner felt that they are equal and valued participants is important in preventing resentment, of the type the DB&W staff felt, from poisoning relations.

Once WMC discovered the true character of Hanna and determined that the venture was failing, it had to devise a way of extricating itself with minimum damage. This draws attention to the need for participants in co-operative initiatives to develop in advance contingent exit strategies in case an intractable problem arises. WMC had no such plan in place, but the memo of November 1964 suggests that its staff did recognise that terminating a relationship could be managed in a creative manner in order to project specific, desirable signals. (Ellerman understood this, see Chapter 2.) They committed a further mistake in creating a gridlock in the 1967 agreement that prevented them from exploring independently for new iron deposits. Similarly, B&W remained locked into an unsatisfactory relationship with its German subsidiary. Both cases draw attention to the need for those that pursue inter-organisational alliances to consider the various types of exit barriers: those imposed by reputational concerns, legal constraints, and the degree to which their investments are liquid.

Finally, the WMC–H/H episode reveals that time can be important to co-operative initiatives in four ways. First, as we saw in the B&W case, delays in installing a communicating infrastructure obstruct inter-firm learning in the critical early stages of the association. Second, gaps in the continuity of communication provide opportunities for mistrust or suspicion to arise. Third, the longer the venturers haggle over the terms of the initial agreement, the greater the danger that the atmosphere surrounding their relations would be poisoned. Here, culture is important because partners with the same affiliation use and recognise distinct signals which indicate that a crisis point has been reached and decisive steps must be taken to remedy the situation. H/H obviously missed Morgan's signal in May 1964, when he laid out three courses for the future of the joint venture. Once it became clear that distinct approaches to business had created a fundamental misunderstanding, recuperative inter-organisational learning had to be achieved very quickly. Here, the partners failed: they learned only that they could not get along. Fourth, time may be important in light of developments unfolding within the wider business environment. The market would not wait for WMC and H/H to settle their differences and develop their deposits. The relationship between the passage of time and inter-firm learning poses a difficult trade-off for joint venturers. In this regard, the communicating devices, signalling media, and recognised behavioural rules furnished by shared cultural affiliation can serve to accelerate cognitive processes, or alternatively executives' skills in communicating across a cultural divide to promote trust both assume real commercial significance. It is not so much that cultural differences in themselves are significant – indeed they should be expected – but rather how partners deal with them that matters. As the next chapter shows, the J. Walter Thompson Company learned to thrive on such cultural diversity.

10 Contracts based on knowledge

The J. Walter Thompson Company and Unilever – compounding intangible assets, 1900–70

The J. Walter Thompson Company successfully transacted in knowledge and established enduring agency relations with its clients without the aid of an established institutional precedent like the merchant–correspondent model that shipping agents relied upon. This advertising agency had to convince clients that its own intangible assets were valuable so that it could then promote their intangible assets, thereby setting in motion a compounding effect. Examination of JWT's relations with Lever Brothers shows how they developed a common perspective on inter-firm relations and built interconnected systems and structures.

J. W. Thompson began his career in advertising in 1865 when he joined the Carlton and Smith agency in New York as a clerk. He made his mark by convincing Carlton that women's magazines were an overlooked advertising medium. When Carlton retired in 1877, Thompson bought the firm, renamed it the J. Walter Thompson Company (JWT), and expanded its services. In the 1890s, the agency opened new branches in the US and set up its first foreign office in London in 1899.

More decisive overseas expansion occurred after Stanley Resor took over the agency when Thompson retired in 1916. Resor set up JWT's Cincinnati office in 1908 and became general manager of the firm in 1912. Under his direction, JWT formed a stable of foreign branches in the 1920s using its new account with General Motors (GM) – then expanding internationally – as a foundation (West 1988; Kipping 1999). During the Depression, GM reduced its foreign business and JWT closed some offices. Yet, in 1931, the agency was still operating on six continents. After 1945, JWT resumed its overseas expansion to become one of the world's largest agencies.

To support JWT's growth at home and abroad, Resor pursued three related objectives. First, following Thompson's personal lead, he tried to make advertising a credible undertaking. Second, he sought to raise advertising to professional status by developing on-the-job training programmes that would instil high ethical standards and a consultative, team-based approach to advertising work. Third, Resor introduced systematic marketing techniques embodied in the T-square methodology. Named after the mechanical drawing tool, the T-square approach addressed the who, what, where, when, and how of promotional activity to create a structured process for advertising work. This methodology was transmitted overseas, and feedback effects generated improved procedural expertise that flowed back to the US (West 1987). By these means, Resor created a firm-specific foundation for disseminating promotional techniques internationally.

Resor's legacy was the creation of a strong professional reputation for JWT based upon a set of intangible assets. This reputation helped the firm address the basic challenge any agency confronted when it interacted with clients of how it could prove that its advertising techniques increased sales. This problem is essentially the same one that arises when parties try to devise contracts involving knowledge. Using its reputation to smooth these transactions, JWT in turn helped clients to enhance their reputations and brands. Thus, Resor created a foundation for an inter-organisational and international 'compounding effect' for intangible assets.

This chapter examines how JWT initiated and sustained this serial process from 1916 to 1970. The discussion further develops a number of themes considered in other chapters. These include, agency relations, inter-firm communication and learning, and staff development. The first section explores the contracting problem facing JWT and the methods it used to reduce transaction costs. Next, staff training and the development of a professional ethos are analysed. The third part shows how JWT and one of its major clients, Lever Brothers (later Unilever), compounded their intangible assets. Finally, we examine how the two firms created an inter-organisational interface to support their relationship.

The contracting problem

From the time Thompson entered advertising, publishers paid agencies commissions to attract advertisements. On its foundation in 1873, the American Association of Advertising Agencies (4-As) drew attention to large advertisers who dealt directly with publishers to cut out agents and recover their fees. Agents responded by becoming wholesalers, who bought blocks of advertising space that they resold in smaller lots to advertisers for whatever price they could get. By 1900, the proliferation of firms with nation-wide sales, the rise in mass circulation magazines, and a more efficient market for transacting in advertising space threatened the intermediary position of agencies. To survive, increasingly they offered a bundle of services, including copy-writing, artwork, market research, and campaign planning, in addition to space buying.

Pope (1983: 62–4) argues that agencies retained their place between the media and advertisers largely because the commission system (which from 1917 was based on a customary rebate from publishers of fifteen per cent of space prices) satisfied all the parties. Publishers did not have to provide costly services, while advertisers felt that agents offered superior value and had little scope to behave opportunistically. From our perspective, advertising firms, like the shipping agents discussed in Chapter 2, had to establish a knowledge advantage that could enable them to generate higher returns from promotional expenditure than the other parties could obtain at the same cost by internalising the agent's functions. (Clients, for example, would not reach the switch point modelled in Chapter 2.) Advertising agents were disadvantaged because they lacked the support of a precedent, like the merchant–correspondent model. Moreover, they failed to apply the professional template whereby other occupations, such as law and medicine, achieved legitimacy by codifying a body of specialised knowledge, controlling entry by shaping education and accreditation processes, enunciating ethical standards and routines, and gaining the right to self-regulation (Abbott 1988; Perkin 1989; Boyce 1999). The industry had faltered at the first step in this process by 1917, when it and other parties could not agree on a course of professional education (Schultze 1982). Subsequently, the 4-As tried to apply parts of the template informally. Independently, JWT and other agencies set out to develop specialised knowledge through research, formed in-house training schemes, and articulated ethical standards. By publicising these activities, agencies sought to convince clients that they possessed the knowledge required, in turn, to convince consumers to buy goods. Firms like JWT had to establish the value of their own intangible assets before they could initiate a 'compounding effect'.

Stanley Resor was conspicuous among those advertising executives who finessed the problem of contracting in knowledge. In an article he wrote for *Associated Advertising* in 1919 he called for a drive away from 'rule of thumb' methods towards reliance on standardised knowledge like other professions – he cited medicine and law – had developed 'to get the public confidence'. Having studied history and economics at Yale, he believed statistical 'laws' that explained patterns of behaviour exhibited by large numbers of people could reveal advertising principles which if codified would make promotional work more effective. Trying to win professional credibility by association for the agency, Resor publicised the fact that JWT invested resources in this basic research by hiring professors of psychology, statistics, and marketing (Kershell 1989: 98, 264–6).

With such staff JWT could offer services based on a greater *depth* of knowledge than its clients commanded. JWT's facilities included market analysis, distribution studies, product evaluation, demographic investigation, and from 1915 a research department (see Kershell 1989). The agency drew attention to its capability by publishing *Population and its Distribution* (from 1912) and other works (IC4, 1890s to 1980s).[1] The promotional literature JWT aimed at its clients indicates that Resor also emphasised the *breadth* of knowledge the agency could provide. This advantage stemmed from the consultative methods JWT used to mobilise the diverse skills of its personnel. JWT's *Newsletter* described the extensive experience of staff members and how they addressed problems in collaborative fashion (SB7, 17 October 1916).

In later years, the agency claimed that it had a comparative advantage over clients in recruiting such embodied knowledge because it offered creative autonomy. JWT 'provides the working atmosphere and the money to attract the finest advertising brains, the free spirits' (SB4 file 3 'Advertising at its lowest true cost'). Some clients admitted that they could not afford to recruit top talent and recognised that the agency's reputation, history and culture were valuable intangible assets that exerted a strong attraction upon creative people (EW59 'House Agencies', 1958).

Nevertheless, JWT had to strike a workable balance between allowing scope for its 'free spirits' to apply their creative energy and providing a structure for imaginative effort in order to produce effective results for clients. In Resor's time, the T-square provided a methodology for analysing promotion problems. Later, the firm developed more complex team-based routines, consisting of structured interaction among account representatives, creative staff, heads of working groups, and the review board, all of which mobilised complementary view points and enhanced continuity (IC file Case Studies Misc. 'Responsibilities', August 1956).

In later years, JWT made arguments that developed further Resor's basic themes. The agency suggested that it captured wider scope effects than an in-house advertising unit could win because it served clients in many different industries and countries. 'Cross-fertilization constantly stimulates [JWT's] "pool of talent". All creative group-heads, and most writers, divide their time between two or more clients' (SB4 file 3 'Agency Compensation', 1959).

However, the firm made it known that it did not serve clients who were competitors. This and some of Resor's other ethical pronouncements echoed those made by the 4-As and the Truth in Advertising Movement after 1910 (Pope 1983: 184–212). Resor enjoined that JWT would not advertise liquor and eschewed speculative presentations because they were not based on careful study of a client's position and they 'dissipated [JWT's] assets' (Resor quoted in *Advertising Age*, 1962). Like other agencies, JWT advised clients against price competition in favour of indirect forms of rivalry (including, naturally, advertising) typical of oligopoly.

The agency promised clients an objective, independent view of their sales problems and marketing strategies. One customer was quoted in a promotional publication as saying 'I want an advertising agency to be able to say NO when it thinks I am wrong ... Of course, it has to back it up with good sales arguments, but a conflict of views openly expressed generally clarifies the issue' ('House Agencies'). Just how independent a line an agency could take is open to question, but JWT told clients that it could interact with them dynamically to generate mutual learning (EW58 Agency–Client Relationships 1929, 1947–63).

JWT encouraged staff to act like teachers or trustees towards clients in order to build the bonds of trust that support learning. As early as 1916, the firm tried to get employees to see themselves as 'educators' in order to create the type of relationship that arises when one person helps another to discover for themselves a powerful new idea (JWT Newsletter, 12 December 1916).

Even though playing such a role took 'time' and 'resourcefulness', 'nowhere are we more strongly entrenched than where we have been through such a development hand in hand with the client'. The passage was intended to induce staff to think about bonding techniques that could be used to forge enduring ties with clients. With a similar aim in view, JWT encouraged staff to approach client relations with a 'trustee' outlook characteristic of professions that recognised fiduciary duties. As trustees, account representatives should only recommend expenditures that will 'yield the most effective results' for the client rather than those which might boost JWT's short-term revenue. Building a 'long-term relationship with a client' and adopting 'this "trusteeship" attitude inevitably will also produce the best results for us' (IC4 file 1890s to 1980s 'What the J. Walter Thompson Company Stands For', June 1956). Like shipping agents JWT recognised that enduring relationships were founded on trust and mutual growth.

JWT went a step further by creating a formal communicating infrastructure that supported lateral links and structured interaction between agency and client firm staff at various organisational levels. It arranged weekly meetings between teams of JWT and client personnel to harness complementary skills and develop tactical plans. The agency also instituted regular planning sessions for senior executives to devise promotional strategies (EW58 Subject file 'Relationships ...', January 1954). Finally, top staff attended annual review sessions to assess results and develop improved methods. These various meetings opened up channels at various levels in the customer's organisation in order to avoid having ideas being distorted as they moved up the chain of authority and to build consensus. By these means, JWT tried to manage its relations with advertisers.

To convince clients that having a long-standing bond with JWT represented better value for their money than having an in-house advertising department, the firm tried – as Curtis did – to condition how advertisers conceived of the cost of association. Resor encouraged clients to 'look upon advertising as just as definite a factor in his business and his *costs* as materials, labor ..., and personal selling [and to] base ... advertising appropriation on a perfectly definite ratio to sales' (SB4 Client files, 12 December 1916). Although obviously self-serving, this outlook was intended to induce customers to promote their products consistently in order to generate larger sales by building durable brand identity. Nevertheless, as the firm later pointed out, as a result of seasonal fluctuations and new product development 'all advertisers' needs are ... highly variable and flexible, [and] agency services must at all times be in a position to meet these needs' (Agency Compensation, 1959). With a broad client base, JWT could switch staff between different projects in line with variations in demand. In contrast, even large advertisers would find it difficult to justify the cost of recruiting the range of specialised talent they needed, maintaining their promotional capabilities as new forms of media and distribution methods arose, and supporting salaries and overheads during periods of slack demand.

The agency also encouraged customers to see a portion of the commission they paid as an investment in improving advertising techniques. 'Every advertiser pays ... a proportionate share of improving the art [of promoting products] just as does the consumer in the price he pays for each gallon of gasoline ... pay for the cost of improving by research and experimentation the effectiveness of ... gasoline' ('Lowest True Cost'). The inference was that by building a long-term tie with JWT, clients would recoup their investment by having access to enhanced capabilities.

JWT also took pains to emphasise that the fifteen per cent commission did not generate for the agency a profit rate that was high enough to reach the 'switch point'. In 1959, JWT pointed out that agencies with billings of $40 million or more made net earnings of only 1.2 per cent of revenue, the lowest of a sample of seventeen firms in six industries ('Agency Compensation'). Leaving aside questions of how net earnings were calculated, or whether perquisites and the high salaries paid in the advertising industry absorbed a disproportionate share of gross revenue, the argument was intended to show that agency operations were not as profitable as those of clients. Therefore, diverting investment away from producing products to build an in-house advertising unit would reduce a client's profitability.

The commission system was potentially a divisive factor because it did not tie remuneration to results. Indeed, during the late 1950s the traditional framework came under fire. Shell Oil sought a new cost-plus deal from the Ogilvy & Mather agency because the knowledge differential had disappeared: 'experience comparable to that of its own staff in this field is not available in any agency known to them' (EW58 Agency Commission 'Shell–Ogilvy'). In 1958, the 4-As and publishers' groups signed consent decrees that allowed freer negotiation of rates. The agencies criticised the decrees for failing to come to terms with the mechanics of calculating the cost of advertising services. They pointed out that a piece-rate system would lead to under investment in capabilities and quality would deteriorate. Moreover, the commission system ensured that all clients – large and small – paid proportionately the same price for advertising. The fixed commission also reduced the expense and potential harm of haggling. These events of the early 1960s raised once again the issue of what return clients received from expenditure on advertising as one cost item isolated from all others that determined product performance. In *Advertising Age,* M. Harper of the McCann–Erickson agency posed the unanswerable question at the heart of the problem inherent in arranging contracts based on knowledge: 'Ideas – the basic product of advertising agencies – are almost impossible to price'. The best agencies could do to narrow the credibility gap was to cite the arguments above and successful product performances to which their services made some unquantifiable contribution.

Thus, once the function of agencies shifted to offering specialised services after 1900, JWT had to confront the problem of contracting in knowledge. It did so by applying without statutory support the template used by other professional groups. To convince clients of the value of its intangible assets it also built an inter-organisational communicating infrastructure, instilled trust-creating skills in its personnel, and tried to condition advertisers' conceptions of the costs and benefits of promotional activity. The traditional commission system did not link remuneration directly to results. It would have been possible to use a participative contract but this would have been risky for agencies and would have posed high transaction costs because the effectiveness of advertising cannot be assessed directly *ex post* let alone predicted *ex ante*. To avoid market failure, JWT bundled its services to exert influence over the marketing mix and thus contain the risks that its advertising might fail. It also advertised its own intangible assets and its staff to win client confidence and set off the compounding effect.

Staff

JWT had to enhance its staff capabilities to reassure clients at home and overseas. Yet, personnel matters presented formidable challenges. As we have seen, when the movement to provide formal education for advertising professionals foundered in 1917, the agency established its own training scheme. Staff turnover was notoriously high in the industry: thirty-seven per cent per annum in the inter-war period (Marchand 1985: 45) and slightly lower after 1945 (Wilson 67 Domestic Policy, Personnel). In the 1960s, recruits had different expectations, and JWT was compelled to change its personnel policies.

Resor publicised the educational achievements of his staff in order to attract clients. JWT highlighted the fact that by 1919 seventy-one out of its 260 staff had studied at college or university. By the same time, the agency advertised that it had built up a cadre of female graduates of many prestigious institutions to help clients reach women customers, whom it stated made 'eighty-five per cent of all retail purchases' (*Advertising Club News*, 5 June 1918). However, JWT made a point to emphasise that all staff – no matter how well qualified – had to complete 'the regular course of training in advertising which the company gives'.

In *Associated Advertising* (1919), Resor described JWT's rigorous two and a half year programme of instruction. Consisting of prescribed periods working in nine departments and in selling activities, the course was designed to acquaint new staff with the full range of advertising operations. To impart firm-specific knowledge, it provided a comprehensive view of JWT's organisation and how the functions of the various departments were interrelated. Personnel were assigned 'prescribed reading' and had to pass examinations and complete working projects.

After new staff had finished the initial programme, JWT tried to keep them abreast of current developments by means of in-house seminars. The agency's records confirm that these sessions were held regularly from the 1920s onward to discuss patterns of consumer demand, product life cycles, and the application of research findings to promotional strategies (EW60 and 65 Staff Meetings, 1927). These meetings served to disseminate ideas to account representatives who operated at the interface between the agency and its clients.

Seminars were also designed to further each staff member's 'development as an advertising professional', support collaborative decision-making, and enhance firm-specific knowledge (EW70 General Information, Seminars 1960–1). To these ends, sessions examined JWT's philosophy, operations, and procedures. Showing how corporate memory could be used to provide practical instruction, disseminate firm culture, and shape performance perceptions (when precise measures were unavailable), the seminars relied heavily on client case histories. Overseas offices also ran courses, as one manager confirmed, 'to solve [real] problems' and reveal the firm's 'main principles to young and new staff members' (EW10 Frankfurt 2, Carnaris to EW, 15 July 1966).

JWT's weekly *Newsletter* was a supplementary forum for cultivating firm culture, ethical principles, and direct communication. From 1916, it carried articles about the philosophy of advertising, how JWT solved specific client problems, business development, media data, and personnel. Management actively encouraged staff to use the paper to obtain advice from each other (21 November 1916).

From at the latest the 1960s, the agency also used lunch meetings between junior and senior staff as informal fora to promote interpersonal learning and mentoring. This 'very popular' programme furnished a 'friendly link' through which corporate culture could be transmitted through face-to-face contact. 'The purpose ... is to acquaint these men with senior staff and ... allow younger men to ask both advertising and management questions. The senior men, in turn, get a feeling of the kind of talent we have coming along' (SB7 JWT Seminars B. Jimm to M. Keating, 20 November 1963). This informal approach to staff assessment persisted while the company modified its formal appraisal techniques in response to new conditions in the 1960s.

JWT's rapid expansion created increasing demand for new employees while changes in the expectations of younger executives made it difficult to keep and train them in the traditional manner. In 1964, Norman Strouse, who succeeded Resor as president in 1955, estimated that over the next decade the main agencies would have to hire about 2,500 professionals per annum to replace those who retired and to sustain growth (NS35 Writings and Speeches, 'Personnel Projections', 10 November 1964). About the same time, JWT encountered a 'rash of resignations' by recently hired MBAs and new account representatives (EW59 subject files, Evaluation Program, 1965–70). These developments led to a reassessment of 'the nature of our business ... and therefore the kind of people needed to man it.' It caused senior management to return to the traditional approach advocated by Resor: rather than focusing on the client, a trend that had developed in recent years, JWT should concentrate on the consumer. Instead of specialists, this policy called for people with a broad education that made them good 'communicators' whose services, especially as account representatives, were vital in maintaining client relationships. As a result, the firm reduced its intake of MBAs and recruited more arts graduates.

Realising that these types of recruits were 'anxious to move into the main stream of our business', JWT changed its training programme. Because so many newcomers now left the firm before completing the entire two-year rotation through the firm's departments, it devised a shorter course with more hands-on work. The new scheme also included a series of weekly account history examinations involving personnel from many departments who had actually worked on the campaigns. Thus, the firm's tradition of on-the-job, client history based training persisted but in a form that was more appropriate to a new constituency.

In the 1960s, JWT also began to undertake what Strouse called an ongoing manpower inventory assessment to plan for managerial succession (NS35 writings and speeches, 'Agency Management Succession'). The agency sought to manage a portfolio of talent to ensure that the progress of potential leaders was not blocked and that men who had the capacity to become senior figures had opportunities to develop their judgement. Adopting a *15- to 20-year time horizon*, the firm set up an executive committee that delegated tasks to sub-committees consisting of middle managers whom the firm wished to acquire greater experience. However, in keeping with the traditions created by Resor, the plan enunciated that the behaviour of candidates for senior posts must reflect their commitment to the firm's basic values.

To conclude this section, Resor's ideas continued to shape staff development because they remained relevant in helping the agency contend with its fundamental contracting problem. His emphasis on professional values was reflected in JWT's training programme from 1916 to 1970 and in the succession plans developed by Strouse in the 1960s. His legacy did not create rigidity; it was moulded to meet the aspirations of new constituents and to preserve long-standing client relationships.

The Lever–JWT relationship

William H. Lever (Lord Leverhulme), who founded Lever Brothers (renamed Unilever after its merger with Dutch interests in 1929), built Lux soaps into an international brand by 1900. While doing so, he developed formidable promotional skills. Indeed, letters between Leverhulme and his US managers reveal that Lever Brothers transferred very sophisticated sales expertise of its own across national boundaries by 1900 (Unilever 182D).

As a producer of consumer non-durable products, Lever Brothers advertised heavily from the start. Before the emergence of modern full-service agencies in England after 1900, Levers devised their own domestic promotional campaigns and placed their advertisements directly into published media, thereby cutting out the intermediary space buyers. The firm's internal advertising capability was strengthened as part of a cost-cutting drive in 1923, when it formed the Lever House Advertising Service (LHAS) to co-ordinate some of the promotional operations of its subsidiaries. Thus, LHAS bought space for all Lever companies, but the latter were free to buy other services from LHAS or outside agencies. Levers did not pursue comprehensive rationalisation under LHAS but rather sought to reduce costs while retaining access to outside expertise (Sharpe 1964: 14–5). Yet, contracts between LHAS, renamed LINTAS in 1930, and Unilever companies were not symmetrical; although subsidiaries could use outside agencies, LINTAS could not serve non-affiliated clients.

Although unusual and perhaps inequitable, this arrangement was successful. LINTAS expanded overseas and retained about one-half of the Unilever group's advertising business. Concurrently, JWT was one agency Unilever employed to promote its products – including flagship brands – in the US from 1902 onwards, in the UK from the 1920s, and in many overseas markets.

This section and the one that follows examine the JWT–Lever relationship. Specifically, it concentrates on the strong knowledge capabilities of the two firms, inter-organisational transfers of expertise, and learning processes. Attention is also devoted to how JWT applied its advertising processes to Lever products and how it compounded intangible assets by developing an inter-organisational interface.

JWT secured its first account for a Lever product, Lifebuoy hand soap, for the US market in 1902 (IC 3 Lever Brothers 1913–59). Although the agency dropped the Lifebuoy account when it began working for Woodbury, it secured the Lux soap flakes account in 1916. Levers had not had much success with Lux because they promoted it for a limited application (washing woollens, which were not used as widely in the US as they were in Britain) and because the form of the product – soap flakes – was not familiar to customers (most soap was sold as bars). Not realising that Lux was a concentrate, consumers found it expensive, and retailers were reluctant to allot shelf space to what they considered to be just another soap.

JWT applied its standard process to Lux: it conducted research to expose specific problems and opportunities, used the findings to develop themes for copy and art work, identified specific publications to reach the targeted consumer, and then scheduled advertising to enhance cost-effectiveness. Thus, the agency researched the distribution channels used by Levers and investigated Lux's possible uses in order identify specific consumer groups. The agency developed a message designed to work around the retailer by appealing directly to the consumer (middle-class women) who, by demanding Lux, would compel shopkeepers to stock it. JWT sought to change the conception of the product by avoiding any reference to soap and simply calling it Lux: a unique, luxurious, even 'mysterious' product. The idea was to distance Lux from soap, to promote it for washing woollens, and then induce consumers to use it for other cleaning purposes.

JWT's main contribution was to provide a strategy that created a high-class brand image for Lux. The flaked form of Lux could not be patented, and JWT foresaw that success would attract imitators. The agency's aim was to place Lux in a dominant market position and compel rivals to spend 'a fortune and a lifetime to catch up' (IC3 Lever Bros., 1913–59). Subsequently, Lux's brand image proved to be its 'strongest asset', even after dozens of competing products came on the market.

The initial advertising campaign was an unqualified success: sales rose from 10,000 cases in 1915 to over 1 million cases by 1919. The next step was to promote other uses for the product. Working with clothing stores and manufacturers, JWT found in 1919 that Lux was well suited to washing silk, which was becoming fashionable but had to be dry-cleaned at considerable cost. The up-market image created in the first advertisements was used to reinforce this new use and to justify Lux's high price. JWT adjusted its copy, artwork, and media plans to target the new market segment.

In its next campaign, the agency proposed that Lux be used for washing dishes. The attraction here was to reach a market based on thrice daily use, which would bring huge sales. Research revealed that women worried about the effect dishwashing had on their hands, and JWT's advertising emphasised Lux's gentleness. Again, copy, art, and media plans were modified. At each stage, JWT reapplied its basic approach to reach wider market segments. It evaluated feedback on previous campaigns before launching new ones and allocated spending to prevent existing market sectors from becoming saturated and to develop new ones.

Although the Lever records do not provide a overall view of its response to JWT's campaigns, the client did provide important feedback for JWT's plans for advertising Lux Toilet Soap in 1925. In this instance, the agency's copy was not appropriate (it associated the hand soap with the flakes instead of making it distinct) and the thrust of the message was modified. In due course, however, JWT's approach of linking the two products was adopted and proved successful. Overall, Lever's confidence in JWT is reflected in the stream of new product accounts it allotted to the agency. Lux Toilet Soap (1923) was followed by Lux Liquid (1947), Rinso Blue (1954), and Stripe Toothpaste (1956). By the late 1950s, JWT's accounts represented about thirty per cent of Unilever's US advertising spending. Meanwhile, the agency won a considerable amount of this client's overseas business.

Precisely when JWT's London office won the Lux account is unknown, but the introductory tone of a meeting held between Geoffrey Heyworth (later Lord Heyworth and chairman of Unilever from 1941 to 1959) and agency staff in 1927 suggests it must have been about that time (HAT 686 Z4, 14 December 1927). Gaining direct access to a senior executive like Heyworth was important, as the agency's experience had shown, in expediting the approval of campaign elements and avoiding bureaucratic resistance. Moreover, this early meeting laid the foundation for what became a strong, long-term relationship.

Heyworth revealed his commanding knowledge of the British market and Lever's extensive promotional and research activities. For example, he knew that magazine circulation was not large enough to meet the target audience and that Levers had to rely on national newspapers, the broad readership of which did not facilitate efficient targeting. He also knew that the quality of newspaper production made it hard to create the 'quality atmosphere' needed in Lux advertisements. Heyworth described in detail the strengths and weaknesses of each link in Lux's distribution chain, even to the extent of identifying which specific co-operative societies shunned Lever products and which supported them. He gave an in-depth picture of Lever's regional sales and the methods used to win support from distributors in each area. Heyworth also described Lever's research activities.

In light of this executive's expertise and knowledge of conditions in his own home market, what could JWT, as a foreign agency, offer that might justify it having the account for a flagship brand? At this meeting, Heyworth stated that he wanted JWT to produce newspaper advertisements with the right atmosphere for Lux, and he hinted that the agency might help Unilever to develop techniques for correlating sales data from specific territories with media circulation in the same areas. On the first point, JWT's Smith said the agency had sound experience in developing appropriate advertisements. However, in keeping with the fact-based approach laid down by Resor, Smith stated that the London office would have to carry out background research into Lever's business before outlining a concrete plan. Regarding the research issue, Smith said that JWT had suitable analytical procedures.

The most immediate contribution JWT made was to change Lux's image from being 'simply a different form of laundry soap largely for washing utilitarian woolens' to a luxurious product (HAT A720, 1928 a and b). Thus, JWT transferred the product concept it developed in the US to Britain, but in doing so it used a phased approach to build on Lever's existing advertising copy so that the new message would not be inconsistent with Lux's established image. First, it conducted a campaign to extend the uses of Lux. Next, it highlighted the high quality imparted by Lever's manufacturing processes, the firm's reputation, and Lux's purity. (Lux was packaged, whereas other flakes were distributed in bulk and thus susceptible to contamination.) Finally, the advertisements emphasised the product's luxury. Some of these advertisements followed the US practice of including fashion 'news' on coming styles and fabrics to highlight Lux's properties. To support the unfolding campaign JWT forged links with staff at middle levels in the Unilever organisation. From its client's research personnel the agency obtained data about Lux's chemical composition and its effect on fabrics in order to generate copy themes. JWT also developed important ties with Unilever's middle level marketing staff to build consensus and exchange ideas. The campaign as a whole followed JWT's established approach: it was based on market research and consumer investigation, copy was adjusted in light of feedback, and media plans fine-tuned to meet specific market segments. Overall, the agency offered a new product concept and a method to realise this in an adaptive way that was suited to the British market and consistent with previous advertisements. Thus, JWT transferred two intangible assets – skills in formulating brand strategy and systematic promotional methods – from the US to the UK.

Consultations regarding the content of advertising copy show that transfers of expertise gained in the US to the UK did not always proceed smoothly. For example, JWT advocated a message that associated Lux Toilet Soap with Lux Flakes in order to capitalise on the latter's newly founded luxury image. This approach had been effective in America, but Heyworth thought that 'the situation here was not yet ripe for this'. Similarly, when Unilever considered running a special offer on Lux at a reduced price in order to stimulate demand during 1932, JWT again drew on its US experience. It advised that such a policy would destroy the brand leadership that had been built up at considerable cost. JWT argued that 'Lux would simply become what it was twenty or thirty years ago when, in America, at least, grocers refused to stock it and consumers [refused] to buy it because it was just another soap …'. The agency foresaw that sales might increase while the special offer was running but prophesised a rapid fall thereafter. Unilever proceeded with the new approach and sales trends unfolded just as JWT had predicted. Six months after the continuity of the product's image had been broken, the agency recommended expanding Lux's consumer base using a stronger argument based on economy so as to avoid confusing customers further. The incident must have been frustrating to JWT staff but they had to defer to client preferences. Like JSS (see Chapter 3), JWT had to know when to let unfolding events reveal the logic of its position to the other party. When the outcome revealed the accuracy of its predictions, remedial action had to be taken without recrimination, to ensure that a relationship of greater mutual confidence resulted.

To conclude this section, JWT staff established a strong bond with such an experienced, market-focused multinational enterprise as Unilever by demonstrating their superior knowledge and exercising their relationship-building skills. The agency provided an independent view of its client's operations based on its own international experience. By transferring advertising and market research techniques developed in the dynamic American business arena, JWT helped to strengthen one of Unilever's most valuable intangible assets: the Lux brand.

Multinational partnership, 1945–70

After 1945, JWT and Unilever built extensive inter-organisational links to contend with a series of new challenges. Rapid international growth by both firms created tensions within their relationship. The introduction of new brands, the arrival of television, and the spread of self-service retailing increased Unilever's advertising expenditure to levels that concerned its managers (Wilson 1968: 106). Because new trends in consumer demand, media, and advertising techniques first arose in the US and then spread to Europe, JWT and Unilever had to adjust their communication methods and inter-firm links to transfer knowledge and compound intangible assets. This section examines tensions that arose as the two firms charted a course of mutual growth, and how they strengthened agency–client ties.

When Unilever began to reconstruct its European business after 1945, JWT lacked a branch office infrastructure to support its client. As a result, LINTAS rebuilt its continental organisation and won first mover advantages in many countries. JWT gradually reconstituted its branches and began securing individual accounts in specific countries. Colgate Palmolive and Proctor & Gamble also spread into Europe, bringing in their wake other American agencies that also secured work from Unilever. The expansion of multinational soap makers along with that of LINTAS and the American agencies created problems for the JWT–Unilever relationship (EW 6 London General, 1956–8, and Meek's files, 1954–5).

First, the two parties did not uniformly observe the informal elements in the agency–client contract. JWT adhered to the unwritten rule that no agency should handle competing accounts in a given country, but Unilever did not reciprocate (SM4 International Department, 9 March 1955). Some European managers felt that the agency might gain more by working with Proctor & Gamble than by remaining faithful to Unilever. However, Sam Meek, the head of JWT's international operations, did not agree: 'we might ... work ... up a very satisfactory business, but it would be a different kind of business, and without anything like the reputation or stability we now enjoy' (ibid., 1 March 1955, SM to DS). This long-term view, a legacy of Resor, together with concern for the agency's own intangible assets prevented a break from occurring.

Nor did JWT depart from this perspective when Unilever gave other agencies accounts for Stripe Toothpaste, after JWT had developed the product concept. To calm outraged managers, D. Saunders counselled that 'if a Client's performance has been pretty favourable, it is unwise to get too het up [sic] on odd occasions when he seems to fall' short of JWT's expectations (EW6 London Meek's files, 5 August 1958, DS to SM). Citing the basic problem facing any agency, Meek added that JWT had no way to protect its ideas. The firm had to bind clients to it by producing a set of services that 'made the advertising so profitable that the advertiser will invest increasing sums' over the long run (ibid., 6 August 1958, SM to DS).

Differences over business development arose between JWT and Unilever because the latter expected the agency to expand its branches – and thus incur heavy costs – in advance of receiving new accounts. When JWT took an incremental approach by establishing offices with a small, start-up staff, the client expressed disappointment (EW3 Meek's files, 13 April 1954, DS to SM). Regarding the German operation, Meek argued that JWT could not afford to 'build a [complete] team in advance' of getting new business, and Unilever should give the firm new accounts first. 'They would not be experimenting. We have proven our ability' (SM 4 International Department, 26 October 1954, SM to DS). As shipowners and their agents recognised, enduring ties had to be based on equitable mutual growth (see Chapter 2). JWT continued to strengthen its branches in a phased manner (EW 3 *passim*).

JWT had to adjust inter-organisational communication lines and redeploy staff when Unilever adopted a new decentralised policy of allowing subsidiary firms to select agencies for their own territories. Although JWT had strong links with senior Unilever executives, these men could not influence the decisions of subsidiaries. However, working through Ivor Cooper, Unilever's advertising manager, the agency was able to forge ties with executives at the client's European companies. JWT also seconded London staff who had strong relationship-building skills to continental offices in the hope that these men could gain the confidence of local Unilever managers (EW 3 Meek's files, 14 April 1954, DS to SM and EW6 *passim*). The agency accepted the logic of Unilever's policy for its experience with General Motors had revealed that a centralised approach to overseas advertising could create resentment at the local level (EW6 London, 12 July 1956, DS to SM). Working within the constraints posed by Unilever did bring JWT a string of new accounts.

Unilever's product policies and its decentralised approach highlighted more fundamental communicating deficiencies that induced both parties to make a series of far reaching improvements to their inter-organisational interface starting in 1960. When Unilever reorganised its British operations on the same lines as its American business, JWT's London office asked the head office in New York for information about Unilever's US structure and how JWT had adjusted its American set up to streamline inter-firm transmissions (EW4 Meek's files ,9 March 1960, T. Sutton to SM). New York furnished charts of Unilever's US organisation, its largest division, and the account teams JWT had formed to 'put against the Lever account' (ibid., 17 March 1960 A. Butler to TS). These diagrams showed that the key contact points were Unilever's Product managers, a Merchandise Manager, and the Advertising Vice President, 'an extremely important man' who devised the advertising budgets for all products. [LINTAS also copied JWT's Product Team structure in 1938 (Sharpe 1964: 53).] Thus, both client and agency transferred organisational knowledge across national boundaries, and JWT's transmission also included client specific information needed to fine tune inter-organisational communication lines.

Reflecting the growing importance of Unilever as a source of commissions and prestige for JWT, the agency's European offices began consulting more closely to improve their handling of its accounts. Staff from six offices met regularly to discuss copy, market trends, and the findings of consumer research (EW7, London General, notes on Lux meetings). Also in the early 1960s, JWT set up an international account team, consisting of men with complementary skills from different branches, to work with a World Co-ordinator's office that Unilever formed to pursue global brand strategies (EW23 Lever Lux 1952–6). [To create its own internal flow of knowledge, in

1962 Unilever sent nine executives from various countries 'to study long-term marketing trends and developments in the United States' (Lever Marketing Group Visit, Unilever document, EW23).] The agency took further steps to improve liaison between its research units and Unilever's R&D department. These activities were intended to enhance shared knowledge of national markets and improve Unilever's international brand strategies.

The most important step taken to strengthen the client–agent relationship came after a meeting between Unilever, LINTAS, and several agencies was held in New York in 1965. Here, Unilever articulated a comprehensive international policy regarding future relations between its affiliates and the agencies to sustain mutual growth (EW58 Agency Compensation, Unilever and its Advertising Agencies, 7 July 1965). Unilever assured the agencies – and informed its subsidiaries – that it did not intend to take advantage of its size or play off outside agencies against each other or against LINTAS. The Unilever group would use LINTAS as its chief agency, and it would give a sufficient amount of business to outside multinational agencies to ensure that the group remained an important client without relegating any agency to a position of dependence. In order to remove one source of tension, Unilever announced its intention to allocate an international brand to one agency throughout the world. Also, it would not give a national brand account to an agency that represented a competing product in another country.

To qualify for Unilever business, an agency had to have a base in the US:

> ...the intensity of the competitive struggle for the rich, active, and complex American market is likely to preserve that country's leadership in the skills and tools used in Advertising and in Market Research and other services which Advertising needs. Unilever's companies everywhere must be able to take advantage of American skills and tools.

Moreover, agencies serving Unilever had to have efficient systems for transmitting the superior advertising techniques they developed in the US to their overseas branches, which would then adopt or adapt them to meet local conditions.

Unilever wanted agencies to provide it with an independent perspective and 'to speak for the consumer ...'. In addition, agencies should recognise their 'duty to tell [the] client [Unilever] about new opportunities' to meet consumer needs. Ideally, Unilever wanted forthright, collaborative interchanges with its agencies.

Although Unilever demanded that each agency have 'outstanding creative ability' and believed that this 'must imbue the agency', it expected a disciplined approach to be used. It cited the devices developed by LINTAS to structure promotional work. Unilever knew that independent agencies had similar tools, and although it did not explicitly say so it may have hoped for exchanges of expertise.

Mutual learning about products and promotional activities was, however, a vital feature of the bonds Unilever sought to forge with its agencies. 'The necessary community of purpose and the vast fund of common knowledge will take a long time to build up. Once built up, these *valuable assets* must not be destroyed. That is why the association must be enduring' (emphasis added). Unilever understood that shared expertise built up over the long term helped to compound intangible assets.

Concerning agency remuneration, Unilever recognised that losses incurred on minor accounts and by 'investing' in new brands in the hope that profits would be generated once the product was established were both sources of friction. Its guiding principle was to allow 'a fair profit' on each product account while apportioning 'the rough with the smooth' equitably. Unilever accepted customary compensation formulae but stated that it expected flexibility on overall pricing policy after taking into account the commission and the amount of work required. It wanted to avoid conflict by carefully specifying initial agreements and minimising *ex post* adjustments. Unilever also described the type of research agencies should undertake as part of the work covered by the usual commission (as opposed to extra charges for non-routine research). Knowing that research was costly to agencies, it did not want onerous demands to induce them to cut corners.

Overall, this policy statement mirrored JWT's perspective on client–agency relations, and it reflects some degree of inter-organisational learning by Unilever. The document addressed most of the areas that created discontentment and proposed fairly clear corrective steps to strengthen inter-firm ties. By enunciating basic principles and a spirit to guide future relations the statement reinforced the efforts both parties had made to build interconnected communication lines and organisational structures. Finally, the document articulated how joint learning generated what we have called a 'compounding effect' for intangible assets.

Conclusion

This case shows how Resor created a set of intangible assets that JWT needed to promote its client's reputations and brands at home and abroad. Unlike Curtis, who sought to combine the intangible assets of firms within his pyramid, Resor tried to multiply and magnify the intangible assets of JWT and its clients. To do so, initially he had to legitimise JWT's attributes. Lacking an accepted precedent and unable to apply the professional template with statutory authority, Resor informally adopted some elements of the latter model by prescribing ethical standards, founding in-house training schemes, and attempting to articulate a body of specialised knowledge embedded in clear routines. In so doing he created a legacy that had an enduring impact on JWT's culture and subsequently shaped the way the agency built relational capital with its clients. Resor and other agency executives who pursued similar courses, propelled inter-firm relationships along a trajectory shaped by – as Unilever's statement in 1965 indicates – a common outlook and mutually recognised principles to guide interaction. While JWT's internal culture and that which bound the agency and Unilever provided continuity, it also proved to be flexible enough to accommodate changes in external conditions and an influx of new personnel who had different expectations. Like JSS, JWT had to make crucial adjustments to retain new constituents and sustain growth. These modifications were all the more important for JWT because the people it needed to retain were account representatives upon whom it depended to maintain strong agency–client relationships and to protect the quasi-rents derived from its intangible assets.

JWT was more deliberate in building inter-organisational links than were USS or members of the HSS network, who used more organic means that suited the highly personalised and sometimes private nature of the links in question. JWT not only built inter-firm communication lines at various managerial levels, it also used a more structured approach when working with its clients. (Moreover, the agency also used inter-branch and inter-firm conferences more effectively than did B&W in part because it engineered a common culture and more deeply shared common conceptions.) In the case of Unilever, after 1945 especially, JWT adjusted aspects of its own organisation so that they mirrored those of its client. To cement these structural links it also deployed managers whom it considered relationship building specialists – the equivalent of the skilled team-builders JSS used to bring together PJ and B&S staff at Orient Paint.

By these means, JWT succeeded in maintaining interdependence with a major multinational client for many decades even though the balance of power favoured Unilever, in the sense that it had wider substitution possibilities derived from its link with LINTAS and other agencies. While JWT was able to convince this client of the continued value of association, like the Nickel syndicate, Unilever exercised its latent power in a restrained manner. Unilever also ensured that JWT did not feel that it was in a position of dependence like that of DB&W before 1918. The case that follows shows how overt use of power can create a legacy of mistrust.

11 An Australian supplier chain

The New South Wales Bottle Co., 1909–80

As this chapter shows, supplier chains are not new nor are they unique to Japan. This case explores contract design, the use of power, communicating devises, and environmental conditions as variables that affect the operation of this type of co-operative structure.

Supplier chains are generally associated with Japan; indeed, the *keiretsu* is widely seen as one of the ingredients in the success of that country's car industry. However, opinion is divided whether they represent the outcome of historical patterns of growth and conditioned behaviour, or whether they are simply cleverly designed contractual structures. Gerlach (1992) and Fruin (1991) subscribe to the former view. Along similar lines, Helper (1990, 1991) describes *keiretsu* as the outcome of 'voice' strategies, where parties take a long-term view of relationships and communicate extensively to solve problems that arise (see Chapter 1). Environmental conditions are also important: relatively slow growth and a lack of turbulence are conducive to durable voice relations.

In contrast, McMillan (1989) suggests that Japanese supplier chains represent simply a highly efficient form of contract.[1] They consist of a string of agreements that embody powerful incentives for members to contain costs and innovate rapidly. The elegance of the structure as a whole is reflected in the way it reduces the risks and high capital costs of vertical integration, enhances flexibility, poses market tests for all suppliers, and distributes design and supervisory functions.

A more balanced view suggests that historical patterns of growth, cultural forces, and contract design are all important in explaining the effectiveness of any inter-firm arrangement. How effectively an agreement mobilises incentives to influence specific types of constituents will shape performance, whereas culture and behavioural norms condition how parties respond to these incentives. The crux of the matter is how well participants communicate to learn what influences actuate the behaviour of each other in order to preserve co-operation rather than dependence.

This case examines an inter-organisational framework centred around the New South Wales Bottle Co. [initially called the Brewers' Bottle Association (BBA), but hereafter NSWB], which supplied beer bottles to Australian breweries. By outward appearances the construct, which existed for seventy years, resembled a supplier chain, but its operations were not really voice based. NSWB relied on commercial dependence rather than co-operative interdependence to hold the chain together. When cost-effectiveness declined and the opportunity cost of affiliation rose, specific links broke. Defects in the underlying communications lines and overt use of bargaining power hindered the growth of real co-operation and created a legacy of mistrust.

The history of NSWB highlights issues considered in other chapters. These include contract design, the use of power, developing communication lines to tap local information, and tactics for coping with external shocks. The chapter examines the four sets of contracts and communication lines that linked the breweries, NSWB, bottle manufacturers, and bottle merchants. The first section provides an overview of the contracting chain and the underlying cost structure. The remaining sections analyse each contractual link as it adjusted over time.

The contracting chain and supporting communication lines

Figure 11.1 shows the ownership ties, the transacting links, and flows of cost data within the chain. Sydney brewers, Tooth & Co. Ltd and Tooheys Ltd

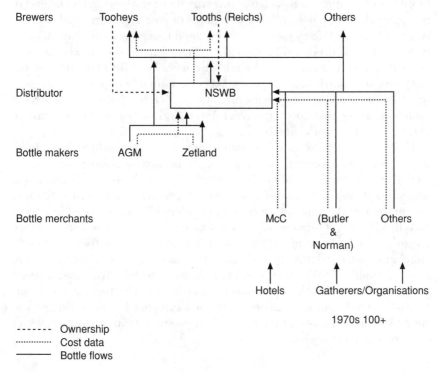

Figure 11.1 Links in NSWB's supplier chain

(collectively, TT), jointly owned NSWB (founded in 1909), which had legal ownership of the bottles. In turn, NSWB hired its bottles to TT as well as Reichs (acquired by Tooth in 1913) and several independent breweries. NSWB purchased new bottles from several local companies, including Australian Glass Manufacturers Co. (AGM), Zetland Glass Bottle Works Ltd, and later Glass Containers Ltd, as well as glass makers outside NSW. To retrieve used bottles NSWB relied on many bottle merchants [in the 1970s, twenty-one in Sydney and ninety-one in the rural hinterland (Z352/48)]. J. J. Field, Lawson Transport, and other cartage firms conveyed bottles throughout the chain. Individuals, dustmen, and charitable organisations (referred to as collectors) gathered and sold bottles to merchants who consolidated them for shipment to NSWB, which cleaned and inspected the vessels. Thus, the chain consisted of multiple contracting links at most levels and ownership ties at its apex. NSWB occupied a central position within the structure because it provided quality control and co-ordinating functions.

Data about the fees received by collectors, bottle merchants, and NSWB, and the price charged by glassmakers in 1921 (the only year for which we have figures) reveal three important points. First, for NSWB the expense involved in recovering used bottles was about forty per cent of the cost of buying new vessels. Second, if it achieved its goal of a seventy-five per cent recovery rate, the firm had to recycle a bottle four times before it made a profit (ten per cent) on its original investment after allowing for the cost of replacing the stock it lost. Third, the overall cost structure made NSWB vulnerable to hold up by merchants who could lower the firm's rate of stock turnover and its profitability. By withholding returns, the merchants (who also collected other containers) could also force NSWB to buy more of the expensive new bottles and, if glassmakers were unable to provide sufficient supply, could also disrupt brewing operations. Merchants did hold up NSWB (albeit at some cost to themselves) on several occasions in the hope of extracting higher collection fees.

Under normal circumstances, maintaining the flow of bottles through the chain was a complex operation. Since beer was perishable before it was bottled, having an adequate rate of bottle delivery was vital. Moreover, demand was subject to seasonal fluctuation, and extra containers were needed to meet the summer peak. To provide a consistent supply of bottles to the breweries, NSWB relied on returns supplemented by purchases of new bottles. Since the firm could not accurately predict the rate of returns from the bottle merchants it carried inventories, as did the glassmakers. When bottles were in short supply, NSWB paid merchants higher recovery fees, and allowed them to raise the fee they paid to collectors to increase the rate of returns. Multiple sourcing of new bottles provided a safeguard against disruptions, but NSWB faced important constraints in inducing glassmakers to accelerate deliveries at short notice.

NSWB–brewery contracts

The link between NSWB and the major breweries was characterised by overlapping operating and financial ties, much like the upper segments of Japanese supplier chains. TT each took up a one-half interest in the company. Later, an independent, Maitland Brewery Co., also made a minor 'dedicated' investment in NSWB, whereas other small, unassociated beer makers simply hired bottles from the distributor but did not own shares (Z223 BBA DM, 26 September 1913).[2] The major brewers signalled their commitment to the joint venture by locking in their investment; since NSWB was organised as a private undertaking there was no public market for its shares. Moreover, the agreement restricted share transfers (Z223/105 Articles of Association, 15 June 1916). TT had equal representation and set policy by consensus.

The operating ties between TT and NSWB were partially exclusive and motivated by profit-sharing incentives. The brewers could hire only NSWB-branded 370- and 740-ml bottles that had moulded upon them 'property of the NSW Bottle Co., Ltd' (Z352/48 Contract, 20 June 1916). TT were free to hire or buy unmarked bottles of these sizes and containers of different capacity from other sources (Z223/105 'NSWB Co.', 19 January 1979). TT and outside breweries shared in the profits or losses of NSWB in proportion to the quantity of the bottles they hired from it and thus had an incentive to maximise their use of NSWB containers.

The earliest surviving hiring agreement concluded in 1916, and renewals arranged in 1922 and 1936, envisioned flexible interdependence between TT and NSWB (Z352, 23 June 1916, draft 1922, and 21 September 1936). These agreements clearly specified the roles and obligations of each party to avoid misunderstanding, but they left items that defied specification for *ex post* resolution. Thus, NSWB alone was to arrange and pay for collecting used bottles and buying new containers. Its officials had the right to inspect the brewers' stocks to confirm that they did not retrieve and re-use bottles without paying a hiring fee. Indeed, TT agreed to 'use every effort ... to maintain and preserve the [property] rights ... of the owners'. Recognising the impossibility of accurately predicting in advance levels of future demand, the agreement did not specify the quantity of bottles TT would hire at particular intervals over the life of the contract. Instead, NSWB agreed to deliver bottles 'in such quantities and at such times as the Hirers shall from time to time require', and the brewers were to 'give the Owner [NSWB] reasonable notice in writing in advance of the Hirers' requirements'. Thus, like Japanese supplier contracts, the TT–NSWB agreement did not set rigid delivery schedules; rather the parties would accommodate each other.

This outlook was articulated in the dispute-breaking mechanisms built into the contracts. TT could withdraw at three months' notice if NSWB failed to comply with 'the terms hereof directly and indirectly' implied. This clause gave TT a means of escape in the event that the supply of containers for their perishable products was seriously dislocated. The wording suggests that the parties recognised the need to observe the spirit as well as the letter of the arrangement. Although this left wide latitude for interpretation, the contract set out a two-tiered dispute-resolving mechanism that initially provided scope for informal, co-operative adjudication and, failing this, legally binding settlement. Thus, the chairmen of the firms would directly seek solutions to matters of difference, and if they failed to reach agreement they would appoint an outside umpire to act in accordance with the Arbitration Act of 1902. These provisions were designed to ensure that this joint venture would not be caught in a deadlock like the one that ensnared WMC and H/H.

The bottle-hiring contracts had flexible pricing provisions. They set a base rate that could be adjusted at six-month intervals in a way 'determined by the Auditor' of NSWB. The agreements did not disclose the adjustment mechanism, but reference to the auditor suggests that it was based on the cost of new bottles or retrieval expenses. Applications for changes in hiring fees were probably supported by cost data that TT could verify through their board members. TT–NSWB contracts covered three years and, reflecting recognised interdependence, they were renewed with few changes.

The contracts also applied built-in incentives for NSWB to contain upward movement in costs. The six-month lags in the hiring fee adjustment mechanism encouraged NSWB executives to control the firm's internal expenses, especially since contracts for new bottles had sliding scales that automatically accommodated changes in specific cost items (see pp. 193–194). If costs fell, the breweries participated in NSWB's augmented profits and thereby recouped a larger part of their net hiring costs. Moreover, organising NSWB as a separate profit centre was designed to provide a spur to its management. Since TT's representatives knew the hiring fees NSWB charged independent brewers (these contracts were discussed at board meetings) and had access to its cost data, they could assess how effectively the subsidiary responded to the market test that it faced when bidding for outside business.

NSWB's contracts with non-shareholding breweries were more contingent than those it arranged with TT (Z203/1 and 26, Z223/105). Agreements with outside firms were of relatively short duration, one to two years. These contracts set a fixed hiring fee and a maximum weekly delivery rate that could be reduced on seven days' notice. They contained dispute-breaking mechanisms similar to those in the TT–NSWB contracts. The only sign of interdependence reflected in the contracts with outside brewers was a provision that they must help enforce NSWB's property rights.

Overall, the link between NSWB and TT resembled those at the top of *kerietsu*. Although based on constitutional authority derived from ownership ties, the tie can be described as one of preferential – but not exclusive – dealing and flexible interdependence. In contrast, NSWB arranged contingent contracts with outside breweries. These latter agreements not only provided a market test but they also allowed scope for the joint venture to build up a larger business. TT benefited from the profits and economies of scale generated by NSWB's specialised operation.

NSWB–bottle manufacturer contracts

Initially, NSWB's contracts with bottle manufacturers were multilateral, market mediated, and contingent. However, during the inter-war period, the firm developed bilateral and increasingly relational ties with one suppler, Australian Glass Manufacturers (AGM), which was then adopting new mass-production technology (Fountain 1996). NSWB forged this link in response to difficulties in coping with wide swings in demand and growing concentration in the glass industry. By the early 1970s, NSWB reverted to multiple dealing because AGM had become inefficient and changes in the law made this inter-organisational link vulnerable. Thus, in contrast to its bond with TT, NSWB's ties to bottle makers were only temporarily characterised by interdependence. Indeed, the firm seemed to waiver between exit and voice strategies. Even during the inter-war period, when NSWB and its bottle supplier seemed to be closest to developing a voice relationship, there were signs that NSWB was able to use its purchasing power to place AGM in a position of some dependence. Real interdependence typical of voice relations proved illusive.

As we have seen, the cost of new bottles was very high relative to both the collection fees NSWB paid to bottle merchants and the hiring price it charged breweries. These price relationships created a strong incentive for the firm to contain the cost of new bottles. Before 1914, NSWB attempted to achieve this end by using competitive tendering and multiple sourcing practices that involved three domestic glass makers and occasionally foreign producers (Z223/105 BBA DM, 23 April 109, 7 October 1910, 21 April 1911). The firm also divided its purchases, particularly between 1909 and 1920, in an attempt to juggle supplies during what was a period of high demand and to provide a hedge against defective bottles that disrupted brewing (BBA DM, 1 July and 9 September 1910, 6 January 1911). Yet, multiple sourcing did not insulate NSWB from serious temporary shortages (BBA DM, 14 June 1912).

In 1916, supply difficulties and price pressure induced management to concentrate purchases. That year, NSWB arranged a very large, exclusive contract with AGM and did not renew agreements with its smaller suppliers (Z203/26 contract dated 26 July 1916). However, by 1920, AGM could not meet NSWB's full requirements and that firm had to turn down business offered by Castlemaine and Woods (DM, 20 August 1920). As a temporary solution, NSWB placed a large one-year contract with newly formed Zetland Glass (DM, 25 June, 16 and 23 July 1920).

By March 1921, however, a precipitous downturn in demand from the breweries forced NSWB to curtail deliveries of new bottles. That year, Zetland merged with AGM to create a single supplier in Sydney. Henceforth, NSWB had to single source its purchases, but it was able to adjust the price-setting mechanisms in its exclusive contract of 1916 with AGM to ensure competitive prices (see p. 194). This automatic adjustment machinery supported a relational form of contract.

The contract of 1916, and all subsequent supply agreements that NSWB arranged from that date until 1938, included a sliding scale that provided a base price which changed according to shifts in the cost of vital inputs. Initially, just two inputs, labour and coal were placed on the sliding scale (Z203/26 contract, 26 July 1916). The next contract, that concluded between NSWB and Zetland on 25 September 1920 (Z203/26), included soda ash within the sliding scale, presumably because this raw material had become a significant or volatilely priced cost item during the interval. All inputs governed by the scale changed in accordance with regulated or market-based indicators that were set by external forces and were visible to the contracting parties.

The use of the traditional sliding scale device was intended to provide flexibility, but the version adopted by NSWB exhibited two defects. First, the 1916 agreement did not specify a maximum price and therefore exposed NSWB to an unlimited cost spiral. As we have seen, NSWB's contracts with TT allowed hiring fees to be revised at six-month intervals, but the bottle makers could raise their prices as soon as their costs rose. The two adjustment mechanisms were not symmetrically designed. Second, unlike Japanese supplier contracts, which included a declining price path over time, NSWB's agreement did not mobilise incentives for the glass makers to contain variable expenses through fuel conservation or labour-saving innovations. As it stood, the sliding scale left NSWB exposed to ever increasing prices.

This defect was partially remedied in later contracts. Rampant inflation between 1917 and 1920 induced NSWB and Zetland to set a maximum price (40 shillings) at which NSWB could suspend purchases and rely on AGM and recycled bottles until Zetland's costs fell (Z203/26, 25 September 1920). All subsequent contracts included a price ceiling and created an incentive for the glass manufacturers to contain costs.

All contracts after 1920 provided scope for adjusting the sliding scale as a whole. A five-year agreement signed on 25 October 1922, after AGM and Zetland merged, allowed the parties to review the base price after three years to accommodate major changes (Z203/26). Similarly, cumulative changes in input costs compelled the contractors to modify the base rates for coal, labour, and soda ash 'so as to bring them into conformity with present conditions' (NSWB DM, 5 September 1927). In these ways AGM and NSWB modified adjustment parameters in response to environmental changes in order to preserve what had become a single sourcing relationship.

During the 1930s, AGM began to display voluntary restraint in passing on higher costs to NSWB (NSWB DM, 25 March 1935, 12 July 1937, and 19 December 1938). AGM's behaviour may have reflected market conditions that moved in NSWB's favour, or it may have stemmed from more transparent information flows (see p. 195). A fundamental change in relations is confirmed by the arrangement in 1938 of a six-year agreement that called for fixed prices with no sliding scale. Instead:

> the vendor company agree[d] to continue on the fixed price determined but if any legislative enactment, governmental regulation, or restriction materially affect[ed] costs or should there be any natural increase in

production costs through war, the prices [would be] reviewed with a view to providing temporarily for an equivalent increase while such conditions prevail[ed].

(NSWB DM, 19 December 1938)

This departure from the sliding scale to informally arranged mutual accommodation occurred as both parties recognised their greater mutual trust and the likelihood that the coming war would undermine the sliding scale. The new informal approach was accompanied by less rigid adjudication procedures and improved communication.

Between 1916 and 1938, the mechanisms by which AGM and NSWB agreed to resolve disagreements over how to apply the pricing formula moved from third-party arbitration to direct communication. The 1916 agreement placed the sliding scale under the same adjudicating machinery that covered all aspects of the contract. In the event of dispute, each party would nominate a separate arbitrator, and these figures would devise a solution. The 1920 agreement enjoined that differences would be referred to a mutually recognised arbitrator whose opinion would be binding except that either party could appeal to the Supreme Court of NSW. The 1929 contract allowed NSWB to examine AGM's cost records, and it did so on one occasion (Z203/26 draft agreement 1929 NSWB DM, 1 May and 12 June 1933). In 1936, AGM agreed to give NSWB quarterly statements covering labour, coal, and soda ash expenses (NSWB DM, 10 and 17 August 1936). Thus, the two firms replaced external arbitration with formal reporting procedures that enabled NSWB to monitor AGM's costs. However, this channel allowed for only a *one-way* flow of information.

Within the contracts that NSWB and AGM arranged between 1916 and 1938, clauses governing relative pricing levels reflected the emergence of an increasingly dependent relationship. These clauses eventually gave NSWB a competitive advantage over rival bottle distributors. Initially, in recognition of NSWB entering into the exclusive agreement of 26 July 1916, AGM bound itself not to sell bottles to other firms at prices lower than those it charged NSWB (Z203/26). The supplementary agreement negotiated with Zetland on 25 September 1920 contained similar terms. By 1922, low-priced foreign-made bottles threatened to give rivals a more significant advantage, so that when arranging a new contract on 25 October 1922 AGM and Zetland, which had just merged, agreed to rebate to NSWB one-half of the difference between the contract price and that of any cheaper imports (Z203/26). Using outside information as the nickel syndicate did, NSWB obtained quotes from foreign manufacturers and producers in Queensland and South Australia to ensure that it obtained competitive prices from its local supplier (NSWB DM, 16 and 30 May, 28 July 1927, and 17 March 1930). The final surviving contract, that of 1 January 1930, stated that AGM would not supply other Australian firms at lower prices and would charge other NSW brewers not less that twenty per cent *more* than what NSWB paid (Z203/26). Thus, over time NSWB's bargaining power relative to its sole Sydney supplier enabled it to secure terms that gave it a price advantage over AGM's other local customers. Such exclusive dealing also compelled the two firms to devise methods of accommodating wide swings in deliveries.

As we have seen, demand for new bottles was derived from demand for TT's products and was influenced by the rate at which used bottles were returned to NSWB. Gradually, NSWB and AGM included more flexible delivery parameters within their contracts. However, in actual practice what sustained a suitable flow of new bottles and, from AGM's perspective, optimal production runs was accurate estimation of TT's requirements and effective communication. NSWB had to process information from TT and bottle merchants in an anticipatory way in order to ensure that it had enough bottles on hand and that AGM could plan its production effectively. Carrying buffer stocks was an expensive alternative that had to be minimised. AGM and NSWB also had to devise ways of ensuring consistent quality.

The first exclusive contract between AGM and NSWB stipulated a delivery rate of at least 230 gross per week with an annual minimum of 12,000 gross. If NSWB required a larger quantity for any year, it had to give AGM two months' notice. Once notice had been given, NSWB had to accept the larger quantity in equal weekly amounts. To facilitate production planning, AGM could manufacture at a higher rate and call upon NSWB to store the bottles on its premises. AGM had to bear the opportunity cost of the capital tied up in the stock. The agreement ensured AGM of a regular weekly cash flow of £300 paid by NSWB on account, with the balance settled at the end of each month. This early contract did not specify an allowable rate of breakage during bottling operations. Subsequent agreements did set a minimum breakage rate above which AGM and Zetland had to compensate NSWB. To ensure that the cause of breakages were fairly determined and to facilitate the implementation of corrective measures, the bottle makers could inspect the machinery at the breweries (Z203/26, 25 September 1920, 25 October 1922, draft contract, 1929).

The post-war boom and slump produced swings in demand that proved to be too wide to be accommodated by the delivery clauses in the exclusive agreement that NSWB and AGM had arranged in 1916 and succeeding contracts. As a result, the firms negotiated new agreements. In 1920, AGM could not meet delivery schedules, and NSWB signed a one-year deal with Zetland calling for 1,000 gross per week (25 September 1920). In the meantime, AGM improved its deliveries and NSWB scaled back its purchases from Zetland in a new three-year contract dated 21 January 1921. The new arrangement allowed for variations of between 450 and 500 gross per week, but it also created a strong incentive for Zetland to maintain a delivery rate of at least 450 per week. If Zetland failed to supply this amount, NSWB had the option of taking the shortfall in succeeding weeks or declining it altogether, not paying for the bottles, and deducting them from the total called for in the contract (75,000). For Zetland, any shortfall could mean a permanent reduction in sales.

Early 1921 witnessed further wild fluctuations in demand with which the new agreements could not cope, and both AGM and Zetland requested yet another set of new contracts (DM, 27 May and 10 June 1921). The new agreements set minimum delivery rates for six- and twelve-month periods but allowed for increasing supplies up to a maximum level on four weeks' notice (Z203, 15 July and 10 August 1921). NSWB could cancel the increased rate and revert to the original quantity at six weeks' notice. The contract between NSWB and AGM also allowed the latter at its own expense to stockpile bottles on NSWB's premises up to a specific level ahead of the summer peak. NSWB could use this reserve at two weeks' notice. These agreements provided greater flexibility in meeting seasonal demand and set parameters for delivery rates that did not exceed the capabilities of the two bottle makers.

Finally, when Zetland and AGM merged in 1922, they arranged a new five-year contract with NSWB. This agreement was much simpler than its predecessors and provided for smoother sequential adjustment. The combined bottle maker agreed to provide a minimum of 600 gross per week, and if it failed to do so NSWB could refuse to take up the shortfall later. NSWB could request AGM to supply bottles at a rate above 600 gross per week before the start of any quarter. The agreement also provided for the storage of a buffer stock at AGM's factory. This simple agreement was routinely renewed and operated successfully for the rest of the inter-war period. The two firms communicated effectively to modify seasonal delivery rates in line with demand conditions that had become more predictable and more stable than those that prevailed earlier (DM, 24 October and 19 December 1924, 7 August 1925, 13 August 1926, 10 September 1928, 14 September 1931, and 25 July 1938).

The shift from a multiple sourcing, market-mediated contract to one that was more relational in character was supported by increasingly flexible delivery scheduling and pricing procedures as well as improved communication. The parties gradually refined their contracts to eliminate most of the initial defects, but they could not devise means of eliminating costly buffer stocks through some form of just-in-time delivery system. Wide swings in demand conditions eventually forced the parties to recognise some degree of interdependence. However, one-way information flows and NSWB's use of its bargaining power to extract a price advantage indicate that its relationship with AGM was tinged with a degree of dependence.

Nevertheless, adjustments made during the inter-war period proved to be sufficiently effective to maintain the bilateral relationship for nearly fifty years. In the 1970s, NSWB 'encouraged' the formation of Glass Containers Ltd by giving that firm initially twenty per cent and then thirty per cent of its business. NSWB allocated one-half of its requirements jointly to AGM and GCL and invited tenders from the two firms for the remainder. This competitive tendering arrangement saved NSWB $1,667,000 in 1975 alone (Z352/48). The resumption of multiple sourcing was induced by new competition laws and the declining efficiency of AGM, but it indicates that NSWB and AGM had not perfected their voice strategy.

NSWB–bottle merchants contracts

The final link in the chain, that between NSWB and the bottle merchants, showed no signs of interdependence. This is surprising since NSWB relied on organisations like the Victoria Bottle Merchants Association which had 'the prime function of protecting the property rights of the owners of bottles' (Z203/34). In the 1920s, there were signs that NSWB and some merchants began to communicate more closely, but in general NSWB took a cavalier attitude towards them as a group.

After 1945, environmental change radically altered the economics of recycling, and belatedly NSWB tried to strengthen its ties with merchants. As Butler & Norman (B&N), a large Sydney bottle merchant, put it:

> over the past ten years or more, the method of bottle collection has altered considerably. During the depression years some collectors worked part time to augment the 'dole' ... Better wages, shorter working hours, and more liberal conditions for employees are responsible for the gradual disappearance of the old-time collector.
>
> (Z203/29 B&N to NSWB, 16 August 1954)

The assessment of income tax on rubbish collectors also discouraged them from recovering bottles for NSWB, and although charitable organisations became more active they did not make up for the loss of traditional recycling agents. Brewers began making increasing use of non-recyclable containers with the advent of the 'throw away' society. Finally, soaring urban real estate values increased the opportunity cost of tying up capital in collection yards, and Sydney bottle merchants began selling their properties and leaving the business. These factors eroded NSWB's profits and induced it to experiment with new incentives in an attempt to preserve a recovery system based on independent merchants.

Although two merchants, B&N and McCarthy, built up large, specialised businesses in the inter-war period, NSWB relied extensively upon small firms that retrieved branded bottles as part of a wider recycling operation. NSWB's relations with small operators remained highly contingent. For example, NSWB assigned each merchant a collection territory and thus controlled the range of his operations. So great was NSWB's confidence that it could easily replace any merchant that it entered into hiring agreements with country brewers for one to two years, but retained the right to cancel contracts with the merchant it appointed to the same locality at one month's notice (Z203/26). NSWB also determined the gross margins of the merchants by dictating not only the fees that it would pay them, but also the fees that they would pay collectors, householders, and public houses. NSWB's contracts with small merchants did not leave scope for any type of direct dispute resolution but rather envisioned only legal recourse. Thus, lacking any trace of interdependence, these agreements gave NSWB the power to restrict merchants' operations, terminate relationships unilaterally and at short notice, and to influence the merchants' profitability.

These one-sided contracts did not include any automatic adjustment mechanism like the sliding scale that governed the price of new bottles. Merchants applied to NSWB for changes in the fees paid to them or the fees they paid to collectors, and NSWB usually required supporting cost data. NSWB paid higher rates or imposed decreases in either collection fee according to the state of trade (Z223/105 BBA DM, 10 May 1911, 7 July 1911, and 28 February 1913). It aimed to set fees paid to collectors at levels that stimulated an adequate rate of returns to the merchants, while it tried to prevent the latter from swelling their profit margins. Merchants who paid collectors fees that differed from those set by NSWB had their contracts terminated (Z223/105 BBA DM, 6 August 1909).

Bottle merchants tried to exert countervailing bargaining power by forming an association that is mentioned in NSWB's records from 1909 to 1930, when it seems to have ceased operations. In any case, this organisation was too weak to prevent NSWB from conducting business with non-members (DM, 19 January 1923 and 11 April 1924).

NSWB paid different rates to merchants operating in specific geographic areas and particular market sectors partly in recognition of the distinct cost conditions they faced and partly in recognition of their bargaining power. Thus, McCarthy, who served Sydney hotels using a fleet of trucks and a large workforce, received a higher rate than small merchants who relied upon collectors to bring bottles to their yards. How NSWB prevented arbitraging is unknown. But overall it showed no willingness to make its actions more transparent in order to avoid recurrent haggling with merchants.

NSWB could not treat large operators, like B&N and McCarthy, in the same off-handed manner that it used when dealing with small merchants whom it could easily replace. Recognising that it had greater need for the services of these large firms, for which there were fewer substitution possibilities, NSWB set rates to protect these firms from incursions by smaller merchants (DM, 27 July 1923). Nevertheless, when McCarthy or B&N applied for a fee increase, they had to provide very detailed cost data. McCarthy complained that this information gave NSWB the capacity to determine what was a 'reasonable rate of profit' for the merchant (Z203/32 McCarthy to NSWB, 1 May 1967). In one instance, NSWB used this information to evaluate the possibility of running McCarthy's hotel trade itself, but decided not to do so. Overall, NSWB's dealings with large operators were characterised by hard bargaining.

Moreover, large operators had to obtain NSWB's permission to acquire other merchants' businesses. As a result, NSWB could control the size of their operations and their bargaining power (DM, 5 May and 18 August 1941).

Nevertheless, B&N and McCarthy grew large with NSWB's permission because they were efficient operators who provided valued service. Despite the growing strength of these firms only once did NSWB nest a contract with a large operator by loaning funds (DM, 20 April 1942).

Thus, until World War II, NSWB relied overwhelmingly on price incentives, which it manipulated arbitrarily, to stimulate returns and to contain the cost of recovering bottles through a chain of itinerant collectors and merchants. Its contracts with small merchants remained highly contingent. Although it obtained information about the operating costs and expansion plans of McCarthy and B&N, NSWB took no steps to develop reciprocal or wider information channels with them. Nor did it signal any interdependence with these firms even though they played key roles in the collection system. Consequently, NSWB remained vulnerable to any new conditions that might make unilateral control over price incentives inappropriate. After World War II, NSWB's recovery organisation was disrupted as declining bottle returns eroded the firm's profits and undermined the viability of B&N and McCarthy. NSWB belatedly tried to develop closer ties with all merchants and to devise new incentives.

Serious problems first arose in the 1950s when carters, bottle merchants, and glass makers encountered relentless cost increases, which they could pass on to NSWB under the provisions of the government price commission. Although NSWB raised its hiring fees, declining collections, especially from rural areas, forced it to buy large quantities of new bottles. In 1959 came the first sign that NSWB was starting to communicate in a meaningful way with constituents within its collection system.

That year, acting on NSWB's behalf, McCarthy surveyed the recovery organisation in NSW and recommended that differentials in collection fees be used systematically to provide an incentive function. In addition, McCarthy's hired a country representative, whose expenses NSWB agreed to share, to police bottle use and maintain 'a liaison between agents (merchants) and the company' (DM, 9 February 1959). This marked the first substantive attempt to draw upon complementary expertise from within the collection system. A suggestion from Randwick council that NSWB implement a deposit charge on bottles to encourage returns by final customers was apparently not acted upon (DM, 27 February 1961).

A series of financial losses suffered from 1963 to 1966 forced NSWB to undertake a comprehensive re-examination of its recovery procedures. The firm's records showed that the number of vessels lost in rural areas, where the breweries sold the most bottled beer, amounted to nearly twice that not retrieved in metropolitan Sydney. Although recovery rates fell in both areas, they remained persistently lower in the countryside (Z03/32 memo, 14 August 1967). A report by John Kenny, assistant to general manager G. Gray, proposed two solutions to the problem of deficient rural recoveries which were as low as seventeen per cent of sales made in some areas (Z203/32 memo, 11 July 1966). First, Kenny outlined a plan to appoint representatives to promote collections, to liase with local government, and to motivate merchants. The $72,000 cost of the scheme would be covered if returns could be increased from sixty-four to sixty-eight per cent of rural sales. If the representatives could boost recoveries to seventy-five per cent of state-wide sales, NSWB would save a staggering $800,000 per annum. Second, Kenny suggested an incentive programme whereby local merchants would get a one per cent increase in their fee on *all* bottles they recovered for each one per cent increase in collections above a minimum target. If the scheme achieved a seventy-five per cent recovery rate, NSWB would save nearly $0.5 million after allowing for the extra fees.

Kenny indicated that the programme might be difficult to implement because it required a detailed knowledge of sales in each merchant's territory. The cost-effectiveness of the representative scheme depended on how well the firm contained the associated administrative expenses. Kenny recommended a phased approach of first hiring the representatives, second, if this did not produce an adequate result, retaining the representatives and adding a moderate incentive fee, and third discontinuing the representatives' activities and raising the incentive payments to the maximum envisioned in his report. In effect, what Kenny outlined was an experiment to determine, while containing the cost to NSWB, whether improved communication channels, monetary incentives, or a combination of the two produced the best results.

In the event, the ingenuity of Kenny's plan was only partially appreciated by his superiors. NSWB went ahead with the representative scheme but allowed an across-the-board increase in the merchants' recovery fees without any incentive payment (Z203/32, 14 August 1967). Next, Kenny's manager, Gray, recommended an incentive payment that was modified to an increase in the fee plus an incentive payment on all bottles if merchants achieved a thirty per cent increase over the average quarterly returns recorded during the past three years (6 February 1968). Finally, Gray suggested that a system of zoning be put in place. Although it is not clear which of Gray's recommendations were adopted, his memos indicate that he did not fully appreciate the intent of Kenny's scheme, and collections did not improve sufficiently.

In 1969, NSWB's metropolitan collection system was thrown into disarray when B&N withdrew from the trade. The growing use of non-returnable containers and the assessment of income tax on dustmen who gathered bottles had reduced the volume of B&N's business to the extent that it was uneconomic to continue (Z203/29 B&N file, 3 September 1969). At a stroke, NSWB's Sydney organisation was deprived of seventeen of its thirty-four collection yards (Z203/32 memo, 23 February 1970).

NSWB convened a working committee including officials from the breweries to discuss a mass collection system that Brambles Ltd proposed to set up and run (Z203/32, 1 April 1970). However, the committee wished to preserve independent merchants 'rather than allow a situation to develop where Brambles dominated collections or where Brambles and McCarthys were the dominant collectors, as was formerly the case with Butler & Norman and McCarthys'. Fearing the possibility of a hold up or the effect of another major merchant withdrawing from the business, the committee decided to seek the views of a cross-section of merchants to determine how collections could be improved in the context of the existing organisation.

These consultations revealed that merchants needed higher fees, better supplies of trays, and improved service by carters. The committee agreed to raise fees and decided to discuss the situation with two cartage firms. From one of the carters, P. Field, the committee obtained a wealth of hitherto untapped expertise. Straight away, Field suggested that NSWB provide a much stronger incentive to stimulate bottle returns. Having been in the business for over thirty years, he stated that until recently there had been 'no real liaison' between NSWB and the merchants. As a remedy he proposed monthly 'round table' meetings between NSWB, merchants, and cartage firms. (As an indication of the low regard in which NSWB held the merchants, the latter upon visiting the firm's offices were not invited into the manager's office, but were left standing in the reception area.) Field criticised the slowness with which NSWB responded to requests for increased fees and for not giving reasons for its decisions. He also thought traffic handling at the breweries and the organisation of deliveries were both deficient. When Field proposed that the company form a large centralised collection yard for co-ordinating returns from the country and the city (NSWB's facility was too small), the committee requested him to consider whether he could form and operate such a facility (12 May 1970).

Field submitted a comprehensive report (Z203/32, no date) that hit upon the source of NSWB's problem: it lacked the means to consolidate bottles for delivery to the breweries. Owing to their location and size, B&N's yards had acted as nodes that served this purpose for a large part of the collection system; a logistical fact that apparently NSWB had not understood. McCarthy's yards were too small for the purpose. As a long-term solution, Field proposed that a 3- to 5-acre collection yard, equipped with cleaning and sorting facilities, be established and operated by an independent contractor. This arrangement would leave NSWB officials free to concentrate on policy, marketing, and co-ordinating, while the contractor could handle the distribution system at a lower cost using non-union labour.

Field argued that this framework would provide a suitable division of responsibilities, something which NSWB had never achieved even though TT had set up the firm as a separate unit to exploit decentralised initiatives:

> In all the years of my association with the company, it has never had efficient management. This has been the case for the managers have either been incapable or so fettered by the Directors or the employees of the breweries that they have become incapable.
>
> (Z203/32, no date)

Field suggested that the management of NSWB should be accountable only to its own board and deal with the breweries as supplier to clients. Overall, he proposed a new division of collection and marketing functions and for a more autonomous relationship between NSWB and TT. NSWB's records do not disclose what actions the firm took in light of Field's assessment. At this point, their attention was directed with some urgency to another quarter.

Perhaps sensing their advantage, McCarthy placed the entire system in jeopardy by threatening to discontinue operations unless NSWB raised its fees. NSWB's W. E. Graham stated 'I don't like McCarthy's attitude, but since we can hardly afford to lose the bottles they collect at this time' he recommended that NSWB meet the request. The firm caved in and gave McCarthy the increase he asked for.

Indeed, for the next few years, NSWB continued its established practice of negotiating rate changes with McCarthy and the other merchants. In 1974, the firm considered introducing an incentive scheme once more in response to a request from McCarthy for a higher fee (Z203/31nd, 1974). The plan established a monthly target (19,800 gross) on which McCarthy received a specific rate. NSWB agreed to pay progressively higher fees if returns exceeded the base target by specified increments. (To receive additional payment for any particular month, McCarthy had to have reached the target during the preceding month; this provision was designed to prevent the merchant from holding back deliveries from one month to win an extra payment the next month, as the Nickel Syndicate restrained purchases to increase its rebate.) The subtlety of the plan lay in the fact that although marginal costs rose rapidly, average costs rose more slowly and still represented a substantial saving over the cost of buying new bottles. Moreover, the additional payments were designed to be a substitute for the rate increase requested by McCarthy: achieving a recovery rate seventeen per cent above the target would yield the same increase that they had asked for under the old scheme. Finally, NSWB planned to adjust the monthly target in line with seasonal fluctuations in demand. The records do not confirm whether NSWB implemented the scheme, but McCarthy did begin withdrawing from the trade. NSWB considered buying the merchant's facilities but did not proceed (Z203/31, 26 March 1976, 27 January, and 3 May 1978, 24 February 1979, and 1 July 1980).

During the later 1970s, the firm applied a variation of this plan to twenty other merchants. Initially, NSWB gave the broader scheme a one-year trial. Yet, it reserved the right to discontinue an arrangement with any individual merchant. This tentative approach signalled NSWB's lack of commitment to an incentive-based system. In the absence of a determined effort by NSWB to build co-operative relations, bottle merchants continued to leave the industry.

After 1950, radical environmental change revealed deficiencies in NSWB's market-based inducements. The firm began to experiment with new incentives, but it did so in a half-hearted manner. NSWB's reluctance to act more decisively can be attributed perhaps to interference from TT but more fundamentally to patterns of behaviour that were conditioned by its long-term possession of preponderant market power over small bottle merchants. Its officials seemed to have resented the countervailing strength of larger operators and did not build interdependence with them. The history of NSWB's relations with the bottle merchants reveals how hard it can be to establish voice-based ties after an atmosphere of mistrust has been created by recurrent use of an exit strategy and contingent contracting. Profoundly adverse environmental conditions made the task more difficult at the same time that they made it imperative to change the nature of inter-firm relations.

Conclusion

In its general outline, NSWB's contracting chain resembled Japanese supplier frameworks. Both combined multiple sourcing, internal competition or market tests, and some investment ties. However, whereas NSWB's agreements with various constituents exhibit interesting features (some of which were clever and others that created weaknesses), the firm did not establish a suitable mix of contractual elements. Overwhelmingly it relied on detailed specification and monitoring devices. The key ingredient missing from NSWB's chain was a cultural bond that could engender a comprehensive spirit of interdependence. At each link in the chain, NSWB failed to develop and maintain the necessary two-way communication lines. (Nor did it create a forum like the one Field suggested or those established by the *keiretsu*, JWT, and B&W.) Without a strong inter-organisational communicating infrastructure, NSWB lacked the means, similar to those developed by USS and the HSS network, to mobilise lower-level knowledge. Without timely access to vital logistical expertise, such as that commanded by McCarthy and Field, NSWB could not in an anticipatory way respond to environmental conditions that threatened the entire chain. Nor did NSWB use the power inherent in its position to develop effective communication channels. Instead of using its strength in a creative or even a restrained manner to signal that it invited trust, it exercised its power overtly, and, as bottle merchants in particular could observe, in an arbitrary way. The resulting legacy of mistrust created rigidities and left the firm without the means to respond effectively when the pace and degree of environmental change suddenly increased. Without the type of long-term perspective on inter-organisational relations that communication and co-operation can create, short-term commercial dependence alone determined the opportunity cost of affiliation. Yet, as the next chapter shows, in some contexts, contingent relations and a culture that reveres opportunism can support discrete, project-based ventures.

12 Hollywood networks, 1970–99

Film makers' networks provide a series of contrasts with those analysed in earlier chapters. The contractual forms, the communication channels, and the prevailing culture are unique. The peculiarities of Hollywood contracting have cost a series of uninitiated investors billions of dollars.

Movie making involves linking specialised talent with investment capital needed to support production and distribution. Like other knowledge-based businesses, the film industry relies on people who have production experience and the strategic capacity to provide new products (or images, in the case of actors) that meet rapidly changing patterns of demand (Powell 1990: 308–9). In film companies, administrative officials face high levels of uncertainty concerning what ingredients make a movie successful, and so they are compelled to delegate responsibility for production to creative executives (Hirsh 1972: 644). In formal terms, creative personnel possess specialised, tacit knowledge, and given the project-based character of the industry, they work under temporary contracts for different production units (firms or individuals). Harnessing such talent and wedding it to investment capital is a formidable challenge.

Film makers face high fixed costs in producing and distributing movies, and they must meet these expenses before any revenue flows in. Average negative costs (the cost of a completed film ready for printing) rose from $9.4 million in 1980 to $52.7 million in 1998. During the same period, average theatrical distribution costs (the expense of making prints and advertising) escalated from $4.2 to $25.3 million (MPAA, March 1999). Advertising costs alone soared from $3.5 to $22.1 million per picture as movie firms increasingly promote directly to the final consumer; moreover, each product must be publicised individually. The risk of failure is high, and audience response is hard to predict. 'Flops' are immediate and visible.

Since the difficulties involved in contracting with talent and supporting production and distribution are so daunting, we might expect that, within Williamson's (1975, 1985) framework, a high degree of uncertainty would result in market failure. Yet, the industry successfully finesses the contracting problem and delivers a growing stream of movies [233 in 1980 and 509 in 1998 (MPAA, March 1999)]. It does so, not by using market mechanisms, but by relying on networks.

Faulkner and Anderson's (1987) study of 2,430 films made between 1965 and 1980 revealed the operation of networks characterised by repeat dealing among elite directors, producers, and cinematographers. Faulkner and Anderson show how individuals with strong track records create informal webs and how successes reinforce these constructs. Talent that performs poorly gets marginalised.

Faulkner and Anderson (1987) identified only the top segment of the networks that permeate the film industry. There is also a spectrum of low to middle level webs that harness other talent and technical specialists. In financing, ties among brokerages, banks, insurance firms, and other investors are important. Distribution chains include different combinations of participants. Contracts among all these parties are interdependent. Moreover, shifts in technology, distribution outlets, and sources of capital have caused contracting patterns to change almost continuously since 1980.

Behind these networks, a rating system, based upon highly visible awards and financial performance, supports the formation of operating links. This system is also embedded in a hierarchy of contractual arrangements that distribute rewards with acute asymmetry. These agreements unfold within a low-trust, litigious, high-stress culture. Participants observe zero sum perspectives, collective memory is short, and opportunism is expected. As a reflection of these cultural forces, the industry-specific terminology used in agreements serves to conceal contracting processes from outsiders and to reinforce an artificial but very necessary hierarchical reward structure. For our purposes, these contractual gradients, their supporting terminology, and systems for reputation rating provide, on an exclusive basis to 'insiders', the information needed to reduce uncertainty surrounding the transactions that sustain film-making operations. The following sections examine in sequence, producer networks, contractual forms, distribution, and finance.

Producer networks: context, mobility, and rating

The image of wheeling and dealing in Hollywood is not far from reality. Effecting display and socialising at the city's numerous fora can lead to an entrée. Once entry has been secured, participants build track records and develop wider contacts. Getting a 'break' may be difficult, but it happens. Jon Peters began as a hairdresser, became Barbra Streisand's lover, and emerged as a joint head of Columbia (Griffin and Masters 1996). The huge rewards stemming from 'making it' constantly replenishes a pool of prospective participants. Who are the players?

The *executive producer* (acting as an independent contractor or working for a studio) arranges the business side of film making, in particular financing and distribution. Next, the *producer* selects the script and hires the principal talent (director, cinematographer, and the main actors). *Talent agents* often assemble and sell packages, including talent, a script, and director, but increasingly studios put together combinations themselves. The *director* is responsible for all creative aspects of the project and for observing the producer's budget constraints. The *cinematographer* plans the sequence of film shots. The *screenwriter* produces the story, which becomes a screenplay giving the layout of the sets, actors' movements, and the lines. The *actors* include stars ('A' talent) supporting players ('B' talent), those who play minor roles, and 'extras'.

The main participants have sub-networks of trusted specialists with whom they have worked before. Producers (firms or individuals) have a range of business contacts, whereas directors have ties with particular actors and cinematographers. Cinematographers maintain ongoing relationships with chief camera men and set designers. Technical supervisors have sets of specialists with whom they work (McGuiness 1999). Thus, members of the elite cadre analysed by Faulkner and Anderson (1987) and other parties act as intermediaries who mobilise other personnel. Indeed, the quality of these principal contractors' connections, as well as their own particular skills, in part makes them attractive as members of the main network.

What makes three figures – directors, actors, and cinematographers – crucial, however, is their ability to attract an audience and generate sales. Directors, who are more important to audiences in Europe than in the US, acquire reputations based not only on their drawing power but also on their ability to make films on time and according to budget, thereby increasing the chance that profits will be made. Their track records are also important to independent producers because they are advantageous in arranging pre-sales (raising money to make the movie by selling distribution rights in advance) and completion bonds (see p. 218) (*The Hollywood Reporter,* 20–26 October 1998). Well-known directors also attract cinematographers and star actors, both of whom can boost revenues and facilitate financing. Thus, contracts between talent, distributors, and producers are linked.

Yet, star actors and directors, in particular, command large fees which push up costs and increase the risk that a film will not be profitable. Thus, producers face a trade-off between these fees and the pulling power, in terms of financing and sales, of these participants. Some take the view that 'A' stars reduce risk, while others hire new talent to keep costs low and to limit downside risk; if a film becomes a hit, the upside potential is immense. Pursuing a hybrid strategy, Eisner, after taking over at Disney in 1984, used his directors' contacts to hire well-known actors who had fallen out of favour, were anxious to revive their careers, and accepted modest fees. Thus, while there are ways to limit risk, informal links are crucial in assembling interrelated contracts.

Networks are formed in a variety of ways. Anecdotal evidence indicates that prospective members establish a presence in Hollywood venues and that third parties provide introduction services. The large number of relatives of successful figures (for example, the Fondas and Julia Roberts) suggests that newcomers can gain entrance using family reputations and contacts. Talent agents also provide intermediary services. At Disney, producers and talent drew on contacts that they had made working for other studios (Grover 1991). Dreamworks, an independent film-producing firm, was set up by Spielberg (ex-Universal), Geffen (ex-MCA/Universal), and Katzenberg (ex-Disney), all of whom had previously worked together. Many actors have capitalised on their names and contacts by setting themselves up as directors and then producers. Thus, network formation is shaped by patterns of upward and sideways mobility.

Anecdotal sources reveal the dynamics of downward mobility in Hollywood. Although an individual's standing is based on his/her long-term track records, the adage that 'you're only as good as your last credit' still holds with some qualification. All parties gain reputation by being associated with a successful movie. One 'flop' does not, however, impair a participant's career. But, being affiliated with a series of three or more unsuccessful films can badly damage one's contracting possibilities as the power to attract an audience recedes, contacts dry up, and successful allies distance themselves. It is unusual for 'A' stars to recover premier status after a few failures have relegated them to 'B' stature. John Travolta is a notable exception.

Jerry Weintraub's difficulties at WEG reveals important aspects of the Hollywood culture (Lowell 1999). Confirming that 'anyone can make it', Weintraub started out working in the mail room at a talent agency and became a music promoter. He was hired as chief executive of United Artists and then fired for allegedly not consulting with the board. After this setback Weintraub had sufficient funds and contacts to set up his own studio, WEG. After a series of flops, industry gossip came out into the open: Weintraub's management style was criticised, his ambitions were characterised as grandiose, and the chattels he used for self-publicity were interpreted as tasteless display. Finally, a columnist hinted he was involved in drug use. Although a few people expressed confidence in Weintraub, the gleeful reaction to his difficulties shows a vindictive dimension to Hollywood's contracting culture. Rather than closing ranks, as the shipping community did when Lord Kylsant fell on hard times (Davies 1981), some in the film fraternity derived gratification from Weintraub's problems. Nevertheless, after WEG failed, Weintraub's contacts saved him: he set up as an independent producer working with Warner Brothers. The episode also reveals the operation of a variety of reputational arbiters.

The function of rating participants in film productions is carried out by a variety of institutions. These include Star Power and Director Power, which quantitatively rank the financial performances of actors and directors each year, Academy of Motion Picture Arts & Sciences, the Directors Guild, and others. Film reviewers assess artistic performance while gossip columnists play a role in shaping public images. Finally, there is 'street talk' that circulates informally among people in the industry and sometimes provides timely clues of developments in progress before these become public knowledge. Frequenting Hollywood venues provides access to this type of information, and having the capacity to filter the vast quantity of it accurately can yield contracting advantages.

Contracts

Actors, directors, and producers with good track records can negotiate potentially lucrative contingent compensation contracts that serve a private rating function. Based on a share of either gross revenues or net profits generated by a film, these agreements can also provide the funds needed to support upward mobility; for example, from actor to director to producer. Those who rise through these ranks secure greater creative control as well as more influence over the financing of a film and the distribution of rewards. But this was not always the case.

In the heyday of the studio system, before 1956, actors were hired on an exclusive basis and received a weekly or per-picture salary. Performers had little say about which films they appeared in and were lent or rented out by their studio to others. In effect, the studios controlled their career development.

During the industry recession from 1946 to 1956, which was caused by the spread of TV and a reduction in discretionary expenditure due to high rates of household formation, the 'star system' declined as studios cut overheads by avoiding long-term contracts with talent (Balio 1987: 319, 376–7). Increasingly, the studios arranged agreements that offered actors potentially high contingent payments but compelled them to share risks. For example, in 1950, Universal paid Jimmy Stewart one-half of the net profits earned by *Winchester 73* instead of his usual fee of $250,000 per picture. Thus, to reduce its risk, the studio transformed a fixed cost into a variable expense.

The decline of the star system and the MCA consent decree of 1962 also afforded talent agents greater scope for selling talent and they began to use this new-found power to package scripts, actors, and directors for sale to the studios (Balio 1987: 78). This practice continued into the 1980s, when Michael Ovitz, head of CAA, wielded tremendous power, but increasingly the studios did their own packaging to enhance their flexibility (Grover 1991: 29, 105). In the mid-1980s, competition for talent intensified as independent producers proliferated and as the spread of cable TV and video increased the demand for programming. Studios had to offer stars more attractive deals.

Today, the forms of participative contracts, listed from the most remunerative to the least, are:

1 Gross deals: participation in the gross receipts less 'off-the-top' deductions (taxes, trade dues, and advance payments made to all gross participants)
2 'From the first dollar': participation after off-the-top deductions but before the studio takes its distribution fee and recoups its distribution expenses.
3 'Gross after breakeven' A: participation after the studio has recovered a multiple of a film's negative costs (usually 2.5 or 3 times).
4 'Gross after breakeven' B: participation begins after the studio takes part of its distribution fee (for example, twenty per cent of gross receipts instead of the full thirty to thirty-five per cent usually charged), or before

it deducts the usual ten per cent overhead on advertising or the normal fifteen per cent overhead on production costs.

5   'Gross after actual breakeven': participation after the film starts to earn 'net profits', that is after the multiple of negative cost and distribution charges and fees have been covered.

6   Net profit deals: participation after the studio deducts any further expenses after the film has broken even. This type of deal is vulnerable to cost escalations that cause the breakeven point to 'roll' ('Declaration of Defendant' Superior Court of the State of California C706083, 1990, *Hollywood Reporter,* 17 August 1992).

Deals structured so that the break-even point recedes (a 'rolling break') may result in parties with net profit contracts receiving no contingent compensation. *Batman* earned $253 million in gross revenue but showed an overall deficit of $35.8 million. Net participants Benjamin Meiniker and Michael Uslan, who came up with the idea for the film, did not share in its great success (*New York Times*, 21 March 1991). Indeed, no matter how much the movie earns it is unlikely to generate a net profit.

A 'rolling break' occurs in contracts that allot to stars a larger share of gross receipts as specific targets are met. Thus, Jack Nicholson secured fifteen per cent of the gross, rising to twenty per cent after revenue from *Batman* reached a certain level. Another contributing factor is the studio's practice of charging interest on the full production cost, including escalating payments to gross participants. Finally, clauses allowing distribution costs to escalate also push back the break-even point.

Just because a movie does not generate net revenue does not mean that it is unprofitable for the studio. Doug Lowell has developed a model showing a hypothetical case in which a movie earns over $39 million in gross revenue but shows a net revenue loss. Yet, the studio netted over $8 million for itself (Table 12.1).

In addition to the allocations depicted in the Lowell model, studios may have hidden profit centres to which gains arising from production and distribution are allocated. Substantial profits are buried in the studio's distribution fee that may be excessive. Other earnings arise from the allocation of, for example, just twenty per cent of the income from video to gross revenue, whereas the remaining eighty per cent (some of which represents profit) is allotted to the studio's video division. Often imputed overhead expenses are set against individual films; most of these costs include a profit margin. Studios may also profit from the interest charges they levy on a movie since these are tied to total production costs. Thus, before arriving at a net revenue figure, the studio has levied multiple charges against production and distribution in order to cover costs associated with the film as well as direct and indirect overheads. From these sources, the studio can derive large cash receipts before determining the net revenues in which it, along with other net players, share.

Table 12.1 Revenues and costs (showing points at which gross and net participation begin) for a hypothetical film (Douglas Lowell)

Reported revenue		Studio revenue	
Domestic box office	$30,000,000	Box office	$20,000,000
Rental rate	*45%*	Home video units	200,000
Theatrical receipts	$13,500,000	*Home video revenue*	*$6,500,000*
Home video (net)	$5,200,000	Home video costs	$1,300,000
Cable	$3,675,000	*Net home video*	*$5,200,000*
Free television	$3,770,000		
International (net)	$13,000,000		
Non-theatrical	$300,000		
Total revenues	$39,445,000[a]		
Distribution fee	$6,696,750	Studio keeps	
Remainder	*$32,748,250*	Distribution fee	$6,696,750
Prints and advertising	$18,000,000	Marketing overhead	$1,800,000
Remainder	*$14,748,250*	Interest costs	$2,900,000
Residuals	$626,000	Soft costs	$500,000
Remainder	*$14,122,250*	Studio revenues	$11,896,750
Production cost	$10,000,000		
Remainder	*$4,122,250*		
Marketing overhead costs	*$1,800,000*	Studio costs	
Remainder	*$2,322,250*	Interest costs	$2,610,000
Interest	$2,900,000	Soft costs	$450,000
	($577,750)	Overhead	$720,000
Soft costs	$500,000		
Net receipts	($1,077,750)[b]	Net studio	$8,116,750

Notes
Losses shown in parentheses.
[a]Gross participation starts here.
[b]Net participation starts here.

Defenders of the system point out that not all films fail to generate net receipts. Also, they argue that studios charge a percentage for overheads because these expenses cannot be allocated precisely to individual films (C706083). They contend further that the distribution fee is used partly to cross-subsidise films that really do lose money, and studios must generate a stream of movies – some of which are unprofitable – to maintain access to theatre outlets. Similarly, contingent compensation deals also spread the risk involved in film making.

The formulae used to compute gross and net profits are, according to M. Sattler, 'creatures of contract' associated with a language and a set of conventions peculiar to the industry (C706083). As S. Finger put it:

> 'net profits' and 'gross receipts' when incorporated into a distribution agreement acquire definitions at total variance with the common understanding of these terms by accountants and the financial

community. Thus, such words are merely labels. These terms as specially
defined ... [refer to] simply arithmetic calculations that vary from
transaction to transaction.

(UCCA Entertainment Law Symposium, 1977)

Despite the tendency to define these calculations differently in each contract,
Sattler contends that the terminology is universally understood: definitions
and calculations reflect 'industry custom and practice'.

If Sattler's views are correct and all participants are familiar with the
meaning of terms, methods of calculation, and contract structures, why have
there been a significant number of law suits? The fact that terms used in the
industry do not correspond to recognised accounting concepts makes contracts
vulnerable to opportunistic arguments that a party was misled. There may
have been genuine instances of bad faith, as the judge in the Buchwald case
deemed. (In this instance, the famous columnist was a Hollywood 'outsider'
and knowing he would never be involved in film making again he had nothing
to lose by litigating, whereas an 'insider's' career would be ruined by suing a
producer.) In addition, the increasing use of gross revenue deals to attract
top stars may induce litigation.

To counter the argument that net profit participants can be disadvantaged
when studios afterwards make gross deals with other parties, Sattler argues
that the belated inclusion of a top talent can augment a film's entire revenue
stream and that net participants may thereby derive greater gains. Sattler
again cites 'common understanding' within the industry. He contends that
since studios accept most of the risks, they must exercise control over all
deals connected with a project. Moreover, the cost of arranging interrelated
contracts among a large number of parties and making *ex post* adjustments to
each deal to accommodate later agreements would give rise to prohibitively
high transaction costs. He also argues that there are 'very real constraints'
on studios in granting gross profit deals that might reduce the level of net
profits in which the studios themselves participate. The studio must balance
this consideration with the need to offer gross deals to attract top talent that
can boost gross receipts and ultimately net profits. The studio directly bears
some of the consequences if it miscalculates.

Contingent remuneration contracts serve many purposes. First, the
industry-specific nature of the underlying conventions may expedite deal
making by furnishing a 'short-hand' of sorts that speeds up communication
and by offering models that can be employed off the shelf or adapted as
required. Second, these agreements may be useful in obscuring the financial
performance of films to outsiders. Third, for those within the industry these
deals support mutual monitoring and act as ranking devices. For these reasons,
such long-standing precedents are resistant to change from within the
industry. Fourth, it may be that these contractual forms offer flexibility and
wide scope for sequential adjustment, features that are important given the
project-based nature of the business.

Distribution

In the 1930s, Warner Brothers, MGM, Paramount, 20th Century Fox, and RKO produced films in their own studios, controlled distribution channels, and owned or were allied to theatre chains. Vertical integration ensured the big five access to exhibition and thus reduced risk. In 1948, the Paramount Decrees forced the majors to detach themselves from theatre chains, but they retained their distribution operations. Today, the major studios are Sony-owned Columbia, Disney, Seagram's Universal, Viacom's Paramount, MGM/ United Artists (UA), News Corp-owned 20th Century Fox, and Time Warner. All of the majors are parts of entertainment conglomerates that include some combination of publishing, cable or network TV, and music recording. Since the government relaxed the restraints over theatre ownership by the studios in the 1980s, several, including Paramount and Universal, have acquired stakes in theatre companies. There are also a large number of individuals and firms that independently produce films. (Formed in 1919, UA, was the first true independent.)

Independents and major studios differ in several ways. First, independents allow greater scope for creativity and thus tend to produce more adventurous or unusual films that can become huge hits. The studios exert close, sometimes stifling, control over artistic processes. (For example, Universal bought independently made *Babe*, which became a large hit, but failed to generate the same appeal with the sequel *Babe, Pig in the City*, which it made in-house.) Second, studios have closer ties with talent, including in-house writers, directors, and producers, whereas independents use creative people on a freelance basis. Third, studios use equity against which they can borrow to finance film production: their main challenge is to limit balance sheet debt. Independents usually have little or no equity against which to borrow and therefore pre-sell their movies to finance production. Finally, studios possess distribution arms and have much better access to theatres because they spend heavily on advertising, hold films that, through talent, genre or sequels, will generate substantial box office receipts, and have ownership ties to exhibitors. (For example, Warners allegedly compelled theatres to advance it fifty per cent of the fees generated by *Batman* in order to obtain *Batman Returns*.) Independents lack this type of power. This section compares the distribution operations of studios and independents using Disney and New Line as examples.

Disney

Under Michael Eisner, Disney has increased annual production from about four films to between twenty-four and thirty (Grover 1991). As it did so, it had to achieve wider distribution while restraining associated costs. A wide movie release (2,000–4,000 screens) costs on average $20 million in print and advertising costs, whereas a moderate release (300–800 screens) can cost as little as $4–7 million (Lowell 1999). As a diversified entertainment company, Disney has many ways of reducing risk while containing advertising costs by cross-promoting its movies. Indeed, it creates tie-ins with Mattel and McDonalds to promote cartoon characters, including Roger Rabbit, Dick Tracy, and the Little Mermaid, from its movies. The same characters and concepts from other films are used as themes for rides at the firm's amusement parks and for its hotels, thereby creating linked advertising. The Disney TV channel, the Sunday night show *Wonderful World of Disney*, and more recently its purchase of the ABC TV network all provide reinforcing promotion. Moreover, producing sequels, series, and remakes – all proven ways of reducing risk – enables Disney to use recognition by Baby Boomers to tap demand from the Echo Boom generation.

Disney also aggressively exploits ancillary markets to generate publicity and wider distribution. It has a music unit that makes and sells soundtracks from its films. Disney mines its vast film library at little cost by producing videos of its classic movies and cartoons. In order to exploit its synergistic operations into the retail market to recover retailers' margins and improve the effectiveness of its promotional effort, the firm has opened its own highly profitable stores to sell merchandise based on its films. A mail order unit has been set up as well as theme restaurants. The Disney MGM Studios Theme Park serves cross-promotion purposes, and EuroDisney helps the firm expand foreign markets for its films, merchandise, music, and video business.

Independents do not have this type of distribution and promotional muscle, but they often generate better film concepts. To avoid spoiling its image, Disney set up Touchstone Pictures and acquired Miramax Films as studio-controlled quasi-independents to make and acquire art-house films and more adventurous movies. These firms provide Disney with financial benefits, and their movies help its distribution arm win scale economies.

Independents: New Line

Without distribution arms, true independents (as opposed to those controlled by studios) can (1) secure studio distribution support, (2) use independent distributors, or (3) arrange pre-sales. (If they can finance production without pre-sales, they may sell a film outright to a studio as 'a negative pick-up'.) To put New Line into perspective, we need to lay out what is entailed in pursuing each option.

The major studios command eighty-five per cent of US box office sales, and therefore offer independents the best potential theatrical exposure (Prindle 1993: 31). However, the studio will charge up to thirty-five per cent of receipts for its distribution fee, thereby cutting heavily into the independent's potential profits. Independent producers, whether persons or firms, with links to studios occupy positions within a hierarchy of arrangements, the steps of which also serve to rate producers and the people in their networks.

Foremost is a 'put picture' deal in which the studio guarantees to make a movie proposed by the producer. Mel Gibson secured such an arrangement to make a sequel to *Lethal Weapon*.

In a 'pay-or-play' agreement, the studio contracts to pay a substantial fee to a producer whether or not it decides to make one of his or her films.

A 'multiple submission development deal' compels a producer to submit over a period of time a specified number of proposals, one of which the studio agrees to develop and for which it pays the producer a fee.

Under a 'first look' arrangement, the studios contribute to producers overheads on the understanding that they will present their concepts to the studio first. The studio will fund development only if it finds the concept attractive; if it does not, it is not obliged to pay a fee.

The form of payment varies according to the producer's stature; the producer may receive a modest fixed payment, or participation in gross or net profits. The nature of the contract that the producer can negotiate will determine the extent to which the producer participates in the profits generated if the project becomes a hit.

Since studios have such a large share of domestic box office sales, producers who try to use independent distributors are unlikely to secure access to the best screens because they are at a competitive disadvantage relative to the studios' better financed and more effectively designed marketing campaigns. Moreover, they sacrifice profits by paying a heavy distribution fee. In recent years, the number of independent distributors has dwindled with the disappearance of Orion, De Laurentiis, and Cannon, leaving few outlets of this type.

The third option for independent producers is to pre-sell a movie, before making it, to one or more of the following: home video outlets, pay or cable TV companies, television networks, domestic and foreign theatrical distribution firms. (These contracts allow for instalment payments and provide collateral for arranging bank loans that will be used to finance the production.) However, the use of pre-sales presents a conundrum. These contracts are contingent upon gaining domestic theatrical release supported by strong (and costly) promotion. If a producer cannot secure studio support for theatrical distribution at home, his pre-sale contracts will become worth a great deal less. Moreover, by arranging pre-sales, producers usually reduce their chances of securing studio distribution because the majors often demand all distribution rights before they will participate. If the film's potential was not attractive enough to win a studio's interest in the first place, its chances of winning studio support will be much lower after pre-sales have diminished its revenue-generating capacity. Using pre-sales to secure distribution (and to finance production) is difficult but not impossible. However, recent changes in ancillary markets have reduced revenue and pre-sale opportunities (see p. 216).

New Line broke through the distribution constraints facing independent film companies. In 1984, it made a low-budget, quirky movie, as independents often do. *Nightmare on Elm Street* cost just a few million dollars and was sold through some pre-sales internationally and exhibited in the US through independent distributors. Through these outlets the movie came out as a 'narrow release' (it appeared in a few theatres and attracted viewers by word of mouth) to become a surprise hit with over $20 million in domestic box office receipts. The sequel was another inexpensive production that was distributed in the same way, and with an established audience it generated about $26 million. On the strength of these successes, the firm made a public share offer and used the proceeds to set up its own US distribution unit. It produced and distributed *Nightmare on Elm Street Part Three: Dream Warriors* itself and made over $40 million at the box office. In 1990, New Line departed from its policy of making low-budget movies. At roughly double the cost of the *Nightmare* series, it produced two flops, *The Hidden* and *Heart Condition*. Recovery came with a return to low-budget production: *House Party* brought in about $26 million. Then, New Line hit the jackpot with *Teenage Mutant Ninja Turtles*, which made over $120 million in US box office receipts. Success attracted suitors, and the firm was taken over by Ted Turner and ended up in the Time Warner group. Between 1984 and 1990, New Line achieved a return on investment of about twenty per cent a year, a unique record for a firm in the high-risk independent sector. The basis of its success lay in the ability to make unusual films that attracted strong followings and could support sequential hits and in creating distribution networks that allowed it to retain fees (but which also offered a tempting asset for potential acquirers). Keeping production and distribution costs low was also vital. The combination of the two factors enabled the firm to solve the conundrum facing independents and achieve remarkably high returns.

During the 1980s, changes in distribution created strong growth in film output and wider opportunities for independents to arrange pre-sales (see Table 12.2). The most salient development of the decade was the pronounced relative decline in the importance of theatrical rentals from eighty to just thirty per cent of total revenue and the corresponding growth of ancillary markets such as cable TV and home video. Late in the decade, foreign markets became increasingly important (*New York Times*, 28 September 1987). At the same time, mergers involving major studios, theatre chains, and TV networks restricted the domestic distribution options of independents.

In the late 1980s and early 1990s, patterns of contracting adjusted as Europe in particular provided a booming market after the expansion of TV networks through privatisation and the growth of video and cable sectors. The relative inexpensiveness and high production quality of US films enabled them to gain a strong presence in these sectors. By 1990, foreign theatrical, video, and TV sales amounted to thirty-eight per cent of total sales that had reached $13.1 billion.

The boom in foreign sales enabled firms with films targeted specifically to this audience to raise 100 per cent of their negative costs through foreign pre-sales, whereas domestic pre-sales could generate only thirty-five to forty

Table 12.2 Market sectors 1980–98

	US box office ($)	Films released	Video penetration (%)	Video sales ($)	Cable penetration	Cable sales ($)
1980	2.75 bn	233	1.9	136.0 m	17.6 m	NA
1990	5.02 bn	462	70.2	10.4 bn	54.9 m	1.2 bn
1998	6.95 bn	509	84.6	14.0 bn (1994)	67.0 m	20 bn (1996)

Sources: Standard & Poor's 'Movies & Home Entertainment', 27 February 1997; MPAA, March 1999.

Notes
Video penetration refers to percentage of US households having VCRs.
Cable penetration refers to number of US household subscriptions.

per cent (*The Hollywood Reporter,* 23 February 1993). Buoyant offshore sales also created an opening for new companies to specialise in exporting US films made by independents (*New York Times,* 28 September 1987). Thus, Filmstar made a public offering of equity to raise funds, which it used to pay producers for pre-sales agreements tied to overseas distribution. In this way, the firm offered the services of both a financial and distributing intermediary specifically to independents.

Recently, independents have faced a further squeeze as the Asian crisis and currency instability have reduced foreign sales. Moreover, as European TV operations have matured, they have begun making their own low- to medium-budget programmes and relying on the US major studios for fewer, higher-quality films. The independents' problems are aggravated further by increasing production and distribution costs and new challenges in their domestic markets.

At home, more mergers among cable, video firms, studios, and TV networks have left fewer outlets for the independents. Domestic box office continues growing in absolute terms, but relative to cable it is becoming less important. Blockbuster, now linked with Viacom Inc. and Paramount Communications, disturbed this key sector by using its market power to halve the price paid for video cassettes by creating revenue-sharing schemes (Lowell 1999). This development has flooded the market with new titles. Moreover, distributors receive minor up-front payments, a share of rental revenue, and a small guaranteed back-end payment up to twelve months later. These arrangements have seriously affected independents, who lacking studio release have trouble generating sufficient consumer awareness to promote video sales, and who now must also wait up to twelve months to secure video revenues that previously were due up front on delivery to the video chains. At the same time, the expansion of the cable business has slowed as more modest growth in new subscriptions induces providers to scale back their bids for outside programming. New technology, such as digital video disks, satellite transmission systems, and the Internet, may provide fresh outlets for the independents.

Finance

As we have seen, the financing options for studios and independents differ. The former have a large equity base, film libraries, and other assets against which they can borrow, but they must limit balance sheet debt. Because they have larger resources – augmented further since their inclusion in the giant entertainment conglomerates – studios can spread their risks over a relatively large number of films. Independents lack significant collateral and rely heavily on pre-sales combined with various credit facilities to support operations. However, distribution expenses as well as interest and fund-raising costs reduce the profit potential of their films. Without extensive resources, independents cannot make the large portfolios of films that are needed to diversify risk. A short string of failures will bring bankruptcy. Still, like New Line, they may be able to stay afloat by juggling financing options long enough to bring in a hit that will secure their position. This section examines the financial dimension of film networks by exploring the changing roles of completion bond firms, banks and brokerages, as well as insurance companies.

Completion bond companies

Completion bond firms are an integral part of independent film producers' networks. These institutions guarantee that the filming of a movie will be completed. The bond is vital to independent producers (the majors guarantee their own films) because it provides a guarantee for pre-sales contracts that act as collateral for bank loans. Without a completion bond a producer will not be able to arrange pre-sales and to borrow to finance filming (*The Hollywood Reporter*, 28 June 1993).

Completion bond firms operate as follows. For a fee ranging from one to eight per cent of a film's production budget, these companies ensure that a film will be made. If a production comes in on budget, the bond firm usually rebates half of its fee. Should a director overrun projected negative costs by more than ten per cent, the bond company will provide the funds needed to finish filming. (Completion bond firms also meet costs that arise because a film is delivered to distributors late.) The bond firm may induce the director to modify scenes to contain further expenditure or expedite filming, and in extreme cases it will replace a director. The completion bond company will have a first claim on the film's earnings to recoup its expenses, and to reduce exposure further it re-insures with Lloyd's of London. Thus, the bond firm plays a key role in supporting an extended chain of contractual links running from the film producer, to banks, distributors, Lloyd's, and other insurance firms.

The successful negotiation of a completion bond and the size of the fee paid depends to a large extent on the reputation of the film director. Bond companies act as a safeguard against opportunists who might deliberately underfund projects. They charge high fees or completely avoid directors who are temperamental, habitually late in finishing movies, or lack a track record. Thus, the contract between a producer and the director is interdependent with the string of agreements with distributors, banks, and bond companies.

However, the relationship between the bond firm and the producer may run deeper than a guarantor–client link. Completion bond companies provide consulting and problem-solving services as well as a monitoring function. For example, at the beginning of a film project the bond company appoints a representative (sometimes a former director) to examine product plans and offer advice, thereby disseminating knowledge of more efficient techniques. When difficulties arise, completion bond firms act as problem solvers for producers and directors. However, if a bond company assumes control of a film, the reputations of participants suffer, and the future viability of the production and talent networks is undermined.

The survival of the completion bond sector itself became problematic in the early 1990s as a result of a series of large claims, intense competition, and the financial problems encountered by Lloyd's of London. As bond firms refused to guarantee movies above a specific budget, independents faced severe financial constraints. While the completion bond business has returned to stability, the events of the early 1990s highlighted the critical role that these firms play in supporting independents' chains of contracts, the mutual monitoring activities that sustain deal making, and the pre-sale agreements on which bank borrowing depends.

Banks and brokerage houses

Historically, banks have lent mainly to studios, a relatively low-risk, low-profit operation, because these clients furnish security and because the interest they can charge is close to market rates. Risk was reduced further by high-quality information that flowed through close links between studio executives and long-serving bank officials. For example, just two people ran the Bank of Boston's entertainment unit from 1926 to 1983, and Bank of America management had great continuity, which in part explains a fifty-year link it had with Disney.

In the mid-1980s, studios contained balance sheet debt by creating quasi-independent companies that issued equity to support bank loans. For example, Disney and the Betts interests set up Silver Screen as a limited partnership and provided equity against which the venture could borrow. Silver Screen had the additional attraction of enabling Disney to reduce its risk, generate distribution business, and secure payments for its overheads (Grover 1991: 92–3). In 1989, when Japanese funds were flooding into Hollywood, Disney arranged another limited partnership supported by a consortium of banks.

Again, the debt did not appear on Disney's balance sheet and inflate its leverage (Grover 1991: 234–5).

In the mid-1980s, banks displayed a growing tendency to offer more support to independent film companies. The shift in the direction of lending was brought about in part by a decline in demand for facilities from the majors that were making large profits and had other financing options as a result of affiliation with entertainment conglomerates. Bank deregulation also facilitated the shift in lending focus. Another factor that made independents more attractive as creditors was the injection of equity capital during the stock market boom. (Until 1986, the availability of US tax incentives that assisted film making also attracted funds to the industry.) Before October 1987, Wall Street brokers supported independents that required an amount of capital large enough to support the brokerage fees, accounting costs, and legal expenses. However, by 1990 this source of funds had dried up as brokers' information lines proved to be inadequate.

Developing business ties to firms below the studio level required the banks and brokers to establish sound information channels and strong personal ties. Despite the learning and time costs involved, lending to non-studio companies was very profitable because the banks charged high fees and interest rates to cover a significant risk premium. The banks' staff costs were low as long as their clients performed well and required little monitoring. In 1987, however, banks that had lent to independents found that a number of clients encountered financial difficulties and absorbed large amounts of the bank officials' time. Staff turnover rates in the banks' entertainment divisions also rose markedly as a result of higher salaries offered elsewhere, with the result that the banks' information channels were disrupted when they were most urgently needed. Moreover, as more banks tried to rein in borrowing, some clients switched to other institutions and thus dislocated links between clients and agent banks and ties among members of lending consortia. By the early 1990s, the poor performance of the film industry and the withdrawal of Credit Lyonnaise, once the leading lender to independents, following the bankruptcy of MGM/UA, subjected the independent sector to a severe credit squeeze.

Dynamic local institutions (including Chanin & Co., Canyon Partners Inc., Dabney/Resnick and Agner, and Libra Investments), with better contacts and information than the Wall Street brokerages possessed, emerged to help the independent sector. Chemical Bank also began conducting merchant banking activities by supporting initial public offerings and investing in film production companies' equity to secure large fees (*The Hollywood Reporter,* 28 February 1993) However, the Chase Manhattan Bank through its acquisition of Chemical Bank and its key entertainment division headed by John Miller, has remained the most important source of funds (Lowell 1999; Shaheen 1999). Chase obtains fees for acting as lead bank for lending syndicates that include other banks and insurance firms. It offers a revolving credit line to firms that develop a small string of movies. Chase lends up to a limit determined by a number of sophisticated criteria, including a ratio between receivables and collateral backing. If the client violates the parameter, the amount it can borrow is reduced until its finances come back within the target range. This automatic adjusting mechanism has proved to be safe and profitable for Chase.

Thus, since the early 1980s relations between banks and film production firms have undergone significant changes as a result of shifting environmental conditions and the formation of new inter-firm communication lines. Information and clever contractual devices, such as the one used by Chase, are vital to the safe deployment of funds. Given the industry's peculiar accounting practices, the high-risk nature of the business, and the importance of assessing participants, a string of newcomers, including Wall Street brokers, Japanese investors (including Sony and Matsushita), who, attracted by synergies between soft- and hard-ware, were misled and fleeced (Griffin and Masters 1996), and foreign banks have lost heavily. More recently, insurance firms have shared the same fate.

Insurance firms

In the 1990s, insurance firms became an important source of funds for Hollywood by insuring banks against loan defaults. The studios use insurance firms to guarantee bonds issued by the quasi-independent units they set up to push debt off their balance sheets. The insurance companies are attracted by high (eight to nine per cent) premiums. Recently, studios securitise the future revenue stream generated by a slate of movies by selling high-yielding bonds to investors. Independents, which have limited equity, pursue the same strategy and rely on the insurance firms' guarantees to support debt. Typically, the insurers guarantee sixty-five per cent of production costs backed by either foreign or domestic distribution rights (*The Hollywood Reporter*, 15 October 1998). Unfamiliar with the risks involved in film making, insurance firms have encountered defaults that left them holding worthless equity. Others accepted net profit positions, which belatedly they discovered to be chimerical. Lawsuits are pending.

With heavy capital requirements, the film industry has been able to juggle financing options by drawing in a series of new investors seeking high fees, huge potential gains, technical opportunities, and perhaps some of the glamour of Hollywood. Those who devise flawed contracts and do not forge sound information channels fare poorly. The question remains: who will be the next supporter – in Hollywood the talk is of internet firms or Silicon Valley's new multimillionaires – and will they learn from the past mistakes of others?

Conclusion

The networks used in the film industry differ from others examined above.

Unlike the HSS construct, which was set up to operate over the long term, the Hollywood networks are temporary and project driven. They also include more extensive sub-networks (based on artistic, technical, distribution, and financial operations) linked by nodal figures who provide screening and implicit guaranteeing services (like TSR's new manager in Chapter 3 but on a grander scale). The underlying contracts are interrelated in a way that goes beyond 'nesting'; the inclusion of artistic personnel with strong drawing power affects the structure of other agreements and influences who participates in them.

As devices for mobilising human capital, the film makers' networks automatically accommodate changes in constituencies, whereas the JSS network and JWT deliberately managed personnel transitions in order to transmit culture, procedural knowledge, and cognitive programming. The Hollywood networks are based on ever-changing ratings, transient images, and shifts in reputational stature within the context of a low-trust culture. As a result, these frameworks do not so much show the patterns of repeat dealing, that Faulkner and Anderson (1987) found before 1980, but rather they operate in a self-adjusting, kaleidoscopic manner to mobilise in serial fashion different sets of individuals with distinct capabilities.

The financial and distribution networks display the same character. Since 1980, changes in environmental factors, including exhibition technology, sources of funds, and market sectors, have called for continuous contractual adjustment. Assembling a matrix of creative and business contracts is somewhat like building disposable structures on shifting sand.

The mix of elements within these agreements consists of complex specifications, numerous mechanisms for mutual monitoring, and what can be described as an anti-culture. The legal provisions used by film makers, like those that linked shipowners to agents and advertising agents to their clients, are based on occupation-specific precedents, but these appear to be far more esoteric. The specifications provide considerable flexibility for *ex post* adjustment and provide wide scope for disadvantaging parties who entered into earlier agreements. The most interesting feature of the legal provisions, perhaps, is the way they serve a rating function and thus overlap with other monitoring instruments. Combined with numerous public rating devices that assess specific aspects of individual performance, this private ranking system transmits powerful signals on an exclusive basis to 'insiders'. Together, private and public rating frameworks facilitate contracting activities aimed at wedding human capital to investment funds.

When considering the Hollywood culture, we come full circle from the high-trust context in which British shipowners operated. In an antithetical way, players in the film industry are opportunistic, observe zero sum scenarios, and attach utility to deceiving others, especially 'outsiders'. Indeed, opportunistic behaviour if manifested in an innovative way may confer additional renown upon the perpetrator. Even the language used in the industry – and especially in contractual agreements- is intended to serve a divisive function. Unlike Curtis and the Swires, who attempted to use language for integrative purposes, film makers adopt an esoteric vocabulary to confuse 'outsiders' who are drawn to the fame, glamour, and high stakes in Hollywood. For 'insiders' the terminology provides a shorthand needed to accelerate communication and deal-making to meet the rapid pace set by constantly changing fads, images, and markets. Thus, as in the other cases above, the passage of time is important in Hollywood, but perhaps more so because the pace is so frantic. Having timely and accurate information and building contractual safeguards are vital. 'Outsiders' who lack the required contacts and familiarity with contractual forms find themselves caught in a voracious vortex.

13 Conclusion
Inter-firm relationships

This book brings together business history and economic theory to show how communication, knowledge transfers, and learning activities can unfold across corporate boundaries. In the process of doing so, it identifies a set of principles that may be useful for institutional analysts and business people. Hopefully, the exercise as a whole has demonstrated that history is a valuable resource and knowledge of the past can provide competitive advantage.

As Curtis recognised, history provides us with a map that can guide decision-making by disclosing courses that were effective, some which led people astray, and others that proved to be dead ends. Knowledge of the past also teaches us that this cognitive map can be very suddenly and profoundly altered by unexpected developments that make patterns of action which were hitherto discarded as ineffective worthy of careful consideration. In other words, what has not worked in the past might work in light of new conditions.

Thus, history is much more than a record of objective facts. Events are subject to the organising influence of those who recount them. Theory and present-day concerns offer useful guidance to the direction of inquiry and investigation. Yet, those who program the cognitive map must remain faithful to the context in which events unfolded so that their significance to those affected can be understood in terms meaningful to them. History requires us to step outside our own frame of reference and sympathetically apprehend the meaning of actions that took place within another social and cultural milieu. Aware of this, we can see more clearly what has changed and what has not; we can see how our frame of reference differs from that of others who have gone before us. The capacity to understand other people on their own terms and the judgement to determine how we differ from them are both vital skills for those interested in evaluating and using co-operative relationships.

The first section below presents my broad findings and directions for future work by business historians and theorists. The final part of the conclusion lists variables and techniques according to how they relate to the components of contracts, contracting capability, and the communicating infrastructure.

Findings and future directions

The cases above explored a range of co-operative structures, some of which have hitherto escaped investigation. Undoubtedly, there are many other forms awaiting discovery and analysis by historians. The sheer variety of inter-firm frameworks alerts us to both the wealth of choices available and the scope for innovative design.

Many of these co-operative forms do not have a hierarchical substitute; most are unique and are not amenable to internalisation. Indeed, to merge and subject the constituent parts to authoritative instruction would violate transaction cost economising, but more importantly to do so would in most instances defy the underlying logic of communicative rationality. Consolidation would sacrifice those gains that stemmed from mutual growth, joint learning, enhanced reputation, resource sharing, and having access to diverse information sets. By proceeding beyond transaction cost concerns to take into account these attributes, the analysis is thrown open to reveal dynamic, growth-inducing variables that influence institutional selection.

Each form considered here had its own integrity. This is not to say that all of these frameworks were distinct: the B&W group and the HSS network consisted of a combination of different forms. Nor, of course, were they unchanging. The HSS network evolved, as did OP and JWT, whereas the Hollywood networks exhibited rapid and almost continuous change. However, there was no tendency for mode shifts to unfold in a particular direction, either towards the market or towards a hierarchy. Indeed, shipowner–agent ties changed in every conceivable way. Each framework also had its own integrity in the sense that it was formed within a particular context to motivate specific participants to work towards an initial goal.

Although our evidence does not enable us to identify how all parties in the cases made contact, it has revealed specific mechanisms (such as fora), agents (especially intermediaries), and a variety of informal links (based on family, occupation, transactional, regional, educational, and national affiliation). In addition, PJ and JSS knew of each other, indicating that reputation acted as a beacon to potential partners. Apart from recognising the importance of reputation, transaction cost economics largely ignores how partners meet; bargainers are taken as given. This is one area in which further historical research is needed to provide a foundation for generalisation. Managers who develop 'intelligence systems' to cross-reference their contacts may discover some telling connections and some gaps that require exploration.

Mutual assessment processes are not always revealed in firm records; the JSS–PJ and WMC–H/H cases are exceptions. Management scientists have drawn attention to both partner- and task-specific variables, and they rightly suggest that assessment is not a discrete activity, it is continuous. Our findings confirm that complementarity can develop over time as inter-firm learning unfolds; indeed, it may expose new opportunities in serial fashion as the history of the HSS network reveals.

Strangely, transaction cost economics does not explore negotiating processes, although it recognises that costs are involved. Several of our cases reveal negotiating processes in action (Chapters 2, 3, 4, 9, 10, and 11). Further historical investigation may discover devices, conventions, and techniques that help to reduce negotiating expenses and accelerate the pace of discussions.

Principal–agent theory and transaction cost economics focus closely on the details of contracts, especially the legal specifications and monitoring devices. The cultural component receives less thorough treatment despite its obvious significance. Our cases reveal nearly every possible combination of the three elements. Specific mixes suited the context, the parties involved, the aims pursued, and degree of trust as reflected by the extent of interpersonal and inter-organisational knowledge. Moreover, any combination could prove effective in a particular set of circumstances. For practitioners, the point here is that there is almost unlimited scope for creative design. The only constraints are imposed by the limits of imagination or the failure to establish the legitimacy of a specific configuration.

Whereas Williamson's framework directs attention primarily towards reducing the *costs* of arranging transactions, this study has tried to highlight *benefits* derived from exchange. As suggested by the logic of communicative rationality, the more astute participants in the co-operative ventures studied here recognised that any agreement was just a basic initial framework that could be adapted to pursue growth-related objectives that might become apparent as future events unfolded. One of the objectives of this book is to direct attention to the communicating and learning activities that underpin co-operation and to encourage a more balanced analytical approach with regard to assessing transaction costs and benefits.

A central insight arising from this study is that communication directed towards assessing these expenses and advantages can be, and indeed is, *structured*. To be sure, some transmissions can be incidental and specific channels may evolve almost naturally. Nevertheless, these occurrences do not prevent communication – in all its ramifications – from being the object of deliberate design. In some contexts (recall the shipping industry in Chapter 2), a communicating infrastructure was already installed and available for immediate use. As in 'single-loop' learning (operating within a given system), players, like Ellerman and Stephen Furness, exhibited considerable imagination in communicating to arrange transactions. In cases where parts of the established, public good type of communicating infrastructure were not amenable to the pursuit of a particular type of exchange, economic actors changed one or more elements. In 'double-loop' fashion (by which one adjusts the system), Resor at JWT introduced a different model in the form of the professional template and he shaped (what was in the advertising business) new human resource attributes to support transactions aimed at compounding intangible assets. Similarly, JWT and B&W built new fora, many firms cited above created new channels, HSS devised new communicating conventions, and JSS (like JWT) cultivated personnel suited to occupy positions at interfaces between firms. When a public type of infrastructure was not available, firms like PJ and JSS proceeded further with 'double-loop' learning to build a customised infrastructure to sustain transfers of existing expertise and the creation of new knowledge. The components of their framework were in general the same as those incorporated within public constructs used at the time. Our research did not reveal a 'triple-loop' response, manifested as a completely unprecedented form of inter-organisational systemic construct, but this of course remains a possibility. Perhaps further historical research or the study of cybernetics will discover one.

The realisation that inter-organisational communication can be structured to support the transfer and creation of knowledge exposes the profundity of Richardson's insight that firms are *not* 'islands of planned co-ordination in a sea of market relations'. With porous frontiers, organisations are subject to manifold organising influences projected through deliberately contrived mechanisms intended to evoke co-operation. As is confirmed by some of our cases (especially Chapters 2, 6, and 10) inter-firm collaboration involves to some degree strategic, structural, systemic, and cultural linkage. Perhaps the essence of what Richardson (1972) called 'a willing sacrifice of some sovereignty' is most evident when there emerges an inter-company culture, of the type Curtis tried to create, and an inter-organisational memory, such as the one members of the HSS network developed. When partners programme each other's cognitive processes, develop a shared history, shape each other's conceptions of legitimacy, and create an imagery to influence the receptivity to future transmissions they most certainly enhance communicating and learning activities. However, as JSS knew, by doing so firms risk loosing some of the autonomous capabilities that provide the creative tension needed to sustain innovative collaboration. As the NSWB case showed, creativity can also be undermined by legacies set in train by mistrustful behavioural patterns that lead to information hoarding which, in turn, exposes relationships most acutely to sudden environmental changes.

These insights suggest that both the cognitive 'soft-wares' and the physical 'hard-wares' used for communicating act as 'filters' that screen out potentially significant details. For example, it is important to recognise, as Curtis did, a technology's capabilities in terms of timeliness, security, accuracy, and descriptive capacity relative to the associated costs in their widest sense. Each technology has particular limitations in relation to a face-to-face encounter and each medium generates specific conventions. In both ways, hard-wares may cause salient details to be lost even as they accelerate the pace of exchange.

Similarly, soft-wares in the form of education, culture, and routines help to speed up communicating and decision-making. (When soft-wares are incompatible, as in the B&W case and between Hollywood 'insiders' and 'outsiders' outcomes are obviously unsatisfactory from at least one participant's perspective.) However, soft-wares also filter out 'noise', such as courses of action or choices that have never worked in the past or which lack legitimacy. Managers who develop mapping techniques that help them to recognise what is being filtered out and which details are free flowing (or perhaps too much so, in cases where bounded rationality is heightened) have an advantage in anticipating shocks, and also in structuring improved communicating infrastructures.

Such people are also in a better position to develop a capacity to recognise the most desirable attributes of future soft- and hard-wares. Then, like JSS and JWT, they can tailor human resource development policies to complement the framework and maintain effective communication. Accommodating such change across the boundary of the firm requires the generation of a shared vision to support strategic, structural, systemic, and cultural interfaces. Again, to bring this common perspective into focus poses the same trade-off between similarity and complementarity.

Like other processes aimed at harnessing distinct but related capabilities, the development of shared vision also requires that participants are accorded respect as valued members who can contribute something in their own distinctive way. B&W made the mistake of letting its German unit feel enthralled, with the result that it later became vindictive, whereas NSWB treated some members of its supply chain with complete disregard. In contrast, JSS knew that it had to incur the cost of letting PJ discover for itself the validity of JSS's design for OP's distribution system. Our cases show instances in which the observance of what another party recognised as courtesy, etiquette, and protocols was crucial in building trust and resolving crises. The capacity to *demonstrate* respect by stepping outside of one's own culture and co-operating on terms that are meaningful to another party is fundamental to co-operation. This is, perhaps, what is meant by *dignity*, which, poignantly, is the third behavioural assumption (in addition to opportunism and bounded rationality) that Williamson identified but could not devise a way to include within his framework. Today, business leaders face a formidable challenge in displaying genuine dignity as the pace of decision-making accelerates, communication technology changes so rapidly, and an increasingly global economy brings a more diverse constituency within closer proximity. Yet, this is possibly the most important variable in sustaining co-operative endeavours that maintain the creative tension needed to harness an evolving set of complementary attributes.

Considerations and trade-offs

At the outset of this study I promised to deliver a list of considerations and trade-offs that business people and institutional investigators may find suggestive. I trust they will develop others. One point of this book is to show that there is no one best way to build an inter-firm relationship. What follows is a list of possible ingredients, not a recipe. Practitioners will have to combine the different components in proportions that suit their tastes and especially that of their partners. Cooking time and methods will also have to be varied according to circumstances. Final arrangement and presentation will have to suit the guests and the occasion.

The three basic elements of a contract and the different parts of the communicating infrastructure have already been analysed at length. Space does not permit an extended discussion of the factors that may be considered or those elements that should be balanced. Readers can think about them in relation to the case studies presented above.

Considerations

Contract design: legal provisions, monitoring mechanisms, and culture

- demonstrating dignity
- specification, loose or exacting
- designing monitoring channels (transparency, objective indicators, triangulated links)
- culture and its dimensions
- articulating specific goals
- the use of power
- affiliation, multiple affiliation
- creating structural, system, and cultural interfaces;
- trust building
- winning relationship-specific reputation, relational capital
- bonding techniques
- signalling methods
- creating shared conceptions
- comparative size of partners, difference in substitution possibilities
- learning devices

Ex post adjustment

- continuously confirming dignity
- evolving goals
- accommodating third or outside parties
- creative tension, harnessing and maintaining
- partners' conceptions of gains or costs changes over time
- partners' conceptions of success or failure
- changes in partners' sizes and substitution possibilities
- creating shared vision
- projection of influence (and receptivity)
- requesting and offering reciprocal exchange
- developing feedback mechanisms
- visible or private punishment
- staff development, learning about partner's personnel

- crisis resolution techniques
- legacies
- exit strategies, or managing a graceful or reputation-preserving exit

Communicating infrastructure: models or precedents, fora communicating lines, communicating conventions, people at inter-firm interfaces

- bargaining fora, public and private
- local presence and disparities in parties' local presence
- winning public reputation
- social capital
- affiliations, multiple connections
- legitimacy, behavioural rules, use of informal communication
- communicating channels, triangulating
- communicating aids, cost and efficiency
- signalling media and techniques (private and public)
- knowledge transfers
- types of learning (inter-firm, project-specific, learning capabilities)
- overlapping contracts

Trade-offs or elements requiring balance

- partners' different knowledge bases
- protecting versus sharing core capabilities
- level of trust versus scope for future adjustment
- openness versus exclusiveness
- symmetry of contracts
- balance in partners' dependence
- informal versus formal communication
- visionary, structural, systemic and cultural similarity versus distinctiveness (and flexibility)
- exit cost versus relationship maintenance cost
- trust versus deterrence
- subtle versus direct use of power
- autonomy versus interdependence (also autonomy versus willing sacrifice of sovereignty)
- delegation versus control
- visibility versus obfuscation
- cost of communication versus benefits
- variety versus quantity of experience co-operating

Time-related trade-offs

- rate of growth versus time needed to cement contracts
- speed of contractual adjustment versus pace of environmental change

- speed of mapping out territory to search versus pace of environmental change
- delay in setting up communication infrastructure versus trust building, environmental change, risk of external shock
- haggling time and risk of poisoning a relationship
- recuperative learning, speed of (also crisis resolution)
- gaps in communication
- transforming tacit knowledge into codified form
- managing staff succession at inter-firm interfaces
- managing staff succession to preserve private contacts

While the details of these considerations and trade-offs were especially relevant to the participants in the ventures described above, in a different form they remain important today. Moreover, *how* these variables were used and the ways in which potentially conflicting forces were balanced were vital in determining outcomes.

Notes

1 The theoretical and historical context

1 These expenses arise from spending time finding someone to deal with, arranging an agreement, and monitoring performance to ensure compliance. The cost of carrying out an additional transaction at the margin determines whether the exchange will be effected through market mechanisms or conducted within the firm.

2 For example, aluminium plants are designed to refine bauxite, which has a particular chemical composition. There are usually few sources of supply and a constant flow of raw material is needed to achieve optimal economies during refining. These conditions pose a risk that a supplier will hold up deliveries to extract a 'ransom' from the purchaser. Hence, it is likely that the transaction will be internalised within a firm that owns both the refinery and the bauxite deposit (see Burn 1997).

3 For example, railroads purchase rails infrequently, usually for replacement purposes, and there are many potential suppliers of what is an undifferentiated product. Trains can run on any standard gauge rail so that there is no asset specificity present. The railroad will buy rails in the market place, rather than invest in a rolling mill.

4 The transaction cost approach has influenced some theories of multinational enterprise (MNE) (Buckley and Casson 1976). Caves (1982) and Hymer (1960) emphasise that MNEs win by transferring intangible assets across national borders to exploit quasi-rents (transient above-normal profits) that more than offset the extra costs of doing business overseas. Other theories include Vernon's (1966) locational approach and Dunning's (1973) 'eclectic' model, which combines transaction costs, locational factors, and market power. In the management literature, Porter (1980, 1985, 1986) emphasises strategy and corporate capabilities. Related themes are explored by Doz and Prahalad (1993), Hamel and Prahalad (1994).

5 Williamson (see 1975: 106–8; 1985: 22, 62, 71–2, 120–1) does leave some room for social factors, such as norms of trust and reputation, but he suggests that they explain only exceptional institutional forms.

6 Learning-by-doing effects generate tacit knowledge; this type of knowledge is difficult to articulate because it is learned by performing a task (Penrose 1959; Teece 1982).

7 To make Williamson's approach more fluid, Langlois and Robertson (1995) developed the concept of *dynamic transaction costs*, which reflect the expense a company incurs in persuading, negotiating, co-ordinating, and teaching outside firms so that their capabilities can be contractually linked to those of the initiating company. Thus, information concerns, communicating processes, learning effects,

and knowledge lie at the centre of Langlois and Robertson's framework.

8 These issues are important in the strategy-related works; see Contractor and Lorange (1988) and the management literature cited in note 9.

9 Similar concerns are addressed in the branch of strategic management literature devoted to how firms blend their attributes (Geringer 1988; Bleeke and Ernest 1993; Faulkner 1995) and works on resource dependency (Pfeffer and Salanick 1978; Hamel 1991; Hamel and Prahalad 1994).

10 Powell (1990) rightly suggests that 'trust reduces complex uncertainties far more quickly and economically than prediction, authority, or bargaining'. However, trust does not preclude economic actors from invoking sanctions in the event of default, preparing fall-back positions, or retaining deterrent capabilities. Trust in the sense used here is not of a blind or naive variety; it involves having the confidence (derived from interpersonal knowledge) that another party will act as they speak, rather than the faith that they will do so. In a related way, reciprocity (a key attribute of co-operative relations) is not necessarily based on a precise calculation of benefits gained in relation to favours given. Instead, it entails knowing that one may be called upon by another for assistance or advice and that one may call upon the same person some time in the future and be confident that help or information will be forthcoming. Inviting reciprocity in advance or providing more than was requested are strong signals (Buckley and Casson 1988; Casson 1991)

11 Transactions involving knowledge are often notoriously expensive because the party possessing knowledge cannot divulge it before receiving compensation, while the purchaser will not pay until they can assess the value of the knowledge which may involve absorbing it before making payment. The risk of market failure is high. Moreover, tacit knowledge, which consists of a skill that cannot be articulated in words or knowing how to do something, may be costly to transmit because absorption may entail using it or staff transfers. The problem surrounding such transactions is known as 'the paradox of knowledge' (Teece 1982). Relationships designed to achieve joint learning are also difficult to create and maintain because they pose similar appropriability problems.

12 Intangible assets are non-physical resources, such as knowledge or brand names, that generate an appropriable quasi-rent, or a rate of return above the market rate which is (1) transient because it can be competed away as other firms develop similar knowledge or brands, and (2) appropriable because opportunistic players can acquire knowledge without paying for it, imitate a brand image, or debase the quality standard it represents (Klein *et al.* 1978).

2 Agency agreements in international business

1 These media could, of course, be used to mislead parties (see Armstrong 1986).

2 Figures 2.1–2.4 extend a basic model devised by Hutchinson and Nicholas (1988).

5 A purchasing co-operative

1 In his study of commodity markets, Rowe (1965) refers to only one producer's purchasing arrangement; one that was set up in 1926 by American tyre manufacturers in response to the formation of an international rubber cartel. Consumer co-operatives have been examined more extensively (Hood and Yamey 1957; Birchall 1994).

2 Vickers 1198 Steel Manufacturers' Nickel Syndicate directors' minutes (hereafter SMNS DM) 8/3/1918 and 31/7/1918 refer to an earlier agreement between La Société and INCO and arrangements with Mond but do not disclose details.

However, the records indicate that suppliers allocated specific customers to each other. Wilkins (1970) states that the agreement governed pricing and market allocation.

3 We do not know how much nickel the Admiralty consumed directly or indirectly, but the quantity must have been large before 1918. Vickers 57/61 statement dated 31/7/1935 indicates that the Government expressed its preferences for purchases of nickel from Canada during World War I, but SMNS DM 30/10/1902 reveals that the Admiralty was interested in the nickel question earlier. The Admiralty also explored Canada's potential as an oil supplier in 1905 and pressured the Dominion Government to restrict ownership of domestic oil fields to British or Canadian firms in 1914. Its aim was to safeguard fuel supplies for the Grand Fleet. The relevant legislation had implications for non-British companies that owned mineral deposits (Breen 1981).

4 The syndicate sought assurances from a La Société's official, M. Marchand, who stated that INCO had no interest in his firm. Syndicate members also worried about the possibility that INCO might become a low-cost producer of armour, but from unknown sources they obtained estimates of the new firm's raw material costs and found that these were too high to pose a threat (SMNS DM 7/4/1903).

5 With data about members' consumption Vickers could deduce the size of their order books and thus gain valuable commercial intelligence, but if in fact this was the case it did not create problems within the syndicate.

6 There must have been some expenses that were not apportioned directly to members. For example, Vickers, willingly it seems, shouldered the cost of handling invoices and reports, while officials of the participating firms apparently volunteered their time when attending membership meetings and assisting in negotiations with La Société. These expenses were not reflected by the size of the levy.

7 This calculation does not include some minor expenses (see note 6), and the following benefits: dividends paid by the Anglo-French firm, dividends paid by La Société, and interest earned on the syndicate's small financial reserves.

6 A licensing pyramid

1 Selling the patent would have been difficult because the US had not signed the international patent treaty (it did so in 1921). Moreover, this course would have increased transaction costs and signalled that Curtis lacked confidence in his innovation.

2 Shepherd *et al.* (1985) suggest that behavioural and strategic factors, including the management's desire to build a large international organisation, the need to respond to oligopolistic competition, and risk preferences may encourage direct foreign investment when transaction cost analysis indicates that an alternative solution is more suitable.

3 Because *Lloyd's Register of Shipping* does not provide information about turbines in merchant ships, we cannot estimate Curtis's share of the commercial market.

4 In game theoretic terms, by announcing a specific date when royalty payments would cease altogether, the contract signalled a *definite* time horizon that would induce immediate defection. However, the discovery of patentable improvements would create a game of *indefinite* duration. Co-operation is more likely to endure in this case because participants expect to make future gains.

7 A technology transfer agreement

1 By 1973, inter-firm collaboration had become so formalised and extensive that

an 'inter-organisational chart' was drawn up to illustrate the overall structure of relationships (Babcock Inter Company Collaboration 29 March 1973).

9 A joint exploration venture

1 In 1961, the M. A. Hanna Company controlled assets worth US $500 million (Dougall 1994: 346). In the mid-1960s, Homestake's profits, at US $5 million, were larger than 25 per cent of WMC's assets of $23.4 million (Covell 1994: 244) Other smaller deposits were developed nearby in the Blue Hills to extend the productive life of the main Koolanooka project. (Clark 1983: 175–6).

2 In principal, the partners could have arranged a vertically aligned incentive contract wherein WMC would discover and mine iron ore which H/H would process and sell, but there is no evidence in the WMC papers that they considered this possibility. Perhaps WMC's thinking was influenced by a tradition of joint venturing and sequential dealing within the Australian mining industry, but in any event a vertical contract would not necessarily have provided the firm with funds for exploration and development or a mechanism for spreading risk. Both were important concerns.

10 Contracts based on knowledge

1 Abbreviations: DS, David Sutton; EW, Edward Wilson; IC, Information Centre; NS, Norman Strouse; SB, Sydney Bernstein; SM, Sam Meek; TS, Tom Sutton.

11 An Australian supplier chain

1 Japanese supplier chains consist of a pyramid of firms with a major auto-maker at its apex. A small number of firms in the next tier supply major components (engines), a larger number of companies in the next tier produce subassemblies (carburettors, etc.), and the myriad of small enterprises on the bottom rung make simple parts. For bonding purposes, the auto-maker owns a minority interest in tier one firms and a very small stake in those on the second tier. But it has no investment in companies on the bottom tier. Not only is production contracted out, but so too is design work, primarily to firms in the top two rungs. The auto-maker engages in multiple sourcing even though tier one firms make transaction-specific investments in plant, to harness wider learning capabilities, albeit at the cost of enhanced economies of scale. The supporting contracts lay out quality and delivery rating systems, founded respectively on zero defects and just-in-time principles, that create an incentive for firms to exceed targets and win promotion to higher positions in the chain. The higher their position the larger the profits they will generate by carrying out more sophisticated design work, making more advanced components, and by supervising firms on lower tiers. The price paid for parts is not set at a definite figure; instead, parties agree to a base price that will be raised only if material prices increase or specifications are changed. Suppliers are expected to innovate to contain increases in labour and energy costs. Finally, the base *falls* slightly each year, thereby creating an incentive for suppliers to innovate continuously to cut costs.

2 Theoretically, the breweries could have integrated backwards into bottle distribution instead of setting up NSWB as a separate entity. Independent vertical integration by each brewery would have sacrificed economies of scale and caused the duplication of retrieval systems. TT could also issue NSWB shares to bond other breweries that might wish to use its services. Having a separate unit

generated incentives for NSWB management and provided a basis for building up a larger business that required specialised quality control and co-ordinating skills. Finally, delegating bottle purchasing and retrieval to NSWB enabled TT to focus on its core business, which became increasingly capital intensive and driven by marketing (Merrett 1996). Demand for bottled beer soared in the early twentieth century as the temperance movement limited pubs' trading hours.

Bibliography

Archival sources

Babcock & Wilcox Collection, Business Records Centre, University of Glasgow, Scotland.

Bahamas Airways papers, Merseyside Maritime Museum, Liverpool, England.

Cathay Pacific Airways records, John Swire & Sons, London, England.

China Navigation Co. records, School of Oriental and African Studies, London, England.

English Steel Corporation records, Vickers Collection, University of Cambridge, Cambridge, England.

Furness Withy & Co. Ltd., Redhill, Surrey, England.

General Steam Navigation, National Maritime Museum, Greenwich, England.

J. Walter Thompson Company records, John W. Hartman Centre for Sales, Advertising, and Marketing History, Duke University, Durham, N.C., USA

J. Walter Thompson Company records, History of Advertising Trust, Ravingham, Norfolk, England.

John Scott & Co. records, Business Records Centre, University of Glasgow, Scotland.

John Swire & Sons records, John Swire & Sons, London, England.

City Line and Hall Line records (Ellerman), Business Records Centre, University of Glasgow, Scotland.

Malayan Airline records, Merseyside Maritime Museum, Liverpool, England.

New South Wales Bottle Co. Ltd, Noel Butlin Archive of Business and Labour, the Australian National University, Canberra, ACT, Australia.

Ocean Steam Ship Co. (Alfred Holt & Co.) records, Merseyside Maritime Museum, Liverpool, England.

Orient Paint, Varnish, and Colour Co. School of Oriental and African Studies, London, England.

PAMAS records, John Swire & Sons, London, England.

Pacific Steam Navigation, National Maritime Museum, Greenwich, England.

Royal Mail Steam Packet Co. Ltd, National Maritime Museum, Greenwich, England.

Steel Manufacturers' Nickel Syndicate records, Vickers Collection, University of Cambridge Library, Cambridge, England.

Taikoo Sugar Refinery records, School of Oriental and African Studies, London, England.

Taikoo Dockyard & Engineering Co. records, School of Oriental and African Studies, London, England.

Unilever Archives, Port Sunlight, Wirral, England.

Union Steamship of New Zealand Company records, and Sir John Mills papers,
    Wellington Maritime Museum, Wellington, New Zealand.
WMC records, the University of Melbourne Archives, Parkville, Victoria, Australia.

Interviews and private information

Havilland, C. (1997) Editorial Services Manager, John Swire & Sons (HK) Ltd.
Lowell, D. (1999) MSc, Entertainment Analyst, Los Angeles, CA, USA.
McGuiness, T. (1999) Post Production Supervisor, Los Angeles, CA, USA.
Shaheen, D. (1999) Vice-President, Chase Securities, Los Angeles, CA, USA.

Secondary sources

Abbott, A. (1988) *The System of Professions,* Chicago: University of Chicago Press.
Armstrong, J. (1986) 'Hooley and the Bovril Company', *Business History* XXVIII: 18–
    34.
Arrow, K.J. (1985) 'The economics of agency', in J. W. Pratt and R. J. Zeckhauser,
    (eds.) *Principals and Agents: The Structure of Business,* Cambridge, MA: Harvard
    University Press.
Axelrod, R. (1984) *The Evolution of Co-operation*, New York: Basic Books.
Balio, T (1987) *United Artists the Company that Changed the Film Industry*, Madison:
    University of Wisconsin Press.
Barnard, C. (1958) *The Function of the Executive*, Cambridge, MA: Harvard University
    Press.
Berle, A. A. and Means, G.C. (1932) *The Modern Corporation and Private Property,* New
    York: Macmillan.
Birchall, J. (1994) *Co-op the People's Business,* Manchester: Manchester University Press.
Bleeke, J. and Ernst, D. (1993) *Collaborating to Compete: Using Strategic Alliances and
    Acquisitions in the Global Marketplace*, New York: Wiley.
Boyce, G. H. (1995a) *Information, Mediation, and Institutional Development. The Rise of
    Large-scale Enterprise in British Shipping, 1870–1995*, Manchester: Manchester
    University Press.
Boyce, G. (1995b) 'Accounting for managerial decision-making in British shipping,
    1870–1918', *Accounting, Business, and Financial History* 5(3): 360–78.
Boyce, G. (1995c) 'Communication and contracting: A link between business and
    social history', *Business and Economic History* 24: 287–95.
Boyce, G. (1999) 'A Professional association as network and communicating node:
    The Pharmaceutical Society of Victoria, 1857–1918', *Australian Economic History
    Review* 39(3): 258–83.
Breen, D.H. (1981) 'Anglo-American rivalry and Canadian petroleum policy to 1930',
    Canadian Historical Review 42: 283–303.
Brown, J. and Rose, M.B. (1993) *Entrepreneurship, Networks, and Modern Business,*
    Manchester: Manchester University Press.
Bruland, K. (1998) 'The Babcock & Wilcox Company: strategic alliance, technology
    development, and enterprise control, circa 1860–1900', in C. Bruland and P. Obrien
    (eds.) *From Family Firms to Corporate Capitalism*, Oxford: Clarendon.
Buckley, P.J. and Casson, M. (1976) *The Future of Multinational Enterprise,* London:
    Macmillan.

Buckley, P.J. and Casson, M. (1988) 'A Theory of Co-operation in International Business', in F. J. Contractor and P. Lorange (eds.) *Co-operative Strategies in International Business*, New York: Lexington Books: 31–53.

Burn, P. (1997) 'ALCOA of Australia's role in the transformation of the upstream aluminium industry', in J. Burgess (ed.) *Essays in Honour of Moira Gordon, Gary Keating, Robert McShane, and Kathy Renfrew*, University of Newcastle, NSW Research Monograph no. 1.

Camerer, C. and Knez, M. (1996) 'Co-ordination, organisational boundaries, and fads in business practices', *Industrial and Corporate Change* 5(1): 89–112.

Carlos, A.M. and Nicholas, S.J. (1990) 'Agency problems in early chartered companies: the case of the Hudson's Bay Company', *Journal of Economic History* 50(4): 853–76.

Casson, M. (1987) *The Firm and the Market: Studies on Multinational Enterprise and the Scope of the Firm*, Oxford: Basil Blackwell.

Casson, M. (1991) *The Economics of Business Culture*, Oxford: Clarendon.

Casson, M. (1997) *Information and Organisation A New Perspective on the Theory of the Firm*, Oxford: Clarendon Press.

Casson, M.C. (1990) *Enterprise and Competitiveness A Systems View of International Business*, Oxford: Oxford University Press.

Caves, R.E. (1982) *Multinational Enterprise and Economic Analysis*, Cambridge: Cambridge University Press.

Chandler, A.D. (1962) *Strategy and Structure Chapters in the History of American Industrial Enterprise*, Cambridge, MA: MIT Press.

Chandler, A.D. (1977) *The Visible Hand, The Management Revolution in American Business*, Cambridge, MA: Harvard University Press.

Chandler, A.D. (1990) *Scale and Scope The Dynamics of Industrial Capitalism*, Cambridge, MA: Harvard University Press.

Chawla, S. and Renesch, J. (eds.) (1995) *Learning Organisations: developing cultures for tomorrow's workplace*, Portland, OR: Productivity Press.

Cheng, Chu-Yuan (1986) 'The United States petroleum trade with China, 1876–1949', in E. R. May and J. K. Fairbank (eds.) *America's China Trade in Historical Perspective The Chinese and American Performance*, Cambridge, MA: Harvard University Press.

Child, J. and Faulkner, D. (1998) *Strategies of Co-operation: Managing Alliances, Networks, and Joint Ventures*, Oxford: Oxford University Press.

Clark, G. L. (1983) *Built on Gold Recollections of Western Mining*, Melbourne: WMC.

Coase, R.H. (1937) 'The nature of the firm', *Economica* (new series) 4: 386–405.

Cochran, S. (1986) 'Commercial penetration and economic imperialism in China: an American cigarette company's entrance into the market', in E. R. May and J. K. Fairbank (eds.) *America's China Trade in Historical Perspective The Chinese and American Performance*, Cambridge, MA: Harvard University Press.

Cohen, J. M. (1956) *The Life of Ludwig Mond*, London: Methuen.

Contractor, F.J. and Lorange, P. (1988) *Co-operative Strategies in International Business*, Lexington, MA: Lexington Books.

Covell, J.L. (1994) 'Homestake Mining Co.', in *The International Directory of Company Histories*, Vol. 12. London, pp. 243–5.

Cox, Howard (1995) 'Learning to do business in China: The evolution of BAT's cigarette distribution network, 1902–41', *Business History* 39(3): 30–64.

Cremer, J. (1993) 'Corporate culture and shared knowledge', *Industrial and Corporate Change* 2(3): 351–86.

Davies, P.N. (1972) 'Lord Kylsant and the Royal Mail', *Business History* XIV: 103–23.

Davies, P.N. (1981) 'Business success and the role of chance: the extraordinary Philipps brother's, *Business History* XXIII: 208–32.

Deloitte *et al.* (1989) *Teaming up for the Nineties*, New York: Deloitte.

Dougall, A.S. (1994) 'M.A. Hanna Company', in *The International Directory of Company Histories*, Vol. 8. London. pp. 345–7.

Doz, Y. (1996) 'The evolution of co-operation in strategic alliances: initial conditions or learning processes?', *Strategic Management Journal* 17: 55–84.

Doz, Y. and Prahalad C.K. (1993) 'Managing DMNCs: a search for a new paradigm', in S. Ghoshal and D. E. Westney (eds.) *Organisation Theory and the Multinational Corporation*, London: Macmillan.

Drage, C. (1970) *Taikoo*, London: Constable.

Dunning, J.H. (1973) 'The determinants of international production', *Oxford Economic Papers* 25: 289–336.

Falkus, M. (1990) *The Blue Funnel Legend*, Basingstoke: Macmillan.

Faulkner, D. (1995) *International Strategic Alliances: Co-operating to Compete*, Maidenhead: McGraw-Hill.

Faulkner, R.R. and Anderson, A.B. (1987) 'Short-term projects and emergent careers: evidence from Hollywood', *American Journal of Sociology* 92(4): 879–909.

Fischer, L.R. and A.M. Fon (1991) 'The Making of a maritime firm: the rise of Fearnley and Eger, 1867–1917', in L. R. Fischer, (ed.) *From Wheel House to Counting House,* St John's, Newfoundland: Memorial University of Newfoundland.

Fletcher, M.E. (1975) 'From Coal to Oil in British shipping', *Journal of Transport History* new series, III: 1–19.

Fountain, H. (1996) 'Australian Consolidated Industries Limited. A case study of transactions in know how', PhD dissertation, University of Sydney.

French, M. (1994) 'Co-ordinating manufacturing and marketing: the role of the selling agent in US textiles', *Textile History* 25(2): 227–242.

Fruin, M.W. (1991) *The Japanese Enterprise System*, Oxford: Clarendon Press.

Geringer, J.M. (1988) *Joint Venture Partner Selection*, New York: Quorum Books.

Geringer, J.M. (1991) 'Strategic determinants of partner selection criteria in international joint ventures', *Journal of International Business Studies* 22: 41–62.

Gerlach, M.L. (1992) *Alliance Capitalism: The Social Organisation of Japanese Business*, Berkeley: University of California Press.

Grabher, G. (ed.) (1993) *The Embedded Firm*, London: Routledge.

Granovetter, M. (1985) 'Economic action and social structure: the problem of embeddedness', *American Journal of Sociology* 91(3): 481–510.

Griffin, N. and Masters, K. (1996) *Hit and Run*, New York: Simon & Schuster.

Grover, R. (1991) *The Disney Touch*, Homewood, IL: Business One Irwin.

Hamel, G. (1991) 'Competition for competence and inter-partner learning within international strategic alliances', *Strategic Management Journal* 12: 83–103.

Hamel, G. and Prahalad, C.K. (1994) *Competing for the Future*, Cambridge, MA: Harvard Business School.

Hannah, L. (1976) *The Rise of the Corporate Economy*, London: Macmillan.

Harrigan, K.R. (1985) *Strategies for Joint Venture Success*, Lexington, MA: Lexington Books.

Heenan, P. (1994) 'Babcock & Wilcox', in *International Directory of Company Histories*, Vol. 3. London. 465–6.

Helper, S. (1990) 'Comparative supplier relations in the US and Japanese auto industries: an exit/voice approach', *Business and Economic History* 19: 153–62.

Helper, S. (1991) 'How much has really changed between US automakers and their suppliers?' *Sloan Management Review* 4: 15–28.

Henning, G. and K. Trace (1975) 'Britain and the Motor ship', *Journal of Economic History* XXXV(2): 353–85.

Hirsch, P.M. (1972) 'Processing fads and fashions: An organisation-set analysis of cultural industry systems', *American Journal of Sociology* 77(4): 639–59.

Hirschman, A. (1970) *Exit, Voice, and Loyalty*, Cambridge, MA: Harvard University Press.

Hood, J. and B.S. Yamey (1957) 'The middle-class co-operative retailing societies in London, 1864–1900', *Oxford Economic Papers* new series 9: 309–22.

Hutchinson, D. and Nicholas, S.J. (1988) 'Theory and business history: new approaches to institutional change', *Journal of European Economic History* 17(2): 411–25.

Hyde, F. E. (1957) *Blue Funnel*, Liverpool: Liverpool University Press.

Hymer, S.H. (1960) *The International Operations of National Firms: A Study of Direct Investment*, Cambridge, MA: MIT Press.

Jensen, M.C. and Meckling, W.H. (1976) 'Theory of the firm: managerial behaviour agency costs and ownership structure', *Journal of Financial Economics* 3: 305–60.

Jones, G and Wale, J. (1998) 'Merchants as business groups: British trading companies in Asia before 1945', *Business History Review* 72(3): 367–408.

Jones, S. (1985) 'George Benjamin Dodwell a shipping agent in the Far East, 1872–1908', *Journal of Transport History* 3rd series 6(1): 23–40.

Jung, I. (1982) *The Marine Turbine*, Greenwich: National Maritime Museum.

Kershell, P.J. (1989) 'Toward a cultural history of advertising research: A case study of J. Walter Thompson, 1908–1925,' PhD dissertation, University of Illinois at Urbana-Champagne.

Kipping, M. (1999) 'American management consulting companies in Western Europe, 1920 to 1990): products, reputation, and relationships', *Business History Review* 73(2): 190–220.

Klein, B., Crawford, R.G. and Alchian, A. (1978) 'Vertical Integration, Appropriable Rents, and the Competitive Contracting Process', *Journal of Law and Economics* 21(2):297–326.

Kreps, D.M. (1990) *Game Theory and Economic Modelling*, Oxford: Oxford University Press.

Langlois, R.N. and Robertson, P. (1995) *Firms, Markets and Economic Change*, London: Routledge.

Lorange, P. (1988) 'Co-operative strategies: planning and control considerations', in N. Hood and J-E Vahlne (eds.) *Strategies in Global Competition*, London: Croom Helm: 370–89.

Lundvall, B-A, (1993) 'Explaining inter-firm co-operation and innovation', in G. Grabher (ed.) *The Embedded Firm*, London: Routledge, pp. 52–64.

McKay, J. (1986) 'The House of Rothschild as a multinational enterprise 1875–1914', in A. Teichova, M. Levy-Leboyer and H. Nussbaum (eds.) *Multinational Enterprise in Historical Perspective*, Cambridge: Cambridge University Press, pp. 74–86.

McLean, G. (1990) *The Southern Octopus: The Rise of Shipping Empire*, Wellington: New Zealand Ship and Marine Society.

McMillan, J. (1989) *Managing Suppliers, Incentive Systems in Japanese and United States Industries*, unpublished manuscript.

Marchand, R. (1985) *Advertising the American Dream: Making Way for Modernity, 1920–1940*, Berkeley: University of California Press.

Marquart, M.J. (1996) *Building the Learning Organisation*, New York: McGraw-Hill.

Marriner, S. and Hyde, F.E. (1967) *The Senior John Samuel Swire 1825–1898*, Liverpool: Liverpool University Press.

Mechanic, D. (1962) 'Sources of power of lower participants in complex organisation', *Administrative Science Quarterly* 7: 349–64.

Merrett, D.T. (1996) 'Stability and change in the Australian brewing industry, 1919–1920', unpublished manuscript.

MPAA (Motion Picture Association of America) (1998) *US Economic Review*, Los Angeles: MPAA.

Nelson, R.R. and Winter, S.G. (1982) *An Evolutionary Theory of Economic Change*, Cambridge, MA: Harvard University Press.

Nevett, T.R. (1982) *Advertising in Britain. A History*, London: William Heinemann.

Nohria, N. and Eccles, R. (eds) (1992) *Networks and Organisations Structure, Form, and Action*, Cambridge, MA Harvard University Press.

Norris, J.D. (1990) *Advertising and the transformation of American society 1865–1920*, New York: Greenwood Press.

North, D.C. (1990) *Institutions, Institutional Change, and Economic Performance*, Cambridge: Cambridge University Press.

Numazaki, I. (1986) 'Networks of Taiwanese big business', *Modern China* 12(4): 487–534.

Numazaki, I. (1993) 'The Tainanbang: the rise and growth of a banana-bunch shaped business group in Thailand', *The Developing Economies* XXXI(4): 485–510.

Orbell, J. (1978) *From Cape to Cape The History of Lyle Shipping*, Edinburgh: Paul Harris.

Osterhammel, J. (1989) 'British business in China (1860s –1950s)', in G. Jones and R. P. T. Davenport-Hines (eds.) *British Business in Asia since 1860*, Cambridge: Cambridge University Press.

Parkhe, A. (1993) 'Strategic alliance structuring: a game theoretic and transaction cost examination of interfirm co-operation', *Academy of Management Journal* 38(4): 794–829.

Payne, P.L. (1967) 'The Emergence of the Large-Scale Company in Great Britain, 1870–1914', *Economic History Review* XX(3): 518–41.

Penrose, E. (1959) *The Theory of the Growth of the Firm*, Oxford: Basil Blackwell.

Perkin, H. (1989) *The Rise of Professional Society. England Since 1880*, London: Routledge.

Pfeffer, J. and Salanick, G.R. (1978) *The External Control of Organisations: a Resource Dependency Perspective*, New York: Harper & Row.

Piore, M. and Sabel, C. (1984) *The Second Industrial Divide*, New York: Basic Books.

Pope, Daniel (1983) *The Making of modern Advertising*, New York: Basic Books.

Porter, M.E. (1980) *Competitive Strategy: Techniques for Analysing Industries and Competitors*, New York: Free Press.

Porter, M.E. (1985) *Competitive Advantage: Creating and Sustaining Superior Performance*, New York: Free Press.

Porter, M.E. (ed.) (1986) *Competition in Global Industries*, Cambridge, MA: Harvard Business School.

Powell, W.W. (1990) 'Neither market nor hierarchy: network forms of organisation', *Research in Organisational Behaviour* 12: 295–336,

Prindle, D.F. (1993) *Risky Business the Political Economy of Hollywood*, Boulder: Westview Press.

Redding, S.G, (1993) *The Spirit of Chinese Capitalism*, New York: W. de Gruyter.

Richardson, G.B. (1972) 'The organisation of industry', *Economic Journal* 82: 883–96.

Ring, P.S. and Van der Ven, A. (1994) 'Developmental processes of co-operative inter-organisational relationships', *Academy of Management Review* 19(1): 90–118.

Robb, J. F. (1993) 'Scotts of Greenock. Shipbuilders and engineers 1820–1920', PhD Dissertation, University of Glasgow.

Robertson, A.J. (1988) 'Backward British businessmen and the motor ship, 1918–39', *Journal of Transport History* 3rd series IX: 190–7.

Rosenberg, N. (1982) *Inside the Black Box Technology and Economics*, Cambridge: Cambridge University Press.

Rowe, J.W.F. (1965) *Primary Commodities in International Trade*, Cambridge: Cambridge University Press.

Schmitz, C.J. (1979) *World Non-ferrous Metal Production and Prices, 1700–1976*, London: Frank Cass.

Schultze, Q.J. (1982) 'An Honourable Place': The Quest for professional advertising education, 1900–1917', *Business History Review* LVI(1): 16–32.

Scranton, P. (1989) *Figured Tapestry: Production, Markets, and power in Philadelphia Textiles, 1885–1914*, Cambridge: Cambridge University Press.

Scranton, P. (1997) *Endless Novelty Specialty Production and American Industrialisation 1865–1925*, Princeton: Princeton University Press.

Senn, J.A. (1989) *Analysis and Design of Information Systems*, New York: McGraw-Hill.

Sharpe, L. (1964) *The LINTAS Story Impressions and Recollections*, London: LINTAS.

Shepherd, D., Silberston, A. and Strange, R. (1985) *British Manufacturing Investment Overseas*, London: Methuen.

Slaven, A. (1977) 'A shipyard in depression: John Browns of Clydebank', *Business History* XIX: 192–217.

Smircich, L. (1983) 'Organisations as shared meanings', in L.R. Pondy *et al.* *Organisational symbolism*, New York: JAI Press.

Standard & Poor (1997) *Movies & Home Entertainment*, New York: Standard & Poor.

Sturmey, S.G. (1962) *British Shipping and World Competition*, London: Athlone.

Supreme Court of the State of California (C706083) Declaration of Defendant.

Taylor, J. (1972) *Ellerman's A wealth of shipping*, London: Wilton House Gentry.

Teece, D. (1982) 'Towards an economic theory of the multiproduct firm', *Journal of Economic Behaviour and Organisation* 3: 39–63.

Thorelli, H.B. (1986) 'Networks: between markets and hierarchies', *Strategic Management Journal* 7: 37–51.

Trengove, A. (1976) *Adventure in Iron Hamersley's First Decade*, Mount Albert, Victoria: Stockwell Press.

Tsebelis, R. (1990) *Nested Games, Rational Choice in Comparative Politics*, Berkeley: University of California Press.

Tweedale, G. (1984) 'Sir James Kemnal', in *Dictionary of Business Biography*, London: Butterworths.

Vernon, R. (1966) 'International investment and international trade in the product cycle', *Quarterly Journal of Economics* 80: 190–207.

Ville, S.P. (1981) 'James Kirton, shipping agent', *Mariner's Mirror* LXVII: 149–62.

West, D. (1987) 'From T-Square to T-Plan: the London office of the J. Walter Thompson advertising agency 1919–70', *Business History* XXIX(2): 199–217.

West, D. (1988) 'Multinational competition in the British advertising agency business, 1936–1987,' *Business History Review* 62(3): 467–501.

Wilkins, M. (1970) *The Emergence of Multinational Enterprise. American Business Abroad from the Colonial Era to 1914*, Cambridge, MA: Harvard University Press.

Wilkins, M. (1986) 'The Impacts of American Multinational Enterprise on American-Chinese Economic Relations, 1876–1949', in E. R. May and J. K. Fairbank (eds.) *America's China Trade in Historical Perspective The Chinese and American*, Cambridge, MA: Harvard University Press.

Williamson, O.E. (1975) *Markets and Hierarchies: Analysis and Anti-Trust Implications*, New York: Free Press.

Williamson, O.E. (1981) 'The modern corporation: origins, evolution, attributes', *Journal of Economic Literature* 19: 1537–68.

Williamson O.E. (1985) *The Economic Institutions of Capitalism*, London: Macmillan.

Williamson, O.E. and Ouchi, W.G. (1981) 'The markets and hierarchies programme of research: origins, implications, prospects', in W. Joyce and A. Van de Ven (eds.) *Organisational Design*, New York: Wiley.

Wilson, C. (1968) *Unilever 1945–65 Challenge and Response to the Post-war Industrial Revolution*, London: Cassel.

Wrong, D. (1961) 'The over-socialised conception of man in modern sociology', *American Sociological Review* 26(2): 183–93.

Index